Happy 70th

To Bill

Best Wishes

Wilf McGuinness

Wilf McGuinness
Manchester United Man and Babe

Wilf McGuinness
Manchester United Man and Babe

with Ivan Ponting

Foreword by Sir Bobby Charlton

Published by Know the Score

118 Alcester Road Studley, Warwickshire, B80 7NT Tel: 01527
454482 Fax: 01527 452183 info@knowthescorebooks.com
www.knowthescorebooks.com

A CIP catalogue record is available for this book from the
British Library

Mixed Sources
Product group from well-managed
forests and other controlled sources
www.fsc.org   Cert no. TT-COC-2082
© 1996 Forest Stewardship Council

FSC

Printed by Cromwell Press Group, Trowbridge, Wiltshire

ISBN 978 1 84818 503 6

Contents

Acknowledgments Wilf McGuinness would like to thank his family, who mean all the world to him; all his friends inside and outside football for their help and support, particularly Sir Bobby Charlton for his generous foreword; Graham Hales for his attractive design; Andy Cowie of Colorsport for contributing some of the pictures; publisher Simon Lowe.

Ivan Ponting would like to thank his own patient and long-suffering family, and Cliff Butler, the wise man of Old Trafford.

All photographs courtesy of Wilf McGuinness's collection and Colorsport

Foreword by
SIR BOBBY CHARLTON

No one would ever describe Wilf McGuinness as a shrinking violet. Some might call him bubbly or effervescent, but I've known him long enough to make no bones about it – he's loud! But he has been a good friend to me down the years, and I shall always wish him well.

He hasn't always enjoyed the best of luck, either as a player, when his extremely promising career was stopped in its tracks by a horribly broken leg, or as a manager, when things didn't quite work out for him during his short stint in charge at Old Trafford.

But Wilf is nothing if not resilient. He has always bounced back from every reverse, full of zest, ready for his next challenge ... and invariably talking at the top of his voice.

We met for the first time as 15-year-olds in a cup match at Maine Road in 1952, when Wilf was playing for Manchester Boys and I was in the team from East Northumberland. He was immediately noticeable because of the volume of his chatter, and I could understand why they'd picked him to be captain.

After that our paths crossed frequently as we played together at schoolboy level for the North against other regions, and then we were both picked to play for England against Wales at Wembley in front of 93,000 people. Everybody was a little bit petrified at the prospect of performing on such a fantastic pitch in front of that huge, noisy crowd. I suppose even Wilf was nervous, though it wasn't in his nature to show it.

When we discovered we were both headed for Manchester United we started to become pals, and we signed our first contracts at Old Trafford on the same day. But it was when I came down from Ashington in the north-east that our friendship really began to develop.

The best of buddies: Eddie Colman (left), myself and the future Sir Bob outside the front door of the Charlton family home in Ashington, keeping an eye on Bobby's young brother Gordon.

Three amigos: I can't help freaking out to the strains of Bobby's clarinet and the funky saxophone of another pal, Peter Cullen, during one of our many memorable holidays together, this one on the Isle of Man.

Like all the young footballers who didn't come from the Manchester area, I moved into digs, but the families of local lads such as Eddie Colman, from Salford, and Wilf, who was based in Blackley, took me under their wings and looked after me. They would invite me round for my lunch or my tea, and at Christmas time, when I couldn't go home to the north-east because there were always matches, they would never leave me alone in my digs.

It was a lovely warm environment, perfect for a young lad who had moved away from home for the first time, and Wilf's parents were so good to me. They were smashing people who made me feel part of their own family. I liked them very much and I'll never forget them.

Meanwhile it was natural that Wilf and I became close. We did everything together, and in May 1956 he and Eddie came back to Ashington with me for a couple of weeks' holiday. It was the year Manchester City won the FA Cup, and I can recall watching the game at our house.

In those days there wasn't a lot for youngsters to do, and the football facilities were pretty basic, too. It's a different world now, with everything laid on for the boys, but I'm certainly not complaining about the way it was for me.

I *like* to feel that I've played at Denaby Main, a colliery village in south Yorkshire, in a force ten gale with a leather ball so heavy and sodden that you could hardly kick it through the mud. It's all part of growing up in the game. Everything is really quite nice now, with pretty much everything done for the youngsters' comfort and convenience, and it may be that a little bit of the struggle is missing, a little bit that helps to build character.

Back in the 1950s Wilf and I were privileged to be part of a United side that won the FA Youth Cup three times in a row, and to play alongside so many brilliant players, including the incomparable Duncan Edwards. Of course, Duncan was in a class of his own, and it might have been daunting for Wilf to be playing in the same wing-half position, but he just got on with it, always hoping for an opportunity and taking it when it came along.

He was given his first-team debut before me, probably when Duncan was injured or on international duty, and he made a decent impression. Wilf was a promising player, strong in the tackle, full of boundless

Though he couldn't have been keen on flying so soon after the Munich disaster, Bobby and I managed a laugh on this trip. Behind us director and future chairman Louis Edwards (left) and Matt Busby join in with the joke.

enthusiasm, willing to run forever. He wasn't clever with his passing and he was never going to be a great goal-scorer, but he was terrific at breaking up attacks in the middle of the field, an important task in any successful team.

Wilf wasn't on the trip to Belgrade in February 1958, so he wasn't involved in the disaster at Munich, after which the club was in desperate need of high-quality players. My pal seemed to fit the bill. He came in and did so well for United that before long he was in the England team and he looked to have a very big future ahead of him.

But then came that terrible injury, which he suffered in a reserve game with Stoke. I was playing that day, and I saw it at close quarters. It was obvious immediately that it was a bad one and, although he tried very hard to make a comeback, it proved impossible.

It was a cruel fate for a lad who was only 22 and who had just launched his international career. Certainly he could have expected to continue doing well for United, and he might have been part of all the success we enjoyed in the 1960s. Why not? Who knows what he might have achieved?

At such a low point he could have given in to self-pity, but that was never Wilf's way. He remained positive, accepted a job on United's staff and developed into a capable coach. Later there was that difficult spell as manager, but he put that behind him and went on to a satisfying and fulfilling life in the game.

He has a wonderful family, too – Beryl and his four children are all lovely people – and I couldn't be happier that his son, Paul, is now in charge of youth development at Manchester United. He's very good at his work and has become an immensely important figure at Old Trafford.

In recent years Wilf has taken up after-dinner speaking, and it doesn't surprise me that he has been so successful. He's always had a sense of humour, he loved the dressing-room banter and invariably he was in the middle of the fun we all shared as lads together back in the 1950s. Although his voice – how shall I put it? – carries a long way, there isn't an ounce of malice in him, and he would never set out to hurt anyone with his jokes.

Whatever else can be said about Wilf, nobody could deny that he loves Manchester United. Like me, he was hooked into the club by Jimmy Murphy, Matt Busby and Bert Whalley at an early age, and the lessons and values he learned from those wonderful men, about life as much as football, have never been forgotten.

I am delighted to share these memories, and to commend the fasacinating life story of Wilf McGuinness, one of my oldest friends in the game. He was always a man who aimed high, and if he stumbled sometimes on the rocky pathway to the mountain top, he would get up and try again. Who could do more?

Bobby Charlton,
September 2008.

Chapter 1
HEAVEN AND HELL

MANCHESTER UNITED hoisted me to the heavens, not once but twice. First they bestowed on me the pure, unadulterated joy of being a young Red Devil on the threshold of a football career alongside the best bunch of lads who ever drew breath; then they did me the supreme honour of choosing me to succeed the incomparable Matt Busby as their manager.

Sadly, all too soon after demonstrating their faith in my abilities, that same Manchester United were to cast me into the deepest pit of black despair, shattering my whole world as it seemed at the time, by sacking me as the man in charge of the team. Yet through it all, that double dose of ecstasy followed by an interlude of head-banging trauma – and yes, at my lowest ebb I was reduced to nutting an Old Trafford wall in a fit of anguish – what has never been in doubt is that I love the club with every fibre of my being.

That much was true when I was an enthusiastic little lad in short trousers knocking a ball against the side of our house in Blackley, one of the city's northern suburbs, and I'm happy to say it remains true today, when I am lucky enough to be working once more for arguably the most fanatically cherished, downright magical sporting institution on the planet.

Certainly my devotion was total as I worked my way up the footballing ladder, captaining Manchester, Lancashire and England Schoolboys, then signing on at Old Trafford as the proudest young player in the land at the age of 15 in June 1953. After that I graduated to become a professional alongside the likes of Duncan Edwards, Eddie Colman and Bobby Charlton, who all became close friends.

Like the other three, I picked up a medal when United retained the League Championship in 1956/57, and although I had not pinned down a regular place in that most dazzlingly entertaining of sides, at the age of 19 I was still young enough to dream, and believe, that I could cement my long-term breakthrough in the fullness of time.

Less than a year later in February 1958, when the Munich air catastrophe claimed the lives of Duncan, Eddie and six more of my friends, it was like a dagger to my heart. Nothing would ever seem quite the same again. There was no sense of relief that, but for the fact that I had been injured, I would have been on the plane and might have died with my mates. All I felt was this gnawing sense of emptiness and disbelief.

United, of course, had to go on and it was my privilege during the 1958/59 campaign to play my part as Matt Busby, still suffering horribly from the physical and mental wounds sustained on that bleak Bavarian runway, defied the odds to guide our team to runners-up spot in the title race. Aided by his inspirational lieutenant Jimmy Murphy, a man to whom I owed more than I could ever hope to repay as I learned about the game under his often fiery tutelage, Matt achieved a soccer miracle that season, one for which I don't believe he ever received full credit.

Meanwhile I had risen to the rank of full England international – I represented my country every season at all the different levels for eight years after the age of 14 – and, with all due modesty, I believe I could have made a reasonable mark as a wing-half in English football if a broken leg seven weeks after my 22nd birthday had not decreed that I would never play another senior match.

At that point I might have been on the scrapheap, but Manchester United and Matt Busby were immensely good to me, saving my bacon by taking me on as a coach, a position I was delighted to fill throughout the 1960s. During that unforgettable period, in which the club touched new heights by winning the European Cup, I also served England under Sir Alf Ramsey, helping the national youth team taste European success, then joining in the preparation for the ultimately glorious World Cup Finals on home soil in 1966.

But my personal pinnacle still lay ahead. When Matt Busby, fulfilled by reaching the end of his European rainbow but understandably drained by all he had been through, opted to step aside in 1969, he

There may be trouble ahead … but Sir Matt and I are a happy pair on the day we told the world I was taking the reins of the Red Devils.

Look at that classic action …kicking in before a game at Goodison Park at a blissful time when the football world was still at my feet. There's plenty of Brylcreem on my hair – now I use Pledge!

nominated me to take the reins of his great creation. To say I was proud was a gigantic understatement. I was sitting on top of the world.

What followed was not what I hoped. Though I led the side to three cup semi-finals and an improved eighth-place First Division finish in my one complete campaign, we were struggling towards the wrong end of the table by Christmas 1970 and I lost my job.

I was distraught, demoralised, utterly devastated that I should be dismissed with 18 months left on my contract. The shock of that news – delivered to me in the kindest way possible by Sir Matt Busby, my footballing mentor and a man I adored like a second father – hit me with brutal force, the consequences of which I was counting for a very long time. In fact, within 18 months of that terrible day, all of my hair had fallen out, and no doctor has ever been able to say for certain whether that distressing condition was due to my sacking.

I've always been a bubbly sort of guy who has never dwelled on misfortune or been prone to self-pity, but for a while it seemed that the world had stopped turning, and only the love of my family kept me sane. I don't think my state of mind was helped by the fact that some close observers of the Old Trafford scene, not to mention a certain Brian Clough, reckoned that I had been hung out to dry by the club I idolised, but that was never a theory I subscribed to.

Of course I was hurt by United's decision at the time – who wouldn't be? – but even half a lifetime later, having been able to reflect at leisure on the so-called injustices which some people reckoned I suffered, I would not join them in apportioning blame.

They made the case that I was taking over a team in which many of the top players were past their best and that others were carrying debilitating long-term injuries. They pointed out that the latest crop of youngsters, while being decent lads and willing workers, were simply not good enough for Manchester United. They added that, unlike every one of my successors from Frank O'Farrell to Sir Alex Ferguson, I was given no money to spend despite identifying high-quality targets such as Colin Todd, Mick Mills and Malcolm Macdonald before they hit their prime.

It has been said that it was always going to be hard for me to manage footballers who were also my pals, some of whom I had grown up with, and that the continued physical and psychological presence of Sir Matt at Old Trafford undermined my authority. I have always refuted both of these points wholeheartedly, although it is true that there were some grey areas between myself and my predecessor, which I discuss in detail later in the book.

Finally United were accused of being naive for appointing someone with no managerial past, but I feel that viewpoint sells short my coaching experience, which, after all, had been spread over a decade and included some humble input into England's successful World Cup campaign.

My take on all this is that I was overjoyed to be given an opportunity that others might have killed for, and although I'm sorry it didn't work out I'm not the type to beat up myself or anybody else about the outcome. I moved on to further footballing adventures in Greece, York, Jordan, Hull and Bury before returning to Old Trafford, where I am more than happy to be involved in providing corporate hospitality on match days. I must admit, too, that I still get as excited as any schoolboy by Sir Alex's breathtakingly exciting teams. I repeat, I have never stopped loving Manchester United and I never will. I'm overjoyed to have been part of the club's incredibly colourful and uplifting story. I hope you enjoy reading about it in the pages that follow.

Chapter 2
HITTING THE WALL

No one makes the grade in professional football without accumulating a vast collection of debts. In my case I owe more than I could ever dream of repaying to Matt Busby, Jimmy Murphy and the rest of their magnificent behind-the-scenes staff at Old Trafford, the likes of coach Bert Whalley, trainers Tom Curry and Bill Inglis, chief scout Joe Armstrong and physiotherapist Ted Dalton. Before that there was James Mulligan, who doubled as headmaster and sportsmaster at Mount Carmel School in Blackley, north Manchester, where I completed my entire academic education.

Then, of course, there were my parents, Lawrence and May, who could not have been more devoted to me and to my footballing ambitions.

But beyond all those seminal influences on the fledgling career of young Wilf McGuinness, there was another significant contributor, the importance of which it would be impossible for me to exaggerate. I'm not talking here about some unseen fount of wisdom, but a humble wall, the few square yards of windowless brickwork which constituted the gable end of our terraced house at 51 Westleigh Street. Daft as it might seem to many modern youngsters, accustomed as they are to elaborate sports facilities and multiple opportunities at every turn, it was that simplest of training aids which nurtured my emerging passion for the game which was to shape my life.

In that lovely far-off time before our streets were clogged with cars and it was safe for children to venture unaccompanied from their homes, I gave that wall one hell of a battering – kicking, heading and throwing a ball against it for hour after hour, day after day, even year after year as it seems to me looking back across so many decades.

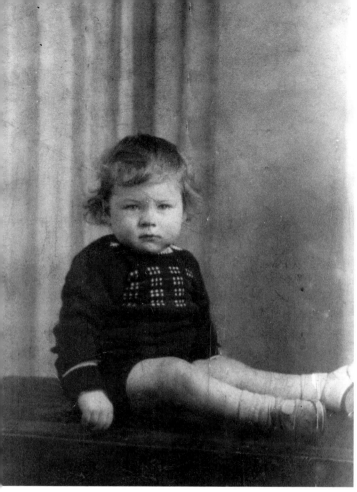

What wouldn't I give for that head of hair now? I'd say I was more of a toddler than a Babe when this picture was taken.

Skipper of Mount Carmel school team, aged 13. I was bigger than the other lads because my mum was the dinner lady!

I captained Manchester Boys to triumph over London Boys in the Coronation Cup at Belle Vue in 1953, and I have the trophy at my feet to prove it. Notice the size of the crowd, and the lad standing on the far right of the back row. It's big John McGrath, who went on to play for Bury, Newcastle and Southampton. Sadly he died in 1998.

I'm the prize-winning ringer in the Old Trafford crowd, chosen by the local newspaper in January 1951. I was there to roar on United in an FA Cup tie with Leeds, and we won 4-0. The cheerleader with the trumpet is Jack Iron.

At the time, of course, in my head I wasn't a little lad in short trousers, often getting in the neighbours' way with my incessant play. No, as my imagination took flight, most likely I was Johnny Carey, my ultimate idol and the captain of Manchester United in the immediate post-war years, playing the key role as my brilliant team lifted the FA Cup at Wembley or won the League title with a last-minute goal. Or maybe I was Stan Pearson or Jack Rowley or Allenby Chilton, all United heroes of that uplifting era when Matt was putting together the first of his three marvellous sides. Then again, and whisper it gently, I might have been Bert Trautmann, the great Manchester City goalkeeper who was such a fantastic performer that he transcended club allegiances. He was a fabulous all-rounder and the first man I can recall who hurled the ball out with a mighty push from his shoulder, which seemed to produce more accuracy than over-arming it cricket-style.

Actually, I ought to point out here that many fans, myself included, used to watch both local clubs as we couldn't afford the travel to away games, though I must also hasten to stress that I have always been United to the core. In most circumstances I wanted both the Reds and the Blues to win, but when it came down to the nitty-gritty of a local derby there was never the slightest doubt in my mind that I was behind Matt Busby's team. Why was I of the United persuasion? Well, though I admired City men such as Big Bert and the dynamic wing-half Roy Paul, overall I thought United had the better, more exciting players. Then there was the fact that my dad leaned towards City, so maybe I just wanted to be awkward.

But to return to that wall at number 51, it enabled me to learn so much – about shooting, chipping, heading, then controlling the ball with either foot, no matter how awkward the angle as it bounced back to me. That might make one or two of my old professional contemporaries smile rather wryly, as I was a wing-half of what might be termed a vigorous persuasion; indeed, I had the reputation in certain quarters of being far more of a destroyer than a creator. They might even take issue, albeit with the best of humour, with the suggestion that I honed my skills to any extensive degree. That doesn't bother me: I'll argue the case that I could play a bit with anyone, and I can put my caps and medals on the table to prove it!

For all my happy memories of Blackley which come crowding in as I write these words, that was not where I first saw the light of day on the 25th of October 1937. I was born in Collyhurst, about a mile from the centre of Manchester and the place which produced such Old Trafford luminaries as Nobby Stiles and Brian Kidd. I left there when I was only an infant, but I know from many subsequent visits to the Twyford Street neighbourhood to see my grandma, aunties and uncles that there didn't seem to be much room, either indoors or outdoors, and that all the small terraced houses were crowded together, just like the ones made famous by *Coronation Street.* For all that, it was a smashing community where most of the people were down-to-earth and supportive. There might not have been a lot of money around, but there were plenty of real honest-to-goodness values, the sort that last you all your life. I always had a great affection for the place, and that remains to this day, even though Twyford Street itself and other of my old haunts have long since been demolished to make way for new development.

Still, I have to admit that Blackley was a more attractive proposition, both in terms of the size of houses and the number of parks where kids could play. I always felt lucky that we were close to a glorious open space called Boggart Hole Clough, where legend had it that a boggart, some kind of ghostly monster, lurked. I never bumped into him, though – and even if I had then probably I'd have asked him if he fancied a game of football!

My oldest concrete recollection, as distinct from those fuelled by photographs, stories or return trips in later years, is of my early days going to Mount Carmel School in Blackley, particularly trudging along the pavements between home and classroom in plimsolls or Wellington boots (depending on the weather), peering through the pea-souper smog which seemed to envelop Manchester so much of the time during the winters. There were a few tears at the outset because I didn't like school. But then, pretty soon, I did like it, mainly because I turned out to be good at sport and school was the place where that ability found its expression.

I was a lad with many blessings, growing up in a secure family envir-onment, with my dad, mum and brother, also named Lawrence, who was four years older than me. In fact, I didn't get to know my father properly in my toddling days because, after serving briefly as an air-raid warden near our home following the start of the Second World War, he was called up to join the Eighth Army in North Africa and Italy.

That meant Mum had to take over the family and we were fortunate that she was such a very strong character. She had to be, not only because of Dad's enforced absence, but because she was completely deaf. I often wonder if my loud voice, which so many people have remarked upon throughout my life, came as a result of shouting at my mother during my childhood, perhaps sub-consciously trying to make her hear me. As it was, we evolved our own code of signals. At first we had a problem with kettles. Understandably she wanted to deal with the hot water rather than leave it to a cack-handed little lad, and I would whistle to tell her it was boiling. Of course, she couldn't hear me, so she showed me how to gesture, waving my hands to indicate steam rising, instead. That worked well enough, and some would say I've been making steam come out of people's ears ever since.

Of course, she was a skilled lip-reader, although sometimes she got it wrong, amusingly so. One of the funniest examples came a few years later, when I was 15 and had just captained England Schoolboys. Mount Carmel School and the local Roman Catholic Church, of which we were staunch members, organised an evening to mark my achievement, and invited my hero, Johnny Carey, to present me with a special football kit. For the ceremony I was up on the stage with my parents and the United skipper, as well as our parish priest Canon Kershaw, my teacher James Mulligan and a collection of councillors and other assorted local dignitaries. The place was packed to the rafters and there were lots of speeches, which my mother followed as best she could by lip-reading as the various worthies rattled on about how marvellously young Wilfred had performed, what great honour he had brought on his parish and school, and how his services were being sought by lots of leading clubs. She seemed to nod and smile in all the right places, but then Canon Kershaw rose to his feet and said there was one person who should take enormous credit for what Wilfred had done, namely Mrs May McGuinness. She had been wonderful, keeping the home going and bringing up two boys while her husband had been away at the war. That Wilfred had come through with such flying colours was clearly due in vast measure to Mrs McGuinness, who also found time to work for the school as a dinner lady; truly she was a remarkable person. Then he sat down, and immediately my mother leapt to her feet and started clapping as loudly as she could. I couldn't believe my own eyes and ears, and went as bright red as my brand new Manchester United shirt. Fortunately pretty well everybody there knew of her disability and understood exactly what had happened, otherwise it would have been even more embarrassing. Still, I had to ask her: 'Why did you just clap Canon Kershaw?' Her reply was to the point: 'What's the matter with you? You must always clap your parish priest!' We soon got over the confusion, but it made everybody smile, including Johnny Carey himself.

Certainly an incident like that wasn't going to faze my mum, who was a formidably courageous woman. She always strove to do what was right in life, and did her utmost to ensure that her sons followed suit. She was an absolute stickler for good manners, not that I always listened to her as dutifully as I should have done. When we passed a lady, if I didn't touch my school cap or my forelock – oh, those were the days, when I had a forelock! – then she would give me a sharp crack.

Looking back now with an adult perspective, I can appreciate how hard she must have worked to keep the family ticking over. To help ends meet sometimes she would clean offices in the centre of Manchester during the evenings. Of course, we didn't have a car, nobody did in our road, so she used to travel in by trolley bus, usually with Lawrence and myself to keep her company and to assure her by our presence that we were not getting up to mischief. Of course, with all the violence on the streets today, it would be a far more intimidating journey than it was for us, especially during the dark winter nights. But during the 1940s we never felt threatened and never had to give thought to our safety.

As for the war, it had very little impact on my life and there was no impression of living in fear. Whenever the air-raid siren sounded in the evening I went under our stairs, where there was a cubby-hole with a big drawer for me to sleep in. It wasn't frightening because I didn't appreciate the danger. To a kid of four, five, six years old, it was all an adventure and good fun. Sometimes we would go to a nearby air-raid shelter, big enough for a couple of hundred people, and practise putting on gas masks. Occasionally, after a real raid, when the all-clear sounded we would go out and look for fires, but we didn't see very many, even though a few bombs landed close by in the park. The Germans would have been aiming for Avro, the aircraft builders near

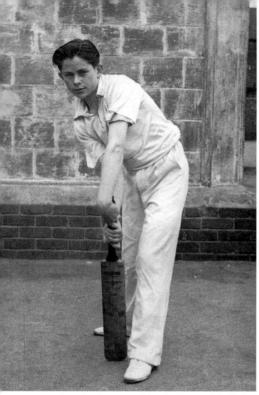

I used to love my cricket and I wasn't bad at it, representing Manchester Boys in the early 1950s.

It was the proudest moment of my young life when I donned my England schoolboy cap.

United skipper Johnny Carey (right) has just presented me with a new kit to mark my selection for England. That's my dad on the left and Canon Kershaw in the centre next to my mum, who made me blush mightily that evening …

Chadderton, or the Trafford Park industrial estate, but missed their targets.

One of my most vivid memories is of being in the Moston Imperial Palace cinema – the MIP as we used to call it – with some mates when they flashed up on the screen the message that the whole country had been waiting for: 'The war is over!' I thought Dad would be coming home at once and I ran home to tell Mum. One day soon the bunting was out and we were waiting for him, but at first he didn't come. We went to bed without seeing him, but he must have arrived during the night because in the morning there was this fella in the house and it was my dad. Obviously I didn't recognise him because I wasn't very old and hadn't seen him for about four years, but we were all very happy.

There was a lot of catching up to do, and it must have been very emotional for him to see how his sons had grown. As for me, I had a pressing question for him: 'Did you kill anybody in the war, Dad?' He told me he had been a lorry-driver rather than a front-line fighter, but he did kill someone, an Italian whom he had knocked down accidentally at the bottom of a hill with his lorry. Somehow that wasn't quite what I had in mind, but I was delighted to have a father again.

Now he started working as a warehouseman in the fruit market in the centre of Manchester, which meant he had to be up at about 4am. The plus side of that was that he would be home by 2pm, so when my football career got under way he was able to watch me play. It was around the time of his return that my passion for the game really ignited, and it grew rapidly as he began to take me to Maine Road to watch both City and United in action. Of course, that ground was City's traditional headquarters, but for several seasons after the conflict United had to play their home games there, too, because Old Trafford had been devastated by the bombs of the Luftwaffe.

As a result, all my most colourful childhood recollections of United feature Maine Road. For instance, there was the afternoon in February 1949 when, together with a bunch of fellow 11-year-olds, I played truant from school to watch an FA Cup fourth-round second replay against Bradford Park Avenue. That was quite an adventure because we couldn't get a bus from central Manchester and had to walk and run to get to the ground on time. Even then it looked as if we wouldn't get in with a crowd of more than 70,000 supporters milling around and most of the

My sportsmaster James Mulligan knew so much about the game and was an early inspiration to me.

Meet the family: that's Dad in the uniform of the 8th Army – he served in North Africa and Italy during the war – while Mum is flanked by me on the left and big brother Lawrence on the right.

turnstiles closed, but we had a stroke of luck. Next to the main stand near the players' entrance there was a gate, perhaps 20 feet long, and that was knocked flat in the crush. Everybody surged inside and it was a miracle there wasn't an horrendous accident – if such a thing happened today there would be a tremendous stink, and rightly so in light of the tragedies that have occurred – but somehow we reached a corner of the terrace, only to find that we still couldn't see. We ended up by taking it in turns to sit on each others' shoulders, ten minutes at a time, and catching glimpses of the game between the bobbing heads of the grown-ups. United won 5-0, with Jack Rowley and Ronnie Burke getting two each and Stan Pearson scoring the other. I saw only a couple of the goals on that rather breathless occasion, but I had a much better view five days later when my father took me to the fifth-round meeting with Yeovil Town, the renowned cup fighters from deepest Somerset. When we reached the packed terrace – and this time there was an attendance of more than 81,000 – I was passed down to the front, as kids often were in those days, and I watched spellbound as United hammered eight past the gallant Southern Leaguers, with Rowley plundering five.

Like me, Dad loved his football. He had always been a sportsman, being a middle- and long-distance runner with St Patrick's Harriers in Collyhurst before we moved house. My big brother was athletic, too, a talented runner and he was always good at swimming, but he was never mad about football and cricket like myself. As we were four years apart we had different friends as we grew up, but even though we tended to fight, as most siblings do, we were basically very close and always knew we could rely on one another. Lawrence was the intelligent one of the family, passing his eleven-plus and going to Xaverian College in Rusholme on the other side of Manchester. Mind, I wasn't slow at school, finishing most terms at the top of the class during my first five or six years at Mount Carmel, but then five other people passed their eleven-plus and I didn't, which was always a bit of a mystery. According to everybody at the time I should have passed easily, but I made the fundamental mistake of thinking the exam paper was too simple. Therefore I tried to do something more difficult than was required, and ended up getting it wrong.

That was disappointing, but there was a silver lining, as my sports-master James Mulligan was quick to point out. Had I passed my exam

I would have had to have changed schools, but now I could stay at Mount Carmel just when I was making massive strides with my football, and he was delighted to keep me in his team. Mr Mulligan, a former left-back who was good enough to play a handful of games for Manchester City and win a full cap for Northern Ireland in the 1920s, was a mentor to me throughout my schooldays. He recognised my burgeoning love affair with the game and he nurtured it. He was a fine man and I owe him a great deal. Coincidentally his son, John Mulligan, was destined to fill a similar role for Nobby Stiles, and then Brian Kidd, at St Patrick's in Collyhurst.

My first memory of organised competitive football, though, is playing for the Cubs at the age of about ten. I never grew tall as an adult, but funnily enough I was quite big for my age at that point. There were a lot of small boys in north Manchester who had been war babies when there wasn't enough nutrition to go around, while I had been lucky enough to be properly nourished.

I didn't realise it at the time, but I suppose I was outstanding in my peer group as a footballer. I was a centre-forward then and I used to score goals by the hatful. I followed Dad and Lawrence in being a decent runner – I had a long-striding, knees-up action – and at that stage of my development I could go past most markers pretty easily. I used to take everything – the corners, the free-kicks, the penalties, the throw-ins. I always had a long, high throw because I used to practise hitting the chimney stack from across the road at home. That developed so that I could reach the six-yard box on a full-sized pitch, which was a bit of a feat for a young teenager.

I did well at cricket, too, and was only 12 or 13 when I got into the Manchester under-15s side as an all-rounder. I was decent enough at both batting and bowling, and I think my fielding was particularly impressive because I would chase everything, never give anything up. That was a long time before the introduction of the one-day game improved general fielding standards, and there were quite a few people who would saunter casually towards the boundary as the ball disappeared over the rope. Not me. I'd be pumping my arms and legs and saying to myself: 'That's not going for four!' I concentrated fiercely, some might have said obsessively, on every ball. I suppose that's just the way I am, and it translated into meticulous study of the rules of any game I played. I was always in a position to tell anybody who wanted to listen exactly what was what, often small but important details like keeping part of both feet on the ground for throw-ins, so I didn't lose many arguments. How they must have loved me!

At football I was always a captain, which means communicating with your team-mates, not so much telling them how to play but giving them pictures, shouting about who was free to receive the ball. In my younger days I guess my approach must have been irritating to some of the older lads, who must have thought I was a loud-mouthed little so-and-so. But that's the way I saw it and I always tried to be true to myself. I made mistakes but I thrived on recovering from them, so not many ended up disastrously, and I was always eager to learn, which helped me tremendously, especially after joining United.

But I'm getting ahead of myself here. The quantum leap in my football development took place when I was 13 and was selected to join Manchester Schoolboys. For my first year at that level I played at inside-forward before moving back to wing-half, and now I was required to learn more about the discipline involved in playing the game properly. For Mount Carmel I had been an attacking centre-back, involved in every phase of play, basically following the ball wherever it went, but that would no longer do. My enthusiasm continued to be overwhelming, and I moved on up to represent Lancashire Schoolboys, but I had to learn to channel all that energy for the common good.

When I was 14 Mr Mulligan, who was the chairman of Manchester Boys, thought I was ready for England trials, and I was sent down to Bournville in Birmingham for a searching training session with lads from all over the country. I must have had something that stood out because, to my untold delight, I was chosen to captain my country's under-14s against Northern Ireland at York City's ground, Bootham Crescent, a venue which was to hold special significance for me much later in life. We won 5-1 against a team which included Derek Dougan, destined to become an accomplished centre-forward, and occasionally a controversial figure, with a host of clubs, including Blackburn Rovers, Aston Villa and Wolves.

Before that 1952 trip my mother had given me a typically stern lecture about how to behave, especially as I was the captain. Among other things, she made me promise to thank the waitresses and all the other people who looked after us in our hotel at Harrogate. So duly I climbed to my feet at the pre-match meal and gave the first, but emphatically not the last, after-dinner speech of my life. Perhaps I spoke rather haltingly but it wasn't too bad for a lad of 14, and whatever else it achieved I am convinced that it helped me retain the captaincy a year later. When I was called up for the 1953 trial at Denaby in Yorkshire I was suffering from 'flu. Even though I felt totally exhausted I was determined not to miss the opportunity, but after enduring a nightmare on the training pitch I felt even more rotten. Certainly the way I played football that day did me no favours. Despite that, though, I was selected to skipper England against Wales at Wembley and I'm convinced that that was due, at least in part, to the positive impression I had made with my thank-you speech to those Harrogate waitresses.

As it would continue to do throughout my life, Mum's advice had stood me in admirable stead. Consequently I experienced the incredible thrill of leading my team out in front of nearly 90,000 people under the famous old twin towers, and although my knees were knocking with nerves at the beginning, I just got on with it and thoroughly relished my part in a thrilling 3-3 draw. Jimmy Melia, who was destined to do well for Liverpool in later years, made a decent impression for us, and a young feller name of Bobby Charlton scored twice. I fancy we might hear a bit more of him as this story progresses …

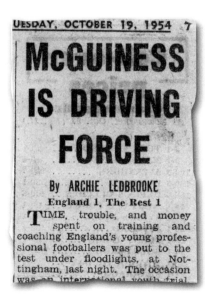

UESDAY, OCTOBER 19, 1954 .7

McGUINESS
IS DRIVING
FORCE

By ARCHIE LEDBROOKE

England 1, The Rest 1

TIME, trouble, and money spent on training and coaching England's young professional footballers was put to the test under floodlights, at Nottingham, last night. The occasion was an international youth trial.

Chapter 3
THE RED FAMILY

IN THE early months of 1953 I was in the enviable position of being chased by many of the leading football clubs in the land. As the captain of England Schoolboys for the second successive season, my services were being sought not only by Manchester United, but also by Wolves, Manchester City, Chelsea and a few more besides. I'm not being big-headed when I say that I had my choice of employers. That's just the way it was.

Given my affection for United stretching back to early childhood, it might seem that signing on at Old Trafford would have been the merest of formalities, but it wasn't. I owed it to myself to weigh up all the many possibilities and, together with my mum and dad, make a cool decision. I tell the joke that I opted for United because of their youth policy and also because they offered my parents the biggest back-hander – but that wasn't true. In the end there were two main reasons why I threw in my lot with the club that I already loved: one involved a cheeky little chap called Eddie Colman and the other concerned the lovely people that made up what I came to recognise as the Manchester United 'family'.

The first time I encountered Eddie he was playing for Salford Boys against my team, Manchester Boys, and he was a joy to watch, a smoothly creative wing-half with a dash of magic about him, pushing and running, always keeping the play moving. When I saw him again he was operating in midfield tandem with Duncan Edwards, my predecessor as the England under-15 skipper, for Manchester United in the newly established FA Youth Cup, putting 23 (yes, twenty-three) goals past Nantwich at The Cliff.

I was captivated by what I had witnessed under the lights of the club's old training headquarters at Broughton, then the point was well and truly rammed home by the first leg of the final against Wolves at Old Trafford. I looked at Duncan's vast and special talent, and I wasn't unrealistic enough to think I was as good as him at that point, but as I had his old England job there was at least some yardstick by which I could compare him to myself. But when I saw Eddie performing so brilliantly, looking like a genius in the making, I thought to myself: 'He's terrific, but he's only played for Salford and Lancashire, he hasn't been picked for England. If joining Manchester United can do that for him, then what might it do for me?' Then I looked at the other youngsters who were thrashing Wolves 7-1 on that May evening, people like Billy Whelan, David Pegg and Albert Scanlon, and I thought how wonderful it would be to play alongside such tremendous footballers. From that moment, the thought of joining United became irresistible.

Then there was the way I was treated by everyone connected with the club, starting with Joe Armstrong, the club's supremely successful scout, a tiny, bright-eyed, friendly character who worked for the GPO, on the telephones, when he wasn't doing his utmost to unearth talent for United. His opening gambit to me, and to all the other lads, was: 'Call me Uncle.' What magnificent psychology that was! Just imagine, every time I was approached by a scout from another club, and there were always plenty of them buzzing around, I would say something like: 'Wait a bit, I've just got to see Uncle Joe over there.' It must have made the others think they had no chance of tapping us up if United's man was so well in that the boys were calling him 'Uncle.' Mind, though Joe was a born charmer, he was no confidence trickster, but a genuinely warm personality who looked after us all to the best of his ability and set the tone for the rest of the Old Trafford community.

In contrast, I'm bound to say, the efforts of some of his rivals were inept. For instance, there was the time when a fellow from Bolton came looking for me but I was out, playing for the school on the local park, so my mother invited him to wait for me in the front room. Mum was an extremely devout Catholic and so there were crucifixes, a holy water font, a statue of Our Lady and images of various saints all over the place. When I got home the Bolton man asked if I had any particular preference among the clubs who were pursuing me, and I told him United were my favourites at that point. His reaction? 'Oh, you don't

I took this snap of Duncan Edwards and Jimmy Murphy when we spent a few days together in Bray, in a lovely part of the Republic of Ireland. It was one of the happiest times in my life.

It was a tremendous thrill to take part in an international youth tournament in Switzerland in 1954, and an even bigger thrill to win it. On the far left it is just possible to discern Billy Whelan, then come Albert Scanlon, Eddie Lewis (barely visible), goalkeeper Tony Hawksworth, Bobby Charlton, myself, Peter Jones, Eddie Colman, John Doherty and skipper David Pegg with the bouquet.

want to go there – only Catholics get on at Old Trafford.' There he was surrounded by all our paraphernalia and he came out with a line like that! What sort of scout could he have been? As for his jibe about religion, while it was true that United employed plenty of Catholics, Matt Busby and Jimmy Murphy among them, there was never any sectarian preference at the club and nowhere near all the footballers espoused the same faith. Some people have tried to give a different impression, but they were wrong.

More convincing than the Bolton approach was one from Wolves, who eventually became the only possible alternative to the club already closest to my heart. In truth, the McGuinnesses did consider the offer from Molineux seriously, not least because the Black Countrymen were vying with United as the most successful club of the day and were also renowned for their vigorous youth policy. Indeed, they had managed to recruit one lad from my own patch, the inside-forward Colin Booth, who had done well for Manchester Schoolboys. But there was another compelling factor: Wolves had offered my father a job as a talent scout, not that he would have had to do anything bar collecting a well-packed brown envelope every now and then.

Certainly the club ruled by manager Stan Cullis with a rod of iron, and destined to become League champions in 1953/54, pulled out all the stops to secure my signature. After being picked up from home in a sparkling, chauffeur-driven limousine, Dad and myself were treated to a tour of Molineux and its training facilities, then we were whisked off to a hotel in the centre of Wolverhampton, where we were given a lavish meal, with no stinting on the drinks for my father. Then we were taken to a smart house, which was to be my digs if I agreed to sign for Wolves, and greeted by a pleasant girl, the landlady's daughter. She ushered us into a lovely lounge which was positively opulent by the standards we were used to, complete with a fitted carpet and French windows opening on to a well-tended lawn – and that's where the script started to go seriously awry. Not being used to so much rich food washed down liberally with alcohol, poor Dad felt suddenly unwell. He didn't make it to the lawn! In fact, he didn't even make it to the French windows before he was sick. Given the circumstances, it really wasn't his fault, but that concluded the business for the day, and the likelihood of my recruitment by Wolves, already remote in view of the increasingly persuasive case for my hometown club, receded still further.

Meanwhile what, if anything, did United offer by way of inducement? In fact, they operated largely by the book, handing over no more than so-called digs money on top of my standard wage. Let me explain. When a youngster from another part of the country, for instance Bobby Charlton from Northumberland, signed for United, the club paid for his digs in Manchester. As a local boy I lived at home, so they paid my parents for my keep, I think it was £6 or £7 a week, admittedly a significant amount in those days. I know it wasn't strictly according to the rules, but it seemed absolutely fair to me. That payment lasted until I turned professional at 17 and, typically, my mum didn't spend it. Instead she saved it up and gave it to Beryl (my future wife) and myself on our wedding day, when she knew it would come in useful.

Boy stars sign for United

By ALF CLARKE

MANCHESTER UNITED today signed on amateur forms two outstanding England schoolboy international players. They are Wilf McGuinness, right half-back, who captained England, Lancashire and Manchester schoolboys last season, and Bobby Charlton, inside left, of Ashington, Northumberland, and England schoolboys. Both players figured in five England international schoolboy games last season.

They are both aged 15 and have only just left school. McGuinness attended Mount Carmel School, Blackley, and I know that League clubs all over the country have been "interested" in him, as well as Charlton, who I saw give some splendid displays last season.

Charlton is a nephew of the

United assistant manager Jimmy Murphy with two former England schoolboy captains—today's signing Wilf McGuinness (right) and Duncan Edwards, who had his

I signed for United as an amateur during the Queen's coronation week in June 1953, straight after leaving school, on the same day as Bobby Charlton. I was photographed in the local newspaper being greeted by Duncan Edwards, two former England Schoolboy captains side by side, and it was a very proud moment for me.

Still, if I figured my life from that moment would consist principally of kicking a football around all day, I had another think coming. My parents were adamant that, at 15 and therefore unable to turn professional for two years, I should get a trade under my belt just in case I didn't make the grade as a player. Bobby Charlton's mum and dad had the same thought and so we were both sent out to work. I was given a job at a textile firm in Chorlton Street, central Manchester, owned by Mr Eric Richardson, a pal of Matt Busby's, while Bobby was required to pass his days in a local engineering factory, Switchgear and Cowans. It didn't please us at the time, toiling away for a couple of pounds a week rather than training during daylight hours with all the other juniors at the club, and maybe it held us back a bit at first. We had to train at The Cliff on Tuesday and Thursday evenings, and the only senior player we encountered there was the full-back Bill Foulkes from St Helens, incredibly enough still a part-time mineworker despite being an England international. Sometimes the United 'B' team for which we played had games on Wednesday afternoons and we were always given time off for them but, like most lads would, we moaned about the arrangements.

Looking back, though, I don't suppose it did us any harm. I learned how to parcel up blankets and sheets, how to tell fibs and get away with what pranks I could with my workmates. In other words I found out something about real life, away from the rarefied atmosphere of Manchester United. Here's another thought to ponder: imagine if things had not worked out for the pair of us – McGuinness Textiles and Charlton Autos might have become icons of British industry. Then again, England would have been deprived of one of its finest footballers and, most likely, victory in the 1966 World Cup. And just think if Bobby hadn't made it either…!

Back in the real world, I was with the company for about 14 months, though in the end I wasn't in a mad rush to turn professional at £5 per week because I was better off as an amateur, working for the textiles company for £2 a week and receiving the digs money on top. I was told it was against the rules to pay me any more than they were offering, but in the end the matter was settled when we met Jimmy Murphy at my dad's works in November 1954, a week after my 17th birthday. Jimmy arrived in a taxi – he never drove – and on the back seat was a television, which was for us. This was something very special at the time as the family didn't have a set, and I duly signed my first contract. The truth is that most big clubs handed out such little perks. That's just the way it was in those days. But I must make it crystal clear that, TV or no TV, I had already agreed to put pen to paper. I was committed emotionally to Old Trafford and there was never any question of holding out for an extra inducement.

I was a lad obsessed with football and overjoyed at the prospect of starting a professional career under the guidance of Matt Busby, the man I believed to be the top manager of them all. His achievements since taking over Manchester United in 1945, with the club short of money and the ground bombed out and unusable, spoke eloquently of both his ability and his ambitions. Though Matt's team had won the League championship only once to date, they were the most consistent combination in the country, finishing runners-up four times in the space of five seasons before finally lifting that elusive crown in 1951/52. In addition they had won the FA Cup in 1948, turning on some of the most breathtakingly beautiful football ever seen at Wembley to beat Blackpool 4-2, and they entertained royally wherever they went.

The players who achieved all that were my boyhood heroes and I'd like to pay my brief tribute to them here. Jack Crompton was one of the smallest goalkeepers in the League, not a spectacular performer but a solid one. In those days the 'keeper used to run around a lot, bouncing the ball and charging into attackers, and as a boy I used to think: 'Who's this little man, pushing people over?' Of course, when I got to know him after joining the club – and I'll talk more about his role as a trainer later in the book – I realised what an extremely tough character Jack was. He might have been quiet, his voice hardly ever seeming to rise above a whisper, but he was very determined and if there was something he wanted to do then he would do it.

During that 1948 FA Cup Final I was listening to the radio at home and cheering United on as Jack made some terrific saves. Mind, I could never be still for 90 minutes. Instead I was running in and out of the house, playing a bit of football against the wall, then nipping back for a score update. I was really disappointed when we went a goal down after 12 minutes – it was never a penalty! – but pleased as punch when we came back to win. A lot of people still reckon it was the best final of all time, and I wouldn't argue with them.

The right-back and captain was the softly-spoken Dubliner Johnny Carey, the cream of footballers. He was the player I looked up to more than any other and one of the main reasons I wanted to join United, though it was a shame he was finishing just as I was getting started. He was such a smooth operator who always seemed to have plenty of time and it seemed that no one could get past him. Even if he was up against a flier, he was able to get his body between his opponent and the ball, and he never looked like he was committing a foul, even if he was. Gentleman John, as he was called so aptly, exuded sheer class. He never flapped no matter what the situation and he was a stylish, straight-backed all-round performer who, at one time or another, filled every position for United except outside-left. Like his manager, he oozed authority and integrity, and was a real father-figure on the field.

Like Jack Crompton, left-back John Aston was a lovely fellow with whom I was to enjoy a terrific relationship when we were coaching together at Old Trafford in later years. He was another vastly accomplished player and he looked certain to enjoy a long run in England's number-three shirt, but selflessly sacrificed his international aspirations as a defender by switching to centre-forward for United during a long-term injury crisis. John had bags of natural skill but he didn't over-elaborate or hog the ball, and he had an almost uncanny knack of always being in the right place. He could take the knocks, too and, boy, could he tonk a football.

As a young supporter I never knew so much about right-half John Anderson, who got his place ahead of the older Jack Warner when the team was shuffled a bit. John seemed to be a quiet, unobtrusive type, but he scored a goal at Wembley and finished up a hero. He was a bit of a late developer and didn't last too long in the team, which can't be said of the big, raw-boned centre-half, Allenby Chilton, an uncompromising north-easterner whom nobody liked to play against. He could be a handful off the field, too, as Les Olive, destined to be the club secretary but then a young office worker and the gentlest of fellows, once found to his discomfort. Apparently disgruntled at being delayed, Big Allenby reached through the window of the ticket office, grabbed poor Les by the throat and growled: 'I want my tickets.' Chilton was sent off a couple of times, which was unusual in those days, and as an impres-

The day I captained England Schoolboys to an 8-0 triumph over the Republic of Ireland at Portsmouth in April 1953. That's me seated second from left in the front row, while Bobby Charlton is on the far right of the same bench.

Matt Busby's first great Manchester United side, which lifted the FA Cup in 1948. Back row, left to right: Matt himself, John Anderson, Jack Warner, Allenby Chilton, Jack Crompton, Henry Cockburn, John Aston, trainer Tom Curry. Front row: Jimmy Delaney, Johnny Morris, Johnny Carey (captain), Jack Rowley, Stan Pearson, Charlie Mitten.

sionable boy I was astonished, thinking that he must have a screw loose or be really nasty.

Alongside Allenby at left-half was Henry Cockburn, a smashing, friendly little fellow who jumped phenomenally well for his size and was superb at positioning. I wasn't the biggest, either, and we filled the same role, so Henry was something of an example for me.

Finally there was that sensational forward line, known as the Famous Five. My word, they were brilliant, every one of them. All of them could play, all of them could score, all of them had a spark to lift them out of the ordinary, something special about them that was going to win a game, whether it was enthusiasm or determination or just plain downright awkwardness. How I loved that in them.

On the right wing was the experienced Scot Jimmy Delaney, who seemed a tough guy. That's what stood out to me, apart from his bald head. He had come up through a hard school with Celtic and certainly knew how to look after himself. Jimmy offered the perfect contrast to Charlie Mitten on the opposite flank, who was a cool customer both on and off the pitch. Charlie played like he talked – smoothly. He always had a story to tell, and he could paint beautiful pictures with his fabulous skill and explosive shooting.

At inside-right was the 'baby' of the team, Johnny Morris; he had everything any footballer would ever need and he told everyone exactly what he thought. Dripping star quality at centre-forward was Jack Rowley, as strong as an ox, with a cannonball shot and a fantastic scoring record. They say that if you whack the ball then you've got a chance, and certainly Jack did that. Looking at him from the terraces I always thought he was a big fellow, but when I met him in the flesh he was only small. As a character he wouldn't be messed about and could be difficult, but I had just started when he was coming to an end and I didn't notice that.

Last, but certainly not least, there was the other inside-forward, Stan Pearson. He didn't have the aggression of Rowley or Morris, but his quality, his timing and his touch on the ball was exquisite. When I was watching from one end of Old Trafford, so often a goal would go in at the other and the cry would go up: 'Who scored that?' Most likely the answer would be Stan, who would have ghosted into the six-yard box and caused mayhem. That was his style: quiet but deadly.

So these were the role-models in whose golden footsteps I dreamed of following, and when I came under the influence of the man who had guided them to glory, I quickly recognised the sheer power of his personality. The first time I met Matt Busby I formed an overwhelming impression of a man accustomed to command. Though he was not particularly tall, he had very broad shoulders and gave off an immense physical presence. His voice was a lovely, deep Scottish brogue, resoundingly strong yet somehow gentle; he looked like a boss and he sounded like one, in total control of himself and the events around him.

Sometimes when we were training we would catch sight of him on the touchline, and his mere presence would galvanise everyone to strive just that little bit harder, making us dig even deeper in our tackling and running. We wanted to show him what we could do; he was that sort of man.

Then there was his attention to detail, which was quite amazing for such a busy person. When I met officials from other clubs, such as Wolves or Bolton, they knew nothing about the McGuinnesses. But when I was introduced to Matt Busby before signing for United, he knew the names of my mum and dad, and even my brother. In a nutshell, he gave off a great, warm feeling of family. He knew all about the McGuinness family and now he was welcoming me into *his* family, the United family. It might sound corny but it was true, and it extended through all the people who worked for him. There was a deep, deep bonding. It built team spirit, and I'm certain other clubs didn't have it to anything like the same degree as Manchester United.

This was an extension of what I had felt from my earliest contacts with Joe Armstrong, and which carried on through my relationships with Matt himself, Jimmy Murphy, Bert Whalley and the rest. They looked after us like surrogate parents, inviting us into their own homes to make friends with their own sons and daughters, a lovely touch which was particularly helpful to lads who weren't from the Manchester area and might easily be homesick.

Jimmy was Matt's first lieutenant, the inspiration to two generations of Old Trafford rookies, and an invaluable mentor. He could be fiery and took no nonsense, but he was always down to earth and you could go to him with any problem, whether it was football-related or not. At times he could make you cry with his scathing criticism – that happened to me more than a few times. Sometimes after a typical Murphy tirade I would think: 'Bloody hell, I've got no chance of making it.' But he knew what was needed with each individual; he knew which ones needed driving and which ones needed cajoling. In my case he knew I could take the flak and not go under, and I like to think I proved him right.

Just as influential in a contrasting way was the coach Bert Whalley, who specialised in picking us up after Jimmy had knocked us flat. Bert, who served United as a dynamic wing-half or centre-half either side of the war, was a kind, gentle fellow, a lay preacher in the Methodist church and as decent a man as ever lived. He and Jimmy knew football inside out and they preached the basics of the game, about working and passing and supporting the man on the ball. They drummed into us that we should get the ball and give it simply, that we should be patient with our passing and wait for gaps to appear. As for tackling, Jimmy was keen on that. He told me there were plenty of inside-forwards who would funk a physical challenge once I had bitten into them a couple of times, and I was good at playing that way. I always tried to do what I was told, even though sometimes I couldn't live up to what he wanted. I think he must have played a bit like me his days with West Bromwich Albion and I have a feeling he identified with my do-or-die attitude, my enthusiasm and my willingness to listen. Even Matt would tell me to put an inside-forward out of the game – not by kicking him, that wasn't Matt's style – but by sticking close to him every step of the match. If you give a talented opponent room he'll run you ragged and score goals so, prevention being better than cure, the idea was not to give him the chance!

Some of the drills might seem basic by today's standards. For instance, at youth team level there was shadow play, where a team would take to the field without any opposition. Then we would pass the ball around, learning how to move it in the right way to the right places at the right time, before someone would kick it into goal. Now it might seem unlikely that youngsters could take that seriously, but Jimmy had the authority and respect to carry it off – and, believe it or not, it was very useful.

Understandably enough, people have always had the idea that life at a top club is unendingly glamorous, but that wasn't the way of it for much of the time, certainly not in the 1950s. For instance, the club was very frugal with money and everything had to last, including the training gear, which was already threadbare. It taught me certain lessons – firstly to look after things carefully, secondly that if you were late for training you would get the worst kit. It wasn't wet because it had been in a drier, but usually it hadn't been washed since the previous session so there would be lots of congealed mud and sweat, perhaps even blood. We had no choice but to wear it, and because of that there were a lot of crawly things going on. Players were getting a case of this and a case of that, and sometimes there was a minor epidemic. If you were last in the bath it was full of mud, sometimes it was black. As I often did extra training that particular short straw tended to be mine, so usually I would opt for a cold shower rather than plunging into my team-mates' foul luke-warm leavings.

Then there was the employment situation, which did not exactly breed security. The clubs always wanted to have the whip hand so they offered only one-year contracts, which was a diabolocal way to treat people. At the end of each May there were always lads waiting in trepidation to see if they had been retained. Sometimes you could get a shrewd idea in January or February, by asking for a new pair of boots. If you were told to wait it was a bad sign, while if they invested in a new pair for you it was a fair indication you were staying. Arthur, our cobbler, would keep the boots mended as best as he could, and each player was supposed to make one pair last a season. He was an important man, Arthur, so much so that he sneaked on to a lot of the celebration pictures when United won the FA Cup in 1948.

Mind, despite such questionable conditions, none of the lads ever wanted to leave United and, thank goodness, I never received the fateful call into the office to be told my services were no longer required – at least, not in my playing days!

Chapter 4

GREAT PLAYERS, GREAT MATES

As my Manchester United adventure continued to gather pace, I became comrades in arms with lads who were destined to be numbered among the greatest footballers the game has ever seen, as well as plenty more who never scaled such Olympian peaks of sporting achievement but who were equally unforgettable characters. How I treasure my memories of the incomparable Duncan Edwards, as I do more than half a century of ongoing friendship with Bobby Charlton. Then there was big, genial Gordon Clayton, who never quite made the grade as a United goalkeeper but remained one of the best chums imaginable until he died prematurely in 1991; and Shay Brennan, one of Matt Busby's European Cup winners in 1968 and, more importantly, one of the loveliest people to walk this earth. Dear Shay was also snatched from us with shocking suddenness. But no one made a bigger impact on me, or left a more gaping hole when his life was snuffed out at Munich in 1958, than that bubbly little genius called Eddie Colman. If Eddie was a star as a footballer – and had he been spared he would have dazzled the world – then he shone even more brightly as a person. I miss him and his wonderful family sorely to this day.

That word 'family'; it keeps cropping up and I make no apology for that because it reflects more accurately than any other exactly what it was like to be part of Manchester United in the 1950s. For instance, shortly after I had signed for the club as a 15-year-old, Jimmy Murphy took myself and Duncan Edwards, who was a year older, to the small town of Bray, just south of Dublin on the east coast of the Irish Republic. Jimmy had some scouting to do and he thought it would be an ideal opportunity for the two of us to get to know each other off the pitch, because he surmised that we would spending a lot of time together in action for United in the not-too-distant future. He spent some time with us, but mostly we were left to our own devices and we enjoyed what amounted to a carefree holiday, further cementing that family ethos. We made a visit or two to the Arcadia dancehall and met two lovely young colleens. After more than 55 years I can't remember their names, though maybe one was called Eileen. Of course, we weren't exactly ladykillers but, like true gentlemen, we did walk the girls home, some three miles into the deep countryside. Still, it was all very polite and proper, right down to the handshakes with which we left them at their doors. Oh that Duncan, he was a modest, unassuming fellow, much quieter than me. Perhaps I should have gone with the effervescent Eddie! Not that Duncan was a stick-in-the-mud. Far from it, he was great fun. But he wasn't particularly assertive in a social group, especially among strangers, and sometimes I wondered if he didn't say too much at first because he was conscious of his strong Black Country inflection, much the same, maybe, as the similarly reserved Bobby Charlton with his pronounced north-eastern accent.

Football-wise, of course, Duncan possessed supreme self-confidence. To spend a short time observing his style was to realise that, deep down, he knew he was the best. There was a glorious certainty about all he did, and he excelled at everything. For example, even though as a wing-half he was usually to be found in midfield, he loved to rampage forward, and any time there was the slightest chance to display his awesome shooting prowess he would take it without fear or hesitation, sometimes even if a colleague was in a better position. No way was Duncan shy or retiring on the field, yet there wasn't a shred of conceit about him. That much is illustrated by his reaction when he was cycling back to his digs one winter's night and he was stopped by a policeman for displaying no rear light. Some less modest characters might have been tempted to adopt the 'Do you know who I am?' approach, but certainly not Duncan, who accepted that he had been caught out and paid the consequent fine with good grace.

He was a truly remarkable individual, and when such a man as Bobby Charlton declares that he wasn't fit to lace Duncan's boots, it emphasises the colossal scale of the talent of our old friend from Dudley. Sometimes

Duncan Edwards with the two comely colleens we met in Ireland. I wonder where they are now …

The likely lads: one of the girls must have taken this snap of Duncan and myself. It's a picture I treasure.

That winning habit: the United party arrive home from Switzerland with the silverware. Left to right are Albert Scanlon, Mr Hartley (a loyal supporter), Eddie Colman, myself (peering over Eddie's shoulder), Billy Whelan, Duncan Edwards and Gordon Clayton, with Tony Hawksworth in the coach doorway.

in the early 21st century, when someone from my generation waxes lyrical about Duncan Edwards, they are met with disbelief but it's a fact that Dunc had everything a footballer could possibly need, except, perhaps, an edge of nastiness. Whereas such mighty modern performers as Bryan Robson, Roy Keane or Liverpool's Steven Gerrard might be seen to 'do' an opponent, that simply wasn't in the Edwards make-up. Oh, he was a supremely muscular physical specimen and he played the game hard – people just seemed to bounce off him – but never with a hint of malice. Only twice did I see him anywhere near losing his temper: once when he dragged a Real Madrid skiver off the pitch at Old Trafford in April 1957 when he believed the Spaniard was feigning injury to waste time after United had wiped out a 2-0 deficit; and again ten days later at Wembley when Aston Villa's Peter McParland butted our goalkeeper, Ray Wood, effectively ending our chances of becoming the first club in the 20th century to lift the League and FA Cup double. When that second incident happened – and it really was an outrageous foul – Dunc took three strides towards the Irishman and for a split second I thought there was going to be hell to pay. But then he stopped and controlled himself, which was a mark of the man. I knew him well, and I'm certain that he didn't have a villainous streak; quite simply, he was that good he didn't need it.

When I think of Duncan it reminds me that football can be a great and sporting game. He proved that you can be strong, determined and skilful, all rolled into one, displaying the level of tremendous talent that we are witnessing today in the shape of Wayne Rooney. Astonishingly, too, he could excel at the back, in midfield or at the front. It just didn't matter; anywhere on the field Duncan Edwards was gold dust.

My connection with Bobby Charlton began when we met in the centre circle at Maine Road as rival captains – he of East Northumberland and I of Manchester – in the English Schools Trophy, and then were picked to represent our country together. At that first encounter Bobby remarked that we'd be seeing each other a week later at the England trials and my initial reaction was one of scepticism. Remember I was an old hand who had played the year before, so I thought to myself: 'Will we really? Just who are you exactly?' It wasn't to be long before I found out!

Like Duncan and I, we were always contrasting personalities – Bobby was reserved and I, er, wasn't! – but a whole lot of rubbish has been said and written about him and we became firm friends for life. So often people have criticised him for being aloof and stand-offish, but if you get to know him then he's brilliant fun to be with, a kind man who loves children and who has a highly developed sense of humour. That doesn't often come out in public. Frequently he wears a serious expression, so I can see where people are coming from when they get the wrong impression. The fact is that while Jack Charlton took after his mother, an effervescent, outgoing lady, Bobby followed his dad, who was quiet, thoughtful, even shy. Complete opposites, but people are different. I don't see why that should be a problem.

I must point out, also, that while Bobby was not the boisterous type, on the field he was never reticent with the verbals, always capable of giving as good as he got. Once I remember him shouting at me to call for the ball because I was free, but when I looked round he was unmarked, too. I told him: 'No, *you* shout for it because if you lose the ball, I'm here to make a tackle. If I lose it, you're never going to win it back.' We had quite an argument – he wasn't very shy on that occasion!

As we signed our United contracts on the same day, it was not surprising that Bobby and I should pal up. In those days the young players would spend a lot of time in the houses of the lads who lived locally, like Eddie Colman and myself, and often the first thing that Bobby would do when he walked in would be to pick up a newspaper and start reading it, rather than joining in the general banter. I thought that newspaper was a shield for him to hide behind, so I used to dig him a bit and say: 'Come on Bobby, snap out of it.' As the years went by, and the adulation mounted, he remained modest, straight and correct, but his wife Norma – a lovely, down-to-earth person with a fantastic memory for people and places – helped him tremendously, bringing him out socially and making him miles better at mixing.

Some of the happiest memories in my life stretch back to a two-week summer holiday at his place in Ashington, Northumberland, along with Eddie Colman when I was 17. I guess it was the Charlton family's way of paying back the Colmans and the McGuinnesses for welcoming Bobby into their homes, and although a fortnight in a sprawling pit village might not sound very exotic to modern youngsters bred on overseas travel, believe me it was quite an adventure for two bright-eyed teenagers, one from Salford and the other from Manchester, in 1955. It wasn't that there was anything spectacular to do – we spent a lot of time playing table-tennis and snooker in the social clubs and youth clubs – but we hung out together and it was part of the bonding process that nurtured a camaraderie so important to the development of a football team. The friendships went beyond the players, too, with most of the parents getting to know each other at the never-ending round of matches, presentations and other functions. My mum and dad became very fond of Bobby's folks, who usually stayed with us in Blackley when they travelled down from the north east. His father, in particular, wasn't keen on hotels and preferred the informality and home comforts of Westleigh Street.

But perhaps the busiest social centre for young United footballers in the early and middle 1950s was the Colmans' house in Archie Street, Salford, which was handily close after training at either The Cliff or Old Trafford. We were always welcomed there by his mum, dad and grandad, Liz, Dick and Old Dick. Just like Eddie, they were all very small. Liz was smashing, kind of round like Queen Victoria with a lovely friendly face. Sometimes Dick would fetch us a jug of shandy from the off-licence on the opposite corner as we played cards, listened to music or chatted into the early hours after a Saturday night out, then probably stayed over. There might be David Pegg, Bobby, Shay, Duncan, Gordon Clayton, myself, various others – it was all very fluid. I can see it now, such a beautiful, welcoming scene and Eddie, as the only child, was the centre of the Colmans' lives. When they lost him at Munich they were utterly devastated. It was unspeakable.

Eddie was absolutely bursting with life, a charismatic personality who just seemed to draw people to him, and he was very dear to me from the moment I got to know him at our first training session together. Just like Tommy Taylor, he always had a huge grin on his face; he was the archetypal cheekie chappy, witty, always with a ready answer to any crack, yet for all that he was amazingly modest – there wasn't an ounce of conceit in him.

Eddie was tiny – even shorter than me, though he built himself up with inch-thick crepe soles on his shoes – and he was the sharpest of dressers, often sporting a long jacket with a velvet collar, the kind of gear I would have killed for but was never allowed to wear at home. In fact, Matt did his best to talk Eddie out of the Teddy Boy stuff, which might have been at the cutting edge of fashion but wasn't exactly the image he wanted for Manchester United. Eddie loved the music of Sinatra and all the emerging rock'n'roll stuff. He was a great jiver, unlike Bobby and myself. To be strictly fair, Bobby wasn't *too* bad, and I tried my best, but I must have cut a ridiculous figure as we jumped about on the dancefloor. Inevitably, Eddie became our social secretary, planning visits to such venues as the Bodega jazz club near the old *Manchester Evening News* offices on Cross Street, where often George Melly was on the bill; the Plaza, where Jimmy Savile was the MC; the Ritz and the Sale Locarno. Nearly all the players socialised most of the time, spending hours at coffee bars such as Lyons and the Kardomah. In those days the shops shut at lunchtimes and on Wednesday afternoons, so we'd be there to meet the shop girls when they went off duty. That led to assignations, of course, often to see a film, and the Odeon cinema had deep doorways where you could try your luck with a kiss and a cuddle. Mind, sometimes I wondered how the girls put up with the smell of us, reeking as we did of liniment, usually an infernal concoction called *Five Oils*, which we applied before kick-off. It was designed to loosen muscles, get the blood moving and help soothe the aches and bruises already accumulated, but it was hardly calculated to attract the opposite sex. No matter how hard we scrubbed ourselves with green carbolic soap in the communal bath after the game, that distinctive odour had an uncomfortable habit of lingering. I suppose we must have made up for that with our natural charm! Those evenings always finished with walking your girl to her bus, seeing her aboard which was the correct thing to do, then catching your own bus home if you were lucky. Many's the time Eddie and I had to leg it back to Archie Street because we missed the last bus.

The two of us had plenty in common, but football-wise we offered a vivid contrast, even though we were both wing-halves. While I was principally a tackler and a runner, Eddie was a creator and a crowd-pleaser, a gifted play-maker who had a knack of making space by throwing a dummy or executing a delicate drag-back, then finding a team-mate with a perfectly directed pass. He had total mastery of the ball, his footwork was twinkling and he was pure joy to watch – no one could ever describe me like that! That said, I never thought that anybody – apart from Duncan – was totally beyond my reach when it came to competing for a place in the side. After all, you have to believe in yourself; if I'd allowed myself to think that lots of others were better than me then I'd never have amounted to anything.

I'm sure it would surprise some people to learn that Eddie was convinced I'd play for England and he wouldn't. It might seem perplexing because at the time of the remark he was lighting up the first team at right-half while, despite being another right-footer, I was Duncan's deputy on the left. I said to him: 'Don't be silly, you're in the first team, you're bound to play for England.' He remained sceptical, saying the FA committee men would prefer my do-or-die approach, but I'm convinced he would have been proved wrong had he lived. Maybe at the time the selectors were waiting for him to get a bit stronger and went instead for more straight-up-and-down performers such as Ronnie Clayton, Eddie Clamp or Ron Flowers, even me eventually.

Mind, Eddie was a truly formidable all-round rival because he was a reasonably good defender for a midfdielder, better in that area than many other attacking wing-halves who let opponents run off them. Eddie would stay with his man, which invariably he could do because he had pace. He didn't have to tackle too much because he read situations so intelligently and intercepted a lot. He couldn't shoot to save his life – there were only two Colman goals in more than 100 first-team appearances – but there were a few colleagues who made up for that.

Despite being a year younger, I made my first-team entrance a month before Eddie in the autumn of 1955, though I didn't retain a regular place, while once he had started he was a fixture. Maybe my opportunity came because of my work-rate, though Eddie was fit and quick, too, perhaps just a trifle chubby at times but nothing to worry about.

A little earlier we had made our debuts for the reserves together at West Bromwich Albion and we both had blinders against two international inside-forwards, Johnny Nicholls and Reg 'Paddy' Ryan. Afterwards everyone was telling us how marvellously we'd done and we were on top of the world, but we were about to learn a lesson. As the following week wore on we couldn't stop talking about our next reserve game, but then Bert Whalley burst our bubble by sticking his head round round the dressing-room door and saying: 'You two boys, Burnage on Saturday in the 'B' team. All right?' Although I was shocked, I would have accepted the decision, but Eddie was having none of it. He piped up: 'No, it's not all right. It's a disgrace.' Poor Bert, a real gentleman, looked uncomfortable and asked if we wanted to see the boss. Eddie said: 'Yes, of course we want to see the boss, don't we Wilf?' What could I say? I had to agree.

So we waited a bit and then went up to Matt Busby's office. Eddie, never shy about saying his piece, plunged straight in. He blurted: 'We had blinders last week, even the West Brom players said we did. We deserve better than this. It's not fair.' Matt let him blather on for a while, then he replied calmly: 'I know, you were magnificent. And both of you play an important part in my plans for the future of Manchester United. But the way I do it with young players is to give them a taste. I don't over-play them in these games, and I want to keep the youth ('B') team together as much as possible. So I'm playing you in that team tomorrow. That's my decision.' Our reaction? 'Oh, thanks very much.' And we left feeling ten feet tall, rather than dejected. He had put us in our place but also he had told us we were part of his plans. We were going to be in his first team. He wasn't a bully; he was gentle with us; and he had boosted our confidence beyond belief. It's called man-management – and Matt Busby was the absolute master of it.

He was the wise, all-seeing patriarch of a footballing family which contained so many disparate members; and when I say all-seeing, that's exactly what I mean. Matt Busby had spies everywhere, a network of informers all over Manchester and beyond who would let him know exactly what his young charges were doing out of footballing hours. And if he didn't like what came to his attention, then the 'culprits' soon heard about it, as I discovered to my own chagrin towards the end of the 1950s.

After training some of the lads used to go into town to have lunch at a place called Snack Time in Newton Street. The place always seemed to be packed, at least partly because Bobby Charlton, Shay Brennan and company were to be found there, so a few of us wondered about getting our own cafe as a business proposition. Then we changed our plan and – years before George Best had ever been heard of – we came round to the idea of a nightclub. Not that we were out to live the high life; our intention was to employ a manager rather than spend too much time there ourselves, but we thought the fact that we were United footballers would attract plenty of punters. The would-be entrepreneurs involved in this cunning scheme were Bobby, Shay, myself and a slightly older fellow called Harry 'Nipper' Leonard, who had once played in the 'A' team for United but was now running a rainwear factory. The property we had in mind was the Queens Club above the Zanzibar coffee bar in Queen Street and one evening we went there to strike a deal. By something like 12.30 am we had agreed to pay the rent plus £1,000 for the business, then we set off for home, happy with our night's work, mission accomplished.

Unfortunately for me, however, next morning I was the first of the three footballers to arrive at the ground and waiting at the players' entrance was a fuming Matt Busby. He pitched straight in: 'What's all this about the Queens Club? You go in enough nightclubs as it is without owning one. You look at your contract and you'll find you can't go into any other business without the United directors' permission. Don't let me ever hear about this again.' At least, that was the gist of it. Despite his gentlemanly reputation, there could never be the slightest doubt that he could be hard at need.

We had no alternative but to accept his decision which, at least in retrospect, made plenty of sense. What we couldn't work out was who had told him what was going on. It was astonishing that he should be acting on the contents of a private meeting within a few night-time hours of it taking place. His contacts were truly remarkable, much like Alex Ferguson's some 40 years later when he raided a party at Lee Sharpe's place and kicked out Ryan Giggs because it was too close to the day of a game. The two managers were very alike in the way they tried to control the lives of their players for the good of the club. Matt looked after you like a father, but there was never the slightest doubt that the interests of Manchester United were uppermost in his mind.

I suppose we felt rather dismayed, maybe even a bit hard-done-by, over the nightclub episode but none of us was the type to let something like that rankle, especially the happy-go-lucky Shay. Born in Manchester but with Irish roots, he was an absolute charmer – tall, dark and handsome with gorgeous big eyes and a lazy grin. When we were young lads, if we were out in the car for the evening and we saw a group of good looking girls, we would pull over and tell Shay: 'Get out and let them see you.' It usually worked, they'd come over and have a chat. We didn't say we were footballers, though on board might have been Bobby Charlton, Gordon Clayton, Bobby English, Johnny Giles and Jimmy Shiels, the last

The class of 1955/56, when we won the FA Youth Cup for the fourth consecutive time, beating Chesterfield in the two-legged final. Back row, left to right: Mark Pearson, Reg Holland, Tony Hawksworth, John Queenan, Joe Carolan, Bobby Charlton. Front row: Kenny Morgans, Alex Dawson, myself, Denis Fidler, Peter Jones.

How young professional footballers used to spend their holidays: Bobby Charlton and I sit down to tea at Butlin's in Pwllheli with Peter Cullen.

two mentioned being rum Irish lads and rascals to boot. We had plenty of laughs but nothing too strong, though there was one incident involving water pistols which was blown up out of all proportion – I'll come to that later. Shay was the top man with the chat-up lines but I must admit I was the close second. Bobby was more of a straight man, though there are one or two stories I'd better not tell because he might read this!

Shay was also a central figure on summer jaunts to the Isle of Man, and to Jersey, where there was one uncomfortable brush with potential aggravation. We were only kids, certainly not famous, but there was one loud-mouth who knew we were United footballers and this fellow took severe exception to Bobby, presumably because our mate from the north-east was just beginning to forge a reputation. As we sat at a table outside a café, he bombarded Bobby with insults, goading him with really subtle stuff along the lines of 'Hey, you ponce.' It was then that Shay decided to get involved. He was never a fighter, invariably preferring to defuse any awkward situation with his amiable charm and easy self-assurance, so it came as a real surprise when, after enduring several minutes of unacceptable behaviour towards his unassuming friend, he stood up and called the oaf's bluff.

'Who are you calling a ponce?' he grated, with just a tinge of unaccustomed annoyance in his voice. Of course, that prompted the trouble-maker to transfer his attention to Shay. 'I'm calling you a ponce, you ponce' he responded, then sprang to his feet to reveal the build of a heavyweight grappler. There was a tense pause during which I feared the situation was going to get out of hand, but suddenly it was over as Shay said: 'So, I'm a ponce' and promptly sat down to a massive roar of laughter from everybody present. In terms of keeping his good looks intact, that was one of the finest decisions he ever made. Shay and I were very close, exchanging best man duties (his first wedding, my only one) and it was a crushing blow when we lost him to a heart attack in 2000. The only consolation was that he died on a golf course, at Tramore in the Republic of Ireland, which wasn't the worst way for him to go.

Another terrific pal was Gordon Clayton, a big man with a personality to match. He played in goal in the first ever FA Youth Cup Final in 1953, when United beat Wolves 9-3 on aggregate, and it looked like he had a real chance of breaking through. But though he had good hands, his knees let him down, and anyway it would have been no cakewalk winning a regular place between the posts with the likes of Ray Wood, Harry Gregg and David Gaskell in the mix.

Gordon was such a warm, welcoming character, the sort who lights up a room when he walks into it, and we hit it off from the start, often going out as a foursome with our respective future wives, Beryl and Pat. The Claytons were very sociable people, lovely to be around. Certainly nobody loved a party more than Gordon, and I can recall a typically enjoyable 'do' one Christmas night in Chorlton, when we were both in the youth team. The trouble was that we were due to play for the reserves against Bury at Old Trafford at 11 o'clock on Boxing morning. The precise details are a little hazy, perhaps not surprisingly, but I know that Bobby, Gordon, Shay and myself walked all the way from the party to the ground and only just got there on time. Were we out of sorts as a result of our overnight festivities? Hardly. We won 8-0, I had a blinder and Bobby scored six. The funny thing was that Les Olive made five of them, and I never found out which party he went to!

Much later, when I was manager at Old Trafford, I was delighted to bring Gordon back to the club as a scout and he proved brilliant with the young lads, instantly putting them at their ease. His sudden death, aged only 54 in 1991, hit me hard, but I will never forget him

Returning to Les, for those who didn't know him I should point out that I'm taking a bit of a liberty regarding that party. There was no way that he would have been out all night before a game. He was far too dedicated for that. Most United fans will remember him as the long-serving secretary of the club and won't even realise that he was once a player, but that does him an injustice. He played twice for the first team as a goalkeeper, and for the reserves and juniors he was a reliable half-back. Later I'll touch on his wonderful work in the wake of Munich, when as assistant club secretary he did so much to keep United ticking over. At the time of his death in 2006, nearly half a century on from the disaster, he was still serving the Old Trafford cause as a director. There was never a more honest and level-headed man in football than Les Olive. He played a gigantic part in the history of Manchester United, and I was proud to call him a friend.

Indeed, that goes for so many of the people I have known during my time in Manchester. For all the glory and the adventure and the passion

Disappointed at losing to Bolton but still smiling, Beryl and I (on the left) at the official banquet after the 1958 FA Cup final with close friends Gordon and Pat Clayton. Well, she was Pat Teal at the time, and Beryl and I were also yet to marry.

Young men of the world: left to right are Kenny Morgans, myself and Bobby Charlton.

I was always very close to Shay Brennan (left) and his lovely family. That's his dad and mum with us at the table.

which I found in the game, unquestionably it is the friendships I forged with the likes of Gordon, Duncan, Eddie, Bobby, Shay, David Pegg, Billy Whelan and so many more marvellous lads that mean the most to me now as I look back.

There is no price that can be placed on genuine comradeship, and I relished it even when I was the fall-guy for the communal high jinks in which we all indulged at every opportunity. For instance, I had to see the funny side, even though I have to admit I was pretty embarrassed, one day when the whole squad had a belly laugh at my expense. There used to be a big plunge-bath in the first-team dressing room at Old Trafford and I was drying myself beside it when Tommy Taylor and David Pegg strolled in. Somehow keeping a straight face Tommy, a renowned wind-up merchant, said to me: 'Bloody hell, Wilf, look at your muscles. They're bloody great. You must be so-o-o fit!' Now, I used to practise my long throw regularly so I did have a bit of a six-pack, although we didn't call it that in those days. So there I was, basking in what, in my innocence, I had imagined to be Tommy's and David's genuine admiration. 'Do you really think so?' I said, and Tommy came back with: 'Yeah, just push your arms up a bit higher above your head, then twist round a bit and it really shows off your muscles. They're fantastic.'

Then, while I was stuck in this ridiculous pose, I happened to half-glance behind me and there were about 20 of the lads, practically wetting themselves to stop laughing out loud. Being the greenest of rookies at the time, I had fallen for the classic set-up by Tommy and David. They had caught me hook, line and sinker, and no one let me forget it for weeks afterwards. But it was all good-hearted, completely harmless fun, and I loved every minute of it. What wouldn't I give today to have the mick taken out of me by Tommy Taylor and David Pegg...

Chapter 5

BRING ON THE BABES

THEY WERE special days. The war was not long over, life was getting back to some sort of normality, a fresh culture was emerging. We looked at the likes of James Dean and Marlon Brando and we gasped at their performances; rock'n'roll was taking off big time. Meanwhile, in sport, it could be said that the new spirit of youth was symbolised by the Busby Babes, who were catching the imagination of fans across the land, playing their football with a precocious swagger that matched the changing times. Not that they were swaggering people, just that when they won – which they were doing with increasing frequency – they did so with such flair and style. I hasten to add that I would never claim to have been stylish myself, but I was part of a thrilling group that was. Most of the players at Manchester United were only just starting out and still had a lot of learning to do, but they were so, so talented and there seemed no limit to what they might achieve.

But what did little Wilf McGuinness bring to the party when he became a Babe in the summer of 1953? I was a wing-half, a midfielder in modern parlance, overflowing with enthusiasm and ready to work until I dropped. I don't consider that I was clumsy with the ball at my feet, but I was no artist, that's for sure. Thus my main job was to win the ball, then give it simply and securely to the creative players – and we had plenty of them – so they could work their magic. After all, if you've got the likes of Bobby Charlton in front of you, what's the point of trying something clever yourself?

When I arrived at Old Trafford I was a right-half, but I switched to the left because of Eddie. I know Duncan was a left-half, but he could

I fly through the air with the greatest of ease, leapfrogging over United's brilliant Irish inside-forward Billy Whelan in training.

play anywhere and I was not cowed by the situation of being up against two such terrific footballers. My standpoint was that I would improve with experience and that Duncan would eventually move into someone else's position. Even if my two pals had lived, that would still have been my view. I had only just turned 20 at the time of the Munich disaster and I wouldn't have dreamed of going anywhere else voluntarily in the quest for a regular place. I was not short of self-belief and I was a good learner. For instance, during one training session Jimmy Murphy told me I needed extra practice with my left foot. So he gave me a ball and directed me to the wall behind the Stretford End, telling me to kick that ball against the brickwork until I began to improve. 'Try using the wall as another player,' he advised. 'Go left, left, right, right, then left, left again. Then mix it up and keep it going for as long as you can. I'll come and tell you when I want you to stop.' Though I had just been through a hard session of running followed by a fierce five-a-side I followed his instructions to the letter. It wouldn't have occurred to me to do otherwise. Trouble was he forgot all about me, and when he happened to walk by a couple of hours later he could hardly believe his eyes because I was still going. At least I knew I had impressed him, though, because he grabbed me by the arm and said: 'Son, that's fantastic. With that sort of determination, I know you're going to make it. Well done!'

I believe it was showing that sort of attitude that made me one of his favourites. I always gave 100 per-cent and I don't believe I ever let anybody down. I was a trier until my last breath. Even if we were three down and couldn't catch up, I saw it as my duty to give everything until the last kick. If I gave a bad pass I wouldn't go missing; making a mistake would never put me off my game, it just made me more determined. I was very fit and I covered a lot of ground, not the most graceful of movers, perhaps, but I tended to reach my destination pretty quickly. On top of that I had a thoroughly professional outlook – I was good at winning and bad at losing. Later Nobby Stiles would come through to help win a World Cup and a European Cup with similar attributes. Not that I was ever as wild as Nobby ... I was much more subtle! To make a more modern comparison, I'd say I'd be something in the order of the Neville brothers ... only I tell better jokes!

So that was me: I couldn't swivel and sway like Eddie, I wasn't a superman in the mould of Duncan and I didn't possess the magical talent of Bobby, but I had a great attitude and some ability; and there were those who reckoned I might be captaincy material. All in all, I reckoned that would do, and I don't think Manchester United were disappointed as I progressed through their junior ranks. Apart from the obvious carrot of forging a career in professional football, there was also the extra huge motivation of the FA Youth Cup, which had been introduced in 1952/53 and won by United. By 1953/54, though still a part-time textile worker, I was in the youth team alongside Duncan, Eddie, Bobby, David Pegg, Albert Scanlon and the rest as we retained the trophy, beating Wolves 5-4 in a two-legged final. Such was the interest in the Busby Babes, and the crying need for a fresh crop of young English footballers in the wake of the senior side's recent Wembley humbling by Ferenc Puskas and his 'Magnificent Magyars', that the second leg at Molineux attracted a crowd of more than 28,000, who watched David score the deciding goal from the penalty spot.

Also in 1954 we all benefited enormously from entering – and winning – the Blue Star youth tournament in Switzerland. For all our young players this was a plunge into the unknown, because I don't think any of us had ever been abroad before so it was a fantastic life experience as well as widening our football education.

For example, none of us were used to hotel life and our etiquette at mealtimes might have left a bit to be desired. Occasionally it was down-right embarrassing, for instance when the waitresses brought us salad and we had no idea whether to eat it before or after our main course! It seems daft now, but we were only young lads out in the big, wide world for the first time.

Football-wise, of course, it was absolutely tremendous, finding out how the game was played in other countries, and discovering, too, that we were good enough to beat the other teams. Crucially, our participation in the tournament tied in with Matt Busby's visionary belief that United should expand into Europe and it was appropriate that the club should take its first step with the youth side, two years before the senior team became involved.

As well as playing the games we met some wonderful people and made friends who are still involved in running the Blue Star event to this day. It is held annually and has become a major strut in United's youth policy, something the club looks forward to every season. Every player who has come up through the ranks at Old Trafford has taken part, and long may that continue.

Bolstered by our Swiss triumph, we won the FA Youth Cup again in 1954/55, this time by the comfortable aggregate margin of 7-1 against West Bromwich Albion. Even better for me, in 1955/56 I was skipper as we retained it yet again, this time overcoming Chesterfield 4-3. The Spireites, who had a promising young feller by the name of Gordon

'But Wolves are so big,' says Mum

EVENING NEWS REPORTER

MRS. MAY McGUINNESS, Wilf's mother, was working at Mount Carmel School canteen, Blackley, serving lunches to children when I took her the news.

"Oh, how wonderful," she cried. Then she added: "I wish it wasn't against Wolves. They're a big side."

Then she rushed home to nearby Westleigh-street, to congratulate Wilf. But she had missed him by minutes. On the table was a hastily-scribbled note: "I'm playing for first team at Old Trafford to-morrow. Gone to Blackpool to join team.—Wilf."

On the sideboard were his wages. Added his mother: "This is the day he has been waiting

Mrs. McGuinness reads the note.

for. He wanted to play for the first team before he was 18 on October 25.

"He has already got seven England caps—five as a schoolboy international, one as an amateur youth international, and one as a professional youth for captaining England against Denmark last Satur...

AFTER THE MAT...

RIGHT: Manchester United's 17-year-old half-back, Wilf McGuiness, takes time off from training at his home in Westleigh Street, Blackley, to read with his mother newspaper reports of his first professional game against Wolverhampton Wanderers at Old Trafford on Saturday.

Banks between their posts, gave us two tremendous games in front of a total of more than 40,000 supporterts before we prevailed. It was a tremendous honour for me to complete my hat-trick of medals, a feat equalled by only four other people, all from United; namely Eddie, Duncan, Bobby and our goalkeeper Tony Hawksworth, a decent performer who went on to make one First Division appearance before drifting out of the picture. I think you might say that Tony and I are keeping pretty impressive company in the Youth Cup record books.

I confess that by then, however, I was already aiming at loftier peaks, having made the quantum leap into first-team football. My promotion came out of the blue as a 17-year-old in October 1955, the day before United, handily placed in the First Division's leading group, were due to meet table-topping Wolves at Old Trafford. Having been groomed as Duncan's deputy, I was pressed into service when he went down with the 'flu on the Friday. It all happened in such a hurry that I didn't even have time to tell Mum and Dad before haring off to join the team, who were preparing at Blackpool. The first they heard of it was when a newspaperman tracked my mother down at the Blackley Institute schools canteen, where she was serving dinners. Her reaction, according to the report, was: 'How wonderful, but I wish it wasn't against Wolves. They are such a big side.' Typical Mum!

Galvanised by the news and wanting to share it with the neighbours – Dad would have been at work – she rushed home to find a hastily scribbled note from me on the table: 'I'm playing in the first team at Old Trafford tomorrow. Gone to Blackpool to join team. Wilf.' Next to that joyous message was that week's wage-packet, unopened.

Meanwhile, Matt Busby, Jimmy Murphy and the lads were doing their best to ensure I wouldn't be too nervous on the big day. I can't say they succeeded, though, and that's hardly surprising as I was due to stride out in front of nearly 50,000 people to face a crack side containing half a dozen England men, including the famous captain, Billy Wright. It was hardly calming, either, to reflect on my immediate opponent, one Peter Broadbent, a sublimely gifted inside-forward and one of the rising stars of the English game, who was destined to make his own international entrance before the decade was out.

Enter Jimmy Murphy, a motivator supreme and always my own personal inspiration. When he spotted me in the corner of the dressing room, eyes on the floor and shaking like a leaf, he took command instantly.

Briskly, he demanded of me: 'How did you get into the first team, Wilf?'

'By listening to you, Jimmy.'

'Well, listen to me today, son. I hate black and gold.'

'Jimmy, I hate black and gold, too, don't you worry!'

'Yes, but it's worse than you think, son,' he gritted in those familiarly passionate Welsh tones. 'The man you've got to mark is Peter Broadbent, and they say he'll play for England soon. He's out to take the win bonus out of your pocket, so you won't be able to go home tonight and treat your mum and dad!'

'Aaagh, give me that ball, Jimmy.'

By this time I was practically foaming at the mouth with eagerness to have a go at Broadbent. I couldn't wait to get on to that pitch. Now, it so happened that Peter was one of the nicest fellows you could wish to meet, an absolute gentleman, and having heard that a 17-year-old was about to make his debut against him, he did a typically decent thing. Just before the referee blew the first whistle, the Wolves man trotted up behind me, patted me on the back and said: 'All the best today, son.'

My gracious reply? 'Sod off, you thieving bastard.' He must have thought he was facing some rabid hooligan, and I must admit that I was so wound up by that nice Mr Murphy that I might have done something stupid there and then, which could only have resulted in my disgrace. I'm delighted to report that sanity prevailed, however, and I acquitted myself pretty reasonably against Broadbent and company in what turned out to be a pulsating 4-3 victory, with Tommy Taylor grabbing a late winner. At one point, though, I did have our supporters gasping when I tapped the ball wide of our 'keeper, Ray Wood. They thought I had nearly scored an own goal, but actually I knew exactly what I was doing and that was playing safe by conceding a corner.

One of our goals was scored by local lad John Doherty, an immensely skilful inside-forward whose career was ultimately ruined by knee trouble. Like me at that point, he was essentially a reserve who enjoyed occasional first-team outings and he was rather in the shadow of the Irishman, Billy Whelan, who had replaced him because of injury in an earlier Youth Cup Final. It was difficult for me to compare the two,

Heads in the clouds: Tommy Taylor (centre) and I on our way home from a European trip. That's Eddie Colman (left) and Mark Jones with their backs to the camera.

The Busby Babes certainly knew how to enjoy themselves. Left to right are Billy Whelan, myself, Tommy Taylor, Bobby Charlton and David Pegg, who seems intent on drowning out Tommy's saxophone solo.

because by then Billy was blossoming on the threshold of his prime and scoring freely while John was struggling with the pain in his knees and, although he could hit a ball beautifully, he was never a prolific marksman. Of the two, I'd have to say I'd have picked Billy for my team and that's not just because John and I argued, good-naturedly of course, for half a century or so. Tragically, our bantering but essentially close relationship was ended by his death in 2007.

John knew football instinctively and could talk a good game as well as play one, so he was always coming up with ideas. Often, even if I agreed with him, I would beg to differ, just for the hell of it, because I didn't want him to get the upper hand. We carried on sparring – someone had to stand up to him, for goodness sake! – and remained the best of friends until the end of his life.

NEW STAR—WILF McGUINNESS

Another Busby 'babe' shocked Sunderland

Sunderland 2, Manchester U. 2.   **By BRIAN WHITLEY**

PRACTICALLY every manager in English football must be wondering how Matt Busby manages to pick up wing half-backs the way he does. Yesterday Duncan Edwards was away playing for England and United brought out 18-year-old Wilf McGuinness, who is still qualified to captain their youth team.

McGuinness showed against Sunderland yesterday that he is a definite promise for the England "B" team a year hence.

Quick into the tackle, he put the ball where it was most wanted; if ever there was a piece of quick thinking shown in this Roker Park game it was when McGuinness scored the opening goal, and his first in top League football.

He fastened on to a rebound, and when he saw the Sunderland defence opened up to meet an expectant wing pass, McGuinness suddenly flashed down the middle and pushed the ball into the net past the advancing Fraser.

United's other goal, scored in the second half by Whelan when Sunderland were a goal in the lead, might have been obtained from an offside position, but Whelan took it coolly though Scottish international Willie Fraser made no sort of a shape to prevent.

A piece of bad luck which McGuinness experienced was that within a couple of minutes of scoring his first goal in his senior

But I digress. Back in October 1955 I was overjoyed at breaking through into the first team, especially as Duncan failed to recover for the next game, at Aston Villa, so I retained my place. But this time I experienced the other side of the coin. My job was to mark Johnny Dixon, the Villa captain, but when we walked into the dressing room at half-time we were 3-1 down, with Dixon having scored twice. Not surprisingly there were a few long faces among the lads, and I thought the skipper, Roger Byrne, and our normally cheerful centre-forward, Tommy Taylor, were staring rather meaningfully in my direction. Being the forthright type, I piped up immediately with: 'Don't blame me for those two goals, I was nowhere near him when he scored.' Roger just shot me a flinty glance and growled drily: 'Well, can you get a bit closer this half, son?' That put me firmly in my place, and I took the point with good grace, but privately I didn't think I was to blame. For both goals I had had to abandon Dixon to cover a team-mate, first Roger himself and then centre-half Mark Jones; but nobody covered for me and so we conceded. Whatever, I thought I had a reasonable game and we fought back to draw 4-4, which meant there had been 15 goals in my first two matches. Fantastically thrilling stuff for the fans, if rather nerve-wracking for the players, but that sort of entertainment was exactly what Manchester United were about.

Of course, there was no way I was going to keep Duncan out on merit, and he returned to hit peak form as United stormed to the First Division title, winning it by 11 points from Blackpool, a resounding vindication of Matt Busby's far-sighted youth policy. I did get one more look-in, being called up for the penultimate game at Sunderland because Duncan was on England duty at Hampden Park – it helped me no end that League games were not postponed because of international calls in the 1950s! It proved a landmark occasion for me at Roker Park because I scored my first senior goal in a 2-2 draw, and a cracker it was, a drilled daisy-cutter from the edge of the box. These days I recall that at one stage of my career I could boast a ratio of one goal to every three games, not bad for a wing-half, but then I have to spoil it by revealing that I had played only three games in total! Being scrupulously honest, too, I must point out that I did not finish the Sunderland match as a hero, exactly, having given away the penalty which enabled wing-half Stan Anderson to claim a point from the spot. Another enduring memory of the day was witnessing the wiles of the dribbling wizard Len Shackleton at first hand. Previously I had been captivated when I'd watched him mesmerise West Germany at Wembley, and now I was just grateful that the great man wasn't my direct opponent.

As the season ended I was feeling pretty pleased with life, being able to crow to Eddie and Bobby that I had made my debut before either of them, though it's possible that their need to do National Service might have had something to do with that. I avoided serving Queen and country because of a suspected mastoid in my ear, which actually came to nothing and was a bit of a ridiculous excuse really. Mark Jones' flat feet got him out of it, while both David Pegg and Albert Scanlon somehow slipped the conscription net, too. It was not down to any lack of patriotism but because none of us wanted to interrupt our careers. Had there been a war on the attitude would have been totally different.

Back on the football front, the United team that lifted the first of two consecutive titles was a truly special one, and my memories of the players, most of them close pals, will always remain precious to me. The captain was Roger Byrne, a natural leader of men. He played at left-back, where he oozed class, and such was his pace and skill that it was easy to recognise that he was a converted winger. When Roger died at Munich he was only 28, in his prime, and had been seen as the obvious long-term successor to England skipper Billy Wright, who wasn't far off retirement. Though he rejoiced in universal respect, Roger was a bit of a loner and a stern disciplinarian which was exactly what some of us needed, as we could be a bit daft and boisterous at times. Certainly he seemed quite fearsome to me as a young reserve. For instance, if you walked into the first-team dressing room without knocking he would order you out, then make you tap politely and wait to be asked back in. Good habit. Then there was the time when I inadvertently pinched his chair and he had no hesitation in pulling me up short. The players were relaxing in the garden of a hotel and Roger nipped away to get something. I hadn't seen him go, all I noticed was the empty chair, so I sat down on it. But when he came back he ordered me out of his seat in no uncertain manner. It was a bit rough on me really because there was no way I had intended to take a liberty, but I wasn't going to argue with the skipper. Looking back I can see that he was right to make sure the youngsters didn't get too cocky, and to make them realise they had a long way to go in the game.

During a lifetime in football, nobody taught me more than Jimmy Murphy. Quite simply, I loved the man.

Roger was older than everybody except Johnny Berry. He was married, and he was studying to be a physiotherapist when his playing days were over, so he had a more mature perspective on life than most of us. He was the first in our group to have a car, which impressed us deeply, but he wasn't in the habit of taking us for joy rides. You could have a joke with Roger but knew you couldn't overstep the mark and Matt Busby must have seen him as an ideal captain. He had authority and he exercised it firmly without ever losing his temper, at least in my experience. Ironically, in his own younger days he had been something of a hothead and there had been disciplinary problems which Matt had been forced to address, but that phase was long gone when I knew him.

Roger's full-back partner was Bill Foulkes, who offered a stark contrast in footballing style. Where the skipper was a smooth, cultured performer, Bill was a rough, raw operator with no pretensions to subtlety. When he was switched to centre-half, some time after surviving the air crash, he proved to be brilliant, filling the new role perfectly and going on to play more games for Manchester United than anyone else in the club's history except Bobby Charlton, and now Ryan Giggs. However, many people reckoned that, as a full-back in the 1950s, he represented the only outfield weakness. Foulkesy was as tough as granite and formidable in the air, which might have been helpful in the box but wasn't always that relevant when facing a winger on the touchline, where often he didn't appear to be the sharpest of movers. His critics couldn't understand why he retained the number-two shirt for so long when Roger, who was right-footed, could have switched sides with either Geoff Bent or Ian Greaves, both a little more comfortable on the ball than Bill, coming in on the left. In fact, Ian did earn a championship medal when he was selected on merit for a spell in the spring of 1956, admittedly at a time when Bill was under pressure through National Service commitments. One thing Foulkesy did have going for him was his utter ruthlessness, a quality which Matt must have wanted some-where in his side. Personally, I would never say Bill *was* a weak link, merely that sometimes he looked one in comparison to his classier colleagues.

Oddly, just as he was something of an outsider in football terms, so he was as part of the social group. I met him first as a young amateur training two nights a week at The Cliff, along with the likes of Bobby and Shay. He was a few years older and a first-teamer, keeping fit through our 'evening class' because he was still holding down a day-job in a coalmine. I think he looked on us as irresponsible little kids. Certainly if we were larking about, and we were from time to time, he would give us a cuff and tell us to get on with our job. Bill was a dedicated trainer, always ready to do that bit extra, a very hard man whom you crossed at your extreme peril. He was ultra-competitive and gave me the impression that he was going to make damned sure that we young whippersnappers weren't going to beat him and take his place. For instance, he was fantastic at head tennis in the small gym, and he was ready to come through the net *and* his opponent if that's what it took to reach the ball.

But as the life and soul of the party, it's fair to say that Bill lacked a little. He was a quiet man, some might say dour, and often it appeared that he liked being on his own. Later, when he married Teresa, he came out of his shell a little more and they mixed as a couple. She was lovely, elegant and charming, a real lady. I was one who always relished an innocent giggle with the girls, even after I married Beryl, so I used to wink at Teresa and she would smile back in a friendly way. Terrific fun.

The other member of that championship team who didn't attract universal acclaim was the goalkeeper, Ray Wood, who was a fabulously athletic shot-stopper with lightning feet, as befitted a man who had once made money as a sprinter, but who was unreliable at claiming crosses. He was very fit and lean, but maybe he didn't have the beef to withstand some of the heavy challenges which were legal in those days. As a character, though, Ray was a charmer, a natural mixer who particularly loved a game of cards.

I have already waxed lyrical about our wing-halves, Eddie Colman and Duncan Edwards, though I should point out that Jeff Whitefoot also collected a gong for his 15 appearances early in the campaign before being ousted by Eddie. As a young fan I had watched Jeff's debut as a 16-year-old at home to Portsmouth in 1950. He was a lovely footballer, an accurate crossfield passer, and he appeared to have a golden future at Old Trafford. But then along came two exceptional rivals and in the end he was allowed to leave, eventually enjoying a tremendous career with Nottingham Forest, whom he helped to lift the FA Cup in 1959.

It's a sobering thought that of the 13 men in this picture, I am the only one left alive. Left to right are Dennis Viollet, Tommy Taylor, David Pegg, trainer Tom Curry, myself, Roger Byrne, manager Matt Busby, Ray Wood, Liam Whelan, Duncan Edwards, Mark Jones, Geoff Bent and Johnny Berry.

Lining up at Villa Park for only my second League match as a 17-year-old in October 1955. The game finished 4-4 and I thought I did okay. Left to right, back row: Jeff Whitefoot, Bill Foulkes, Ray Wood, Mark Jones, Jackie Blanchflower, myself. Front: Johnny Berry, Colin Webster, Roger Byrne, Tommy Taylor, David Pegg.

Ever-present at centre-half in 1955/56 was Mark Jones, a towering, muscular stopper along the lines of his predecessor, Allenby Chilton. He had buckets of detemination and, had he not perished at Munich, he must have had a terrific future in the game. I'm convinced he would have gone on to win England caps, and he might even have kept Jack Charlton out of the 1966 World Cup line-up. Mark was only 24 when he died, so he wasn't that much older than us but it seemed as if he was because he was married. He lived the life of a family man, kept an aviary in his back garden and loved the country pursuits of his native Yorkshire, whereas most of us were out on the town every chance we got. There were times when he was a genial father figure, gently keeping us in line, but he was never bossy. I don't believe I've ever met a nicer man than big Mark.

As for the forwards, the variety of talents and the way they blended together was simply sumptuous. That term there were four regulars in attack – centre-forward Tommy Taylor, his co-marksman Dennis Viollet and wingers Johnny Berry and David Pegg. Responsibility for the second inside-forward position was split between Jackie Blanchflower (18 games), John Doherty (16) and the emerging Billy Whelan (13), while there was more than useful back-up in another outside-left, the young flier Albert Scanlon, plus utility attacker Colin Webster and reserve striker Eddie Lewis.

The most eye-catching of the bunch was big, handsome, fun-loving Tommy Taylor, the free-scoring spearhead. For all his achievement of unseating Bolton's Nat Lofthouse as England centre-forward and accumulating an amazing 16 goals in 19 appearances, he tended to be criminally underrated as a footballer. Tommy's team-mates knew how marvellous he was, but a lot of fans seemed to think he was only good in the air. Rubbish! He led the line better than anyone else I've seen, before or since. Tommy read the game majestically and he had the physique to capitalise on that attribute, constantly roaming to the flanks to open up space for Viollet, Whelan and, from the following season, Bobby Charlton. The big fella's movement was fantastic, extremely unusual in an era in which centre-forwards were either bulky, straight-forward bustlers or more skilful types who could turn cleverly. He was unique in that he would spend loads of time and energy foraging near the touchlines, yet always seemed to be in the box causing mayhem with his trademark headers. Tom would sprint 30 yards on an unselfish dummy run which often panicked opposing defenders, who knew if they chased him they would leave space for Viollet and company, but if they left him he could receive the ball, cut in and destroy them himself. I found it so frustrating that he would get through so much work which benefited the team, yet many fans didn't appreciate the scale of his contribution. They would moan constantly about his lack of control – which wasn't true, incidentally, he had brilliant feet – and seemed to overlook an astonishing tally of 131 strikes in 191 games.

For me Tommy Taylor was England's best centre-forward by a country mile, and it was a travesty that our international selectors didn't pick Dennis Viollet alongside him. Ridiculously, Dennis didn't win a cap until after Munich, yet he was a true thoroughbred at a time when his country desperately needed a classy partner for Tommy. Playing with Dennis was like working with a magnet. You might overhit a pass which seemed to be well out of his reach, yet somehow he'd pull it out of the air. His touch was fabulous and as a finisher he was out of this world, the original sniffer out of half-chances. Tommy and Dennis read each other's game to perfection; as a pair they were peerless. They were both great lads, too, at the heart of our social activities, Taylor the endearingly happy-go-lucky Yorkshireman, Viollet the more subtly charming Mancunian with a bit of a reputation as a ladies' man.

Another player of sublime quality, but contrastingly reserved as a character, was the popular Dubliner Billy Whelan, or Liam as they tended to call him back home in Ireland. Not enough is said about Billy because he was such a quiet person, a very religious boy, not that it stopped him mixing. We could curse and tell risque jokes in front of him, in fact he had a tremendous sense of humour, so nobody could have accused him of being holier-than-thou. Only if he thought things were going a little too far would he step in, saying in his gentle brogue something like: 'Come on, lads. Do you really think that's necessary?' Ironically, though a swear-word would never pass his lips, the one time in his career he was cautioned by a referee it was for abusive language, which we all thought was hilarious. Actually, all he said was 'damn', which just goes to show how standards have changed.

Though naturally unassuming, Billy could be immensely determined, and I think as a fellow Catholic he was a little concerned about my moral welfare – not that I was running wild, you understand, just enjoying life as most young men do! Once, in an attempt to keep me on the straight and narrow, maybe fearing for my soul, he introduced me to Father Mulholland, the parish priest of St Bernard's, Burnage. I have no idea what Billy had passed on about me, but right after saying 'hello' the priest said: 'Let's go for a walk in the garden and I'll hear your confession.' I was taken aback, and said I didn't think that would be necessary. I had nothing against confession as such, but not face to face with somebody I'd just met! For all that, it was an apt illustration of Billy's deeply caring nature.

As a footballer he had the potential to become an all-time great for Ireland, maybe even one of the best in the world. During his all-too-brief career at Old Trafford, he knocked in 52 goals in 98 games – without ever being an out-and-out front-man. That's absolutely phenomenal. Billy was a big, raw-boned lad, a bit rangy and gangly, but he could dribble and he could turn on a sixpence. He wasn't the quickest, but there were plenty of others in the team who supplied pace. When Billy had the ball at his feet he didn't need pace. With the skill he had in his locker he would beat opponents almost any way he chose, sending markers the wrong way with the merest sway of his body. There wasn't an ounce of nastiness about him but he held his own physically, and if anybody bumped into Billy then, believe me, they got hurt.

His most famous goal came in a quagmire of slush and mud in Bilbao in January 1957, when he drifted past three tackles and thrashed the ball into the net from 15 yards. We were 5-2 down at the time and that pulled it back to set up an unforgettable recovery in the second leg. At the time of the air crash he'd lost his place to Bobby Charlton – not a bad replacement – but I'm certain that if he had lived he would have been vying for selection with Bobby and Dennis. Certainly on his day Billy was good enough to command a place in any side, and perhaps Matt might have solved the problem by picking Bobby on the wing, where he had a spell later anyway.

Another quiet man was the team's only southerner Johnny Berry, our right winger and the oldest man in the side by nearly three years. The Babes, in general, were a group of fancy-free singles making hay while the sun shone, but Johnny was married and with a sensible, serious nature. On one level it can't have been easy for him to be surrounded by immature kids, but on another it might have made him feel young. Certainly that's how it's worked for me at various clubs down the years, though some people would say that's because I've never grown up!

Whatever his thoughts about the social side, there was never any doubt that Johnny was one hell of a footballer. He was only small, but a tough nut for a winger and if defenders kicked him he would never lie down, he'd get up and give some back. Darting all over the place at high speed and refusing to take any nonsense, he must have been an absolute pain to mark, but he was a joy to have in your team. I looked up to him not only because of his ability and experience, but also for his willingness to pass it on to rookies like me. Before one game at White Hart Lane in which I was due to play at left-half, he said to me: 'Wilf, if you're ever struggling to find someone within 30 yards of their goal, then just gamble and clip the ball to the far post. I'll be there, just remember that. Sure enough, in the game the ball came to me from Duncan, and Johnny's words were in my mind. So without even looking I lifted it over their defence and he sprinted in, just as he had promised, and whacked the ball into the net. We drew 2-2 and afterwards the reporters were raving about my 'vision', talking me up as an England prospect. Yet I knew that it was Johnny who had made me look good by telling me what to do. My part on this occasion had been little more than having the sense to listen.

On the left flank in 1955/56 was another of my close mates, the easy-going young Yorkshireman David Pegg, seen as something of a dream-boat by the girls with his big eyes and matinee-idol smile. However, by 1957 it was a toss-up between David and Albert Scanlon, another Mancunian, for the number-11 shirt. Both lads were tremendous fun, but their personalities contrasted as sharply as their styles of play. Where David was so laid back, Albert was always chattering, a streetwise character, always the fellow with the latest news and gossip. In fact, he was nicknamed Joe Friday after the detective in the TV series *Dragnet,* because he always knew what was going on. Once as we came off the field at half-time, he announced the winner of the 3.30 at Wincanton. We asked him how he could possibly know that and he said he'd been chatting with fans near his touchline – and that was during a First Division game! Typical Albert.

Who says training can't be fun? That laughing cavalier of a footballer Tommy Taylor leads the way, followed by David Pegg, Dennis Viollet and myself, with Duncan Edwards at the head of the next column.

Cool dudes: Billy Whelan (left), myself and Tommy Taylor on the way home from a European trip in matching headgear, which had been presented free to the whole party.

As players, too, they were chalk and cheese. Albert had pace to burn and he specialised in sprinting to the byline, then hitting the ball across so hard that it would practically knock you out if you got your head on it. David was neither as quick nor as direct, but he had beautiful, fluid skill, being adept at retaining the ball and mesmerising full-backs with his dazzling shimmies. The first time United played Real Madrid in the Bernabeu he ran his full-back so dizzy that, despite winning 3-1, the Spaniards bought a new defender in time for the Old Trafford leg, especially to counter him. David would listen avidly to Jimmy Murphy, soaking up advice about making a yard of space to get in early centres to Tommy Taylor, who was magnificent in the air. In turn that would get the centre-half shouting at the full-back, who would dive in unwisely, thus giving David further chance to work his wiles. Peggy soaked it all up, thinking deeply about the game. Albert, meanwhile, would more than likely be nodding his head to keep Jimmy happy but, in reality, paying precious little attention. He relied on his instincts, and they took him a long way.

In the lead-up to Munich, Albert had claimed the left-wing berth on merit, which makes me ponder which of them might have prevailed in the long term had Pegg not perished so tragically. Based on the fact that David had already been capped by England, and remembering that Albert did not kick on as expected in the early 1960s, I have to plump for the Yorkshireman. Then again, Munich left psychological scars on Albert which might have had a profound effect on his progress, so maybe it's fairer not to offer a judgement. I'd rather just say that if the accident hadn't happened, Matt Busby would have had two scintillating left wingers from which to choose.

Also prominent in the championship squad of 1955/56 was Jackie Blanchflower, who played nearly all his games that season at inside-right, but who went on later to rival Mark Jones for the centre-half slot. Jackie wasn't particularly quick – in fact, he was downright slow! – but his touch and reading of the game were exceedingly fine, and I think he would have excelled in most positions. In fact, he even did well when pressed into action as an emergency goakeeper when Ray Wood was injured in nthe 1957 FA Cup Final.

Like his equally eloquent brother Danny, such a superb captain of Spurs when they won the League and FA Cup double in 1961, Jackie was witty, intelligent and superb company. Like so many Irishmen he was a charmer who could talk the socks off all-comers and it didn't surprise me when he became a wonderful after-dinner speaker later in life. A dark, handsome guy whose wife, Jean, was a nightclub singer, he was a little older than me and always seemed an impossibly glamorous figure. Jackie survived Munich but with horrible injuries which prevented him from playing again.

He was another who was out of the team at the time of the accident, Mark Jones having fought back to reclaim his berth, and there has always been lively debate about which of the pair would have been United's centre-half in the long term. Mark was an iron man, a reliable old-fashioned stopper, while Jackie was easier on the ball in a similar fashion to Bobby Moore, far more of an all-rounder. In the end, possibly, the Irishman might have been a victim of his own versatility, as I think Matt might have opted for the specialist in such a key position. For the most horrific of reasons, that was one verdict which was never to be delivered.

Among other squad members in my debut campaign was the spiky little Welshman Colin Webster, a rumbustious attacker who could hold his own when Tommy or Dennis were absent, but who lacked their class. He could be very aggressive in both word and deed, and defenders did not enjoy facing him. Then there was Eddie Lewis, another stocky, powerful centre-forward who taught me a lot by his readiness to go that extra yard in training. Sometimes he'd ask me to join him after the others had finished, which I was happy to do and we became friends, though he was always a little on the serious side. Eddie managed 11 goals in 24 games as a Red Devil, so he knew where the net was, but it's fair to say he was never going to threaten Messrs Taylor or Viollet for their places. Later he amazed me by playing in the First Division as a full-back with Leyton Orient; I could never have imagined Eddie as anything but a striker.

When the appearances were totalled at the end of 1955/56 I had made three, which meant I didn't even come close to qualifying for a championship medal. But I was only 18, and I had made a start in a very fine side. Now I was determined that the next time the gongs were handed out at Old Trafford, one would be heading in my direction.

Chapter 6
THE FUTURE LOOKED
SO BRIGHT...

FOR MANCHESTER UNITED, and for Wilf McGuinness, I could not imagine a more optimistic scenario than the one which beckoned at the outset of the 1956/57 campaign. Still well short of my 19th birthday, I was living and working in my home-town, part of a vibrant, breathtakingly talented young squad, being guided by the best management and coaching set-up in the business. The Busby Babes were the reigning English champions, about to set off on their great European adventure and ready for a realistic tilt at becoming the first club in the 20th century to lift the coveted domestic double of League and FA Cup. Though I was only on the fringe of the first team I was confident that my future lay at Old Trafford, feeling bolstered by the fact that I had played for England at various levels for the last five years. On top of all that, I had met Beryl, the girl who was going to become Mrs McGuinness. How could life have been better?

The prospect of continental competition was particularly momentous. When the European Cup was launched in 1955, the hidebound English football authorities forbade their champions, Chelsea, to enter, and that short-sighted edict was obeyed by the Stamford Bridge club. However, Manchester United were made of sterner stuff. Matt Busby believed that facing the best that Europe had to offer was the way forward and the message coming out of Old Trafford amounted to: 'Do with us what you will, but we're going in.' We were told that if our travels interfered with our League commitments we would be punished severely. That was a naked threat, but United weren't intimidated. The feeling was that often the hierarchy favoured other clubs over us anyway, so now we would go our own way.

The players felt enormous pride that Matt had stood his ground so courageously and incredible excitement at becoming the British pioneers in the glamorous world of the foreign game. It represented a gigantic step into the unknown, and I suppose we were running a risk of getting egg on our faces if we had fared indifferently. But we got off to a flier, beating the well-respected Belgian side, Anderlecht, 12-0 on aggregate, a result which sent shock waves around Europe. Being Duncan's deputy, I wasn't in the side, but it was a privilege to be among the 40,000 onlookers as we put ten past our shell-shocked visitors in the second leg at Maine Road, which was being used as the Old Trafford floodlights were not yet installed.

NOW GIVE THESE BUSBY BABES A HANDICAP

By BILL FRYER

Manchester U. 4, Charlton A. 2   RATING ★★★★

IT'S no use. We'll have to make this League championship a handicap... United scratch, the rest six points start. At least it would make a race of it.

Take this little affair, for instance. Athletic were really athletic . . . nothing like a bottom-rung outfit. They had a goal start. They were playing against a team with four changes, including three reserves, of whom one hadn't played in the big boys' league before and whose ankle was still a bit wonky.

And Athletic had one of the most dangerous, skilful and enthusiastic chunks of footballer —name of Jimmy Gauld—to be found North, South, East or West of Old Trafford.

Yet they never looked to have an earthly chance.

United, indeed, gave weight to my idea of two weeks ago, that 10 Busby boys and one other would win the World Cup, let alone beat the humble Irish.

It is approach, fitness and skill that wins matches. And the greatest of these is approach. United have it. United reserves have it. And so have United A. B. and what have you.

Bobby Charlton started as if the ball was a grenade in disguise and got rid quickly—too quickly. Then, with a most Colman-like look, he played his own game, beat two men and scored a beauty . . just like an old man of 24. Then he scored again. His ankle plagued him later,

but he did enough to put himself in the £10,000 class at one go. That's if United would sell him. They won't.

Stand-in No. 2 — Wilf McGuinness, like Bobby, aged 18. It is almost incredible that the mighty Duncan Edwards could be replaced by such a going-to-be-mighty boy as Wilf who, like Jimmy Gauld, should be paid time and a-half for overtime.

Stand-in Geoff Bent: Roger Byrne has constantly to be in England class to keep Geoff out . . Bent, the classy kicker who showed he has a full ration of United impudence.

Billy Foulkes played better than when he was an England man . . so did Ray Wood . . . Eddie Colman was Eddie Colman (nuff said) . . . Mark Jones should follow Billy Wright . . . Johnny Berry and David Pegg are as good as any wingers . . . Viollet (below form here) is as good as any other.

This United England must come. Let's have a team for a change.

Misses

Berry scored United's first, and Whelan the last, and United missed a stack of others.

Fred Lucas gave Charlton the lead that brought United to their senses, and Bobby Ayres hit the best of the match—an old-fashioned volley — to make the score 3—2.

And if Charlton had scored six they'd have lost. That's United. They go just as hard as they have to.

We began dominantly in the League, too, storming to the top of the table with a 12-match unbeaten run which included my first outing of the season, at home to Charlton Athletic in early October when Duncan was engaged on England business. We won 4-2 on what proved a red-letter day for English football, as it marked the senior debut of my pal

Bobby Charlton. Most people didn't realise that going into the game he was carrying an ankle problem, but there was no way Bobby was going to pass up such an opportunity, and he made the most of it by hitting the target with two typical thunderbolts. Throughout his career he avoided major injury, which was partly due to good fortune but also due in no small measure to his natural athleticism, enabling him to jump out of the way when necessary. He glided smoothly past the most ferocious of tackles, all style and class; Bobby was exactly what most people wanted their football to look like.

McGUINNESS—LITTLE MAN IN GIANT ROLE

Manchester United .... 3 **Leeds United** 2

EIGHTEEN-YEAR-OLD Wilf McGuinness, stand-in for the injured Duncan Edwards, was Manchester United's " David " to Leeds Uniteds' " Goliath," John Charles, and he stuck to the Welsh international like a leech. Wherever John went there was his little " shadow," worrying and tackling with such effect that it was largely due to McGuinness's efforts that Manchester United won.

My next appearance, about six weeks later at home to Leeds, was particularly memorable for me because my immediate opponent was the great John Charles – and I use the word 'great' advisedly, because there is no shortage of shrewd judges who reckon that when he was in his pomp he was the finest footballer in the world. He could play anywhere, it was part of his greatness; you might even say he was the Welsh Duncan Edwards. Usually Big John would be at centre-half or centre-forward, but on the day we met he was at inside-forward and it was my job to snuff him out of the game. That wasn't the easiest of assignments, considerations of class aside, because he was about a foot taller than me although, with all due modesty, I wasn't bad in the air for my size. At the very least, I was confident of making it difficult for any opponent to reach the ball cleanly, so I jumped with John – possibly the finest header of a ball the game has seen – and I think I got a few.

I won a few full-blooded tackles against him, too, and I can still hear the crowd roaring its appreciation, which gave me the most tremendous feeling of elation. In those days you could challenge from behind and I must admit that sometimes I was late. I must have hurt him once or twice, but never did he utter a bad word in my direction. Instead he would haul himself painfully to his feet, pat me on the back and say:

'Well done, boyo.' I could hardly believe such fantastic sportsmanship. So many of my opponents would be swearing and elbowing and pulling, but John Charles proved to be a complete gentleman. It was a privilege to be on the same field as him. I had an absolute blinder that day and we won 3-2, thanks to two goals from Billy Whelan and one from Bobby. Years later, not long before he died, I was in John's company and I never stopped thanking him for the way he treated me that afternoon nearly half a century earlier.

Of course, Jimmy Murphy, who doubled as the Welsh manager, knew all about John, and he just told me to do my duty. There was no special advice of the type he handed out to his inside-right Reg Davies when Wales were due to face England. Before that game Jimmy went through all the strengths and weaknesses of the England side, but without mentioning Duncan, until little Reg piped up with: 'How shall I play Edwards? What shall I do?' The Murphy reply was succinct: 'Just keep out of his bloody way, son!' Nothing could have better summed up the ethos of both Jimmy and Duncan.

Four days later, buoyed immeasurably by my success against John Charles, I was given my first taste of European action in Dortmund when, with Dennis Viollet injured, the Boss opted to stiffen the sinews of our forward line by deploying Duncan at inside-left, thus creating a vacancy for me at left-half. This was in the wake of the Germans' spirited fightback from three goals down to 3-2 in the first leg at Maine Road, and from their ferocious opening salvos on a frozen pitch at the Rota Erda Stadium it was evident that we were going to have our work cut out in preserving the lead. With our backs to the wall, and the ball bouncing uncontrollably on the icy surface, it wasn't a pretty game. But I relished contests like that and I got stuck in with all my might, giving a particular clattering to one of their internationals, name of Preissler, who had scored in the first leg and wore a hairnet. All the more reason to give him a kick, some might say! Borussia poured forward relentlessly and we were pushed much deeper than we intended, but although we could barely mount a meaningful attack, we defended stoutly, holding out for a goalless draw. Much of the credit for that went to Ray Wood, who played the game of his life, making a succession of point-blank saves which must have driven the Germans close to distraction.

A friendly rival: Jack Charlton of Leeds (second left) welcomes a Manchester United contingent to Elland Road ahead of our First Division encounter in March 1957. The visitors (left to right) are myself, Jack's brother Bobby, Ray Wood and Duncan Edwards.

In safe keeping: Tony Hawksworth takes the ball into custody during an FA Youth Cup encounter with Bexleyheath, Charlton Athletic's junior side, at Old Trafford. That's me on the right with team-mate Reg Holland looking on.

Enjoying themselves at Manchester's Midland Hotel after a European tie, never dreaming what lay ahead: Jimmy Murphy (at back) and journalist George Follows with (left to right) Mrs Follows, my mother and Cissie Charlton, Bobby's mum. Poor George was destined to die at Munich.

Bill Foulkes (foreground) seems to be cleaning up at cards as the Babes relax on their way home from a European tie against Dukla in Prague in December 1957. Their next trip abroad would end in catastrophe. Also pictured in the foreground (left to right) are Roger Byrne, Albert Scanlon, myself looking half asleep, Duncan Edwards, Colin Webster and Eddie Colman. At the back are Freddie Goodwin, Mark Jones (with pipe) Billy Whelan, David Pegg and Tommy Taylor.

I was satisfied with my display, and Matt must have been, too, because I kept my place for the next game, at Tottenham. This time we went two down but recovered to draw, thanks to that sage advice from Johnny Berry which inspired me to set up his strike and Eddie tucking away what was to prove his only League goal about two minutes from time. The build-up down our left-hand side was sweetly precise, with Duncan and David Pegg exchanging passes beautifully. Afterwards some of the more imaginative newspapermen were calling for Eddie and myself to be drafted into the England squad, but all too soon I was back in United's reserves, making just the occasional appearance during the remainder of the winter as United consolidated their status as runaway League leaders.

In March I was in the team at Goodison, where the manager had opted to rest six regulars, but we won anyway, courtesy of a brace from Colin Webster which emphasised the depth of our squad, and I played at home to Villa three days later, when Duncan was used at centre-forward. Despite being similar to John Charles in some ways, Dunc was not such a smooth and subtle mover as the Welshman, rather he resembled the combination of power, pace and control which we are now privileged to witness in the shape of Wayne Rooney. And believe me, when I make that comparison I could not be paying Wayne a grander compliment.

It was not until the end of that month, and my 14th first-team outing, that I was on the losing side, when we lost 2-0 to Bolton in front of 60,000 supporters, with countless more locked out. That vast multitude had gathered on the occasion of Old Trafford's first floodlit encounter, and it was a chronic disappointment to be beaten when we were so keen to put on a gala performance. Truth be told, Nat Lofthouse and company knocked us about a bit that night, and I had a right old tussle with Dennis Stevens, their inside-right and a cousin of Duncan's. I thought he was a vastly underrated player, a dynamic non-stop worker who scored his share of goals, and always made his opponents earn their money. Later he joined Everton, dropping back into midfield and winning a title medal in 1963.

Bolton never needed any extra encouragement to pull out all the stops against United, and I got the impression they gloried in putting one over on their local rivals on such a big night. We were all decked out in special red satin shirts and shorts, which had a sheen and which it was believed would show up more vividly under the lights. Inevitably, having suffered an unexpected defeat, we decided that we didn't approve of the satin, a fascinating parallel with Alex Ferguson's reaction to the grey shirts in which United lost to Southampton in 1996. There's nothing new under the sun!

My next opportunity cropped up in early April when Duncan was playing (and scoring) against Scotland and United were entertaining Spurs, one of the few teams who retained even the remotest chance of overhauling us in the title race. Down the years we had some pulsating clashes with the north Londoners, and this was no exception, despite turning out to goalless. I loved to get in some crunching tackles on Bobby Smith, a tough customer but also more skilful than many people realised, being capable of stunning unwary opponents with unexpected moments of delicacy, but he was missing on this occasion so I turned my attention to little Tommy Harmer, a complete contrast. 'Harmer the Charmer' was a ball-juggling wizard, one of the cleverest I've seen, but I enjoyed jousting with his type because they always gave you a chance.

At this point United were in an enviable position, well clear in the First Division, through to the FA Cup Final and drawn to face Real Madrid in the semi-final of the European Cup. People were talking freely of the treble, never mind the double, and duly we coasted over the line as League champions by eight points. I loved that, particularly as I played in the last three matches of the campaign, against Burnley, Cardiff and West Bromwich Albion as, with a second successive title already in the bag, Matt took the chance to rest a few of his regulars ahead of the Wembley date with Aston Villa. That took my total of First Division appearances for the season to 13, which was enough to earn me a precious medal. But things didn't quite work out on the other two fronts and, although I didn't play in any of the remaining knockout games, I was desperately disappointed.

We travelled to Madrid for the first leg of the European Cup semi-final, and the Bernabeu was awesomely impressive with facilities which footballers of that era didn't dream of. For instance, there was a luxurious swimming pool, a capacious trophy room and even a chapel, which amazed me but also made me understand how thorough Real were in catering for their players' every conceivable need. There were no

The Three Musketeers: Eddie Colman, myself (with trendy little beard) and Billy Whelan heading home from Prague. The sight of that snow on the tarmac seems distinctly eerie now.

Lining up with the 1956/57 League championship trophy and the Charity Shield. Back row, left to right: Eddie Colman, myself, Colin Webster, Ray Wood, David Pegg, Dennis Viollet, Johnny Berry. Middle row: trainer Tom Curry, Jackie Blanchflower, Tommy Taylor, Freddie Goodwin, Mark Jones, Duncan Edwards, Billy Whelan, Bill Foulkes, manager Matt Busby. Front row: Secretary Walter Crickmer, director George Whittaker, chairman Harold Hardman, captain Roger Byrne, director Bill Petherbridge, director Alan Gibson.

This is how I see it, Alfredo ….for some reason Senor di Stefano, one of the greatest footballers the game has ever known, seems a tad sceptical at the latest pearl of wisdom to drop from the McGuinness lips.

I'm happy to listen as that most eloquent of speakers Danny Blanchflower (left), the captain of Spurs and Northern Ireland, holds forth to Duncan Edwards and myself.

substitutes in those days so the reserves did not sit on the bench but were dispatched to the stands, where we joined the rest of the 135,000 crowd in that vast open bowl – I suppose they didn't really need a roof in that climate.

As for the football, we lost 3-1 but I thought we were a trifle unlucky. True, they were a sensationally talented team which had lifted the inaugural European Cup a year earlier, and boasted wonderful players such as Alfredo di Stefano, Raymond Kopa and Francisco Gento. But they weren't all about beautiful football, as I was somewhat shocked to discover when di Stefano deliberately kicked Jackie Blanchflower off the ball. Oh, they could be nasty at need, and Tommy Taylor took some terrible physical stick from their abrasive centre-half, Jose Santamaria. We held them to 0-0 at half-time, but then we conceded a couple before Tommy pulled it back to 2-1. I feel their final goal flattered them and I'd say we were not helped by the refereeing, which was distinctly dubious. Back in Manchester, where the newly illuminated Old Trafford hosted its first European contest, we had planned to attack them from the off, but we were a little naïve and they caught us hopping twice in the first half an hour. Both times they sliced us apart with slick one-two passing interchanges, which left us 5-1 down on aggregate at half-time. After the interval, though, we showed what we were made of, hitting back with strikes from Tommy and Bobby to claim a draw on the night and lay down a marker for the future. As I made my way home I felt three overriding emotions: disappointment that we had been knocked out, pride at our courageous comeback and, the strongest of all, complete confidence that Manchester United would go on to supplant the Spaniards as the continent's top team. I know they went on to lift the trophy five times on the belt, but I don't believe they'd have done that if the Munich disaster had never happened. Real Madrid were both sublimely gifted and staggeringly well organised, but their players were ageing, while the Busby Babes had not reached anything like the peak of their limitless potential. So I wasn't downhearted. The best, I felt certain, was still to come.

Still, any defeat brings inevitable frustration, and we were still smarting from it when we were hit by what I felt was a much more infuriating setback. No club since Aston Villa in 1897 had managed to become League champions and lift the FA Cup in the same season.

Whenever a team had seemed on the verge of it, something had gone wrong at the last moment and the prize had slipped away. Even the mighty Arsenal of the 1930s, replete with the likes of Alex James, Cliff Bastin and Ted Drake, had not done it and the legend grew up that the double was unattainable, that it was protected by some mysterious hoodoo. Well, we had just won the title by a street and, with all due respect to our Wembley opponents, ironically Aston Villa, there seemed little likelihood that we would falter at the last hurdle. We weren't over-confident – Matt Busby would never have allowed that – but we knew we were the best team, simple as that.

However, a mere six minutes into the action, our dreams were in tatters as the result of a grave injustice. Ray Wood caught an easy header from Peter McParland, Villa's Irish winger, who then charged wildly at our 'keeper and there was an almighty clash of heads. They both went down but while McParland soon climbed to his feet, poor Ray was motionless with blood trickling down his face. He had to be stretchered off – later it was discovered he had a fractured cheekbone – and, with no substitutes allowed, centre-half Jackie Blanchflower took over between the posts. That left us with ten men for the rest of the game, apart from a brief period towards the end when Ray returned as nuisance value on the wing, so it's hardly surprising that we lost 2-1.

I was at the match, watching with Beryl, and I could hardly believe my eyes when McParland hurled himself at Woodie. It was utterly diabolical. It might be said that Ray might have been a bit quicker getting out of his way, but that doesn't alter the fact that McParland had perpetrated a reckless attack. Today he would be sent off, but in those days people got away with much more. The Villa man was lucky that none of the United boys sought instant retribution – clearly it crossed Duncan's mind before he thought better of it – but somehow they held themselves in check. What really twisted the knife was that McParland went on to score the two goals which took the cup.

I don't have the slightest doubt that United would have won with a full team, but that's sport, that's life. You have to accept what fate throws at you, no matter how heart-breaking it seems at the time. Matt Busby remained calm, setting a marvellous example, but it was a very sombre do that evening at a big London hotel. I don't mind admitting I was in tears at the thought of such a golden opportunity of making history slipping away in such a cruel fashion. Of course, it wouldn't be long before that mere sporting disappointment would be placed into proper perspective by the starkest of real, life-destroying tragedies, after which Manchester United would never be the same again.

Yet as 1957/58 kicked off, Old Trafford was enveloped once more in an atmosphere of heady optimism. Given an even break, there seemed no summit too lofty to scale and we started off at a gallop, taking 11 points from our first six games (this was the era of two points for a win, of course), scoring 22 goals in the process. But then an astonishing four-goal reverse at Burnden Park heralded a spell of inconsistency, during which I made my first appearance that term, out of position at left-back in a 3-1 defeat at Wolves. Matt had been forced to shuffle his pack because of a 'flu epidemic, but I think he made a mistake in giving me the number-three shirt. With the benefit of hindsight, I'd have played Duncan at left-back – he could excel anywhere – with me at left-half. As it was I didn't have the best of days. I remember trying to let a ball run out but their feisty little winger Norman Deeley managed to keep in it and they scored from his cross. At least that proves I recall my bad moments as well as my good ones! Our only goal at Molineux came from John Doherty, but it was to prove his last for the club as pretty soon afterwards he was sold to Leicester following a difference of opinion with the manager. Nobody won arguments with Matt Busby.

I wasn't getting many first-team games, but I remained optimistic, both that the team could recover to catch League leaders Wolves and that my personal future continued to lie at Old Trafford. I was back at left-half for a 4-1 home win over Villa and for a dismal 3-0 home drubbing by Portsmouth, in which Peter Jones made his only senior appearance for United as a deputy for Roger Byrne at left-back, .

As autumn drew on and results continuing to be variable, the Boss acted decisively with Jackie Blanchflower, Johnny Berry, Billy Whelan and David Pegg making way for Mark Jones, 18-year-old right winger Kenny Morgans, Bobby Charlton and Albert Scanlon. In addition, in December there was the little matter of breaking the world transfer record for a goalkeeper, bringing in the Northern Ireland international Harry Gregg from Doncaster Rovers for £23,500. That was a significant move, not only because Harry was a bold and magnificent performer destined to stamp his fiery personality indelibly on the history of the club, but also because he was the first major purchase since Tommy Taylor arrived from Barnsley nearly five years earlier. That was a measure of the belief Matt Busby maintained in his exceptional crop of home-grown players.

Those radical changes paid an immediate dividend as the revitalised side embarked on an exhilarating unbeaten run which would not end for more than two months, by which time mere footballing matters would be subsumed utterly by the calamity that lay in wait in snowy Bavaria. During this all-too-brief period of grace, United served up some devastating stuff, notably beating Bolton 7-2 at Old Trafford and Arsenal 5-4 at Highbury on the day before we flew out to Belgrade to meet Red Star in the second leg of a European Cup quarter-final.

I wasn't on that fateful trip, but I came perilously close to making it. On the Friday before the team left for London to face Arsenal I was told I would be going to Belgrade the following Monday, so I handed in my passport to the club in readiness. But on the Saturday I played for the reserves against Wolves and I twisted my knee, which locked, and I was carried off. The next morning physiotherapist Ted Dalton had me on the treatment table, and I was diagnosed with a torn cartilage, which meant I could forget all about Yugoslavia and would be out of action for the foreseeable future. At that time cartilage operations were a bit of a worry. There was no keyhole surgery so they had to open the knee, which often led to arthritis later in life, a painful fact for which I can vouch today. At the time, though, that wasn't my primary concern. What upset me, left me feeling inconsolably low as United set off for eastern Europe in winter weather, was not being able to climb up those aircraft steps with my team-mates . . .

Chapter 7
CATASTROPHE

AS I LIMPED along Piccadilly with my pal Joe Witherington on a typically dank, grey late afternoon in early February, my state of mind veered crazily between heady jubilation and sombre anxiety. I was overjoyed that United had reached the semi-finals of the European Cup thanks to a nerve-jangling 3-3 draw with Red Star in Belgrade the previous night, but I was chronically apprehensive about the knee injury which had prevented me from travelling with my mates. At that moment I had no way of knowing that the minor commotion around the newspaper-seller a little further along the Princess Street pavement was the prelude to stark, undiluted misery; and that this was about to become the most traumatic day of my life.

Joe, a sales rep with the *News Chronicle* and a close friend and neighbour of the McGuinness family, had done me a big favour by ferrying me to see an orthopaedic specialist in central Manchester, a Mr Poston, who had examined my ravaged joint and confirmed the fear that I would need a cartilage operation. After the appointment we had a spot of lunch and by about four o'clock we were on our way back to the car when we clocked the feverish activity around the news-stand. Joe wondered why there was so much interest in the late edition and it was only then that I caught the words the young 'paper boy was shouting: 'United in plane crash.' At first I couldn't believe my ears, couldn't take in the potential enormity of the situation, but then I caught sight of a placard which revealed I had not mis-heard the cry.

We bought a 'paper and because it mentioned a crash on the runway, I immediately felt a measure of relief flood through me. I had flown quite a bit for a lad in those days – for instance, I had travelled to the away legs in the previous rounds against Shamrock Rovers and Dukla

Prague – and my instant reaction was that the damage couldn't be that extensive if the aircraft hadn't even left the tarmac. But Joe was more cautious. 'I'm afraid this sounds serious,' he told me, and we went to the *News Chronicle* office to find further information.

As soon as we arrived it was clear that we were talking about a catastrophic accident. People were rushing around the office at top speed, and the Reuters news agency wire machine was spewing out yards of paper carrying the latest facts and speculation as the true position began to emerge. Amid all this frantic activity, Joe sat me down in a relatively quiet corner and brought over some copy from the wire. It revealed the horrifying news that there had been numerous fatalities, although no victims had yet been named. At this point, with an atmosphere close to frenzy continuing to build around me, there was a brief interlude in which I became oddly, unnaturally calm. It was a surreal situation, knowing that there had been deaths, knowing that some of my mates were probably among those who had lost their lives, but not having a clue which ones. That feeling of calmness didn't last long, of course, and pretty soon I was sitting there praying feverishly to myself that my pals had been spared, even as the death toll rose from six or seven to a dozen and above. I stayed at the newspaper office into the evening, and as there were still no details of who had died I phoned home. Dad told me he had seen reports on the television but there had been no names. I was at my wits' end, unable to take in what was happening, and Joe drove me home, where I burst into tears as I walked through the door.

Then, agonisingly gradually, the names of some of the survivors were released. Bobby was one of them, along with Dennis Viollet, Albert Scanlon, Harry Gregg and Bill Foulkes. Duncan, too, though we were told he was grievously injured. Now I started going over all the other names in my mind and I'm afraid I got a bit selfish, just hoping and praying desperately that my best friend of all, little Eddie, would be spared. Just human nature, I suppose. It was Thursday night, when they always held a Novena (a Catholic devotion) at our church and Mum and Dad suggested that I go. When I arrived it was packed, which it never was usually, and I recall vividly a vast outpouring of sympathy mingled with shock. I was part of a tight-knit community and the folks there all knew I was a United player, and they were very kind to me. But I barely heard their well-meant words. It was as though I was in some sort of dreadful fog and such was the emotion that my recall of the exact sequence of events might be a bit imprecise. But I think I got home some time between nine and ten o'clock to find that Eddie's name had still not been mentioned. Now a knot had formed in my stomach and, despite being an eternal optimist by nature, I was dreading the worst. I must have been in a state of shock and the rest of the night passed in a blur. I do remember crying myself to sleep, saying 'Please let this happen, please let that happen' over and over again as I tormented myself with all the possibilities.

By the morning I think I knew in my heart that I would never see the smiling face of Eddie Colman coming through my front door again, and together with Gordon Clayton I went into the ground. There, finally, we were told the terrible news that we had lost Eddie, along with Tommy Taylor, David Pegg, Billy Whelan, Roger Byrne, Mark Jones and poor Geoff Bent, a reserve full-back who had not been expecting to make the trip but who had been added to the party as a precaution because Roger was carrying an injury. Jackie Blanchflower, Johnny Berry and Matt Busby were still alive but in a bad way, while United had also lost dear Bert Whalley, popular trainer Tom Curry and club secretary Walter Crickmer. In addition, most of the journalists had been killed, including former England goalkeeper Frank Swift; also some crew members and others passengers. Altogether, it represented calamity on a scale which I could barely begin to comprehend.

Along with Gordon and some of the other players – I can vaguely remember Ian Greaves, Colin Webster, Ronnie Cope and young Alex Dawson all being there – I slumped in the dressing room in a state of numbed shock. We just sat there, staring dumbly at each other, no one knowing what to say. Then Bill Inglis, the reserve trainer, walked in and broke the spell, telling us to go home and come back on Monday.

There was nothing to be done until then so Gordon and I trailed back outside to my car. I recall that Eddie's girlfriend Marjorie was with us; they had not long been engaged. Then we drove round to the Colmans' house in Archie Street, where the neighbours' kids were outside, kicking a ball around on the cobbles, just like Eddie through all the years of his growing up. His mum and dad and grandad had taken the news with a moving stoicism, but of course they were utterly heartbroken. He was an only child and had seemed to have so much ahead of him, so much

Both Dennis Viollet (left) and I always had a way with the birds! These pigeons in Milan, where we had travelled for the second leg of the European Cup semi-final in 1958, simply couldn't resist us.

The Cromford Club in Manchester was the venue for many a United celebration. From the left are proprietor Paddy McGrath, Shay Brennan, a supporter (with his wife at the front), Kenny Morgans, Mr and Mrs Colin Webster, Ernie Taylor (at back) and his wife, Beryl and myself, Pat (Teal) and Gordon Clayton, and Stan Crowther.

We were always posers! Myself, Bobby Charlton and Dennis Viollet on a pre-season excursion in 1958.

living to do, so much potential to fulfil, and now that was all over. We just hugged each other and cried – what else was there to do? It was the same later when I visited other bereaved families. I couldn't change what had happened, but I could share some of their grief, talk of the happy times I'd known with their boys, just show them how much I cared, too.

On the Monday morning I reported back to the club, but my recollection of what went on is hazy, perhaps mercifully so. It just didn't seem real to be at Old Trafford without the likes of Eddie, Duncan, Tommy and the rest, and I can only picture what it was like through a mist. With Walter Crickmer gone, Les Olive, United's young assistant secretary and a former player, took on the arduous and harrowing task of ensuring the smooth day-to-day running of the club at this most hideously difficult of times. He did a marvellous job in his typically unassuming but efficient manner. Meanwhile it fell to Jimmy Murphy to keep the footballing side ticking over, and his first move was to take the remaining players to the Norbreck Hotel in Blackpool, just to get away from the tidal wave of collective grief that was washing over Manchester. How Les and Jimmy managed to cope is beyond me. I guess they just bit the bullet and got on with it. Real heroes, both of them.

The Football League gave United leave to postpone their next two games, but because I was waiting for my cartilage operation I wasn't directly involved in the team and didn't go to Blackpool. So I was in Manchester when the bodies of my mates came back and were laid out in the club gym, inside the south stand. Then came the funerals, many of which Gordon and I attended. It was an unbelievably stressful time. In no way was I prepared to deal with grief on such a colossal scale. I'd known what it was like to lose a very old grandmother, otherwise death had never touched my life before. Now I was just demoralised at the thought that I would never see my friends again. I suppose it was similar to a war situation, in which large numbers of young people are wiped out.

Then, just when it seemed we were at rock-bottom, 15 days after the accident there was another overwhelmingly crushing blow when Duncan Edwards died. We all knew he was a fighter and I had it in my head that, despite his devastating injuries, somehow he would pull through. That hope had grown with some encouraging medical bulletins from Munich, but in the end he didn't make it. It didn't seem possible, but now the misery had deepened still further.

At the time it didn't occur to me to wonder why I had been spared, although it did later. I also reflected where I might have been sitting on the plane if I had made the trip. Probably next to Eddie, though it could have been Bobby, could have been anybody. I did try to find out who sat where, but then I stopped because I couldn't bear listening to the answer. Most insistent of all, though, as the years have gone by, has been the thought of what lads like Eddie and Duncan and Tommy would have been like at various stages of their lives. It is so painful to contemplate, and I know that really I can't look beyond their football days, which I'm sure would have been fulfilling beyond belief. Truly I think they would have won everything there was to win, would have been the new Real Madrid, but even the thought of losing such superb players doesn't compare to the reality of losing such wonderful people. They were all such fun, bursting with so much life. It was impossible to make sense of what happened at the time, and it's impossible now.

Despite everything, of course, Manchester United had to go on, and the story of the remainder of that season has been rightly dubbed 'Murphy's Miracle.' With Matt Busby initially hovering close to death and then hospitalised for weeks, Jimmy took the helm and somehow kept the club on the rails. He was required to put a team on the field only 13 days after the crash for a fifth-round FA Cup tie against Sheffield Wednesday, and of the previous first-choice selection, only two men – goalkeeper Harry Gregg and right-back Bill Foulkes – were available. Bobby Charlton, Dennis Viollet, Albert Scanlon and Kenny Morgans would all play again, but they were not ready at this point. I couldn't be at Old Trafford for the most emotional night the ground had ever known because I was in hospital for my operation, but I watched from my bed as they showed the highlights of our 3-0 victory on the TV news. I felt so incredibly proud that we got through, although I have to admit that I felt sorry for the Wednesday players, who were on a hiding to nothing with everybody in the country except their own fans rooting for United.

It was a fantastic achievement by Jimmy just to get 11 players on the pitch, the most amazing presence being that of my pal Shay Brennan, who finished up the unlikely two-goal star. It was surprising enough that a reserve inside-forward (as he was then) with no left foot should be given the number-11 shirt, even given our tragic lack of numbers, but it's part of life and sport that heroism can spring from the most un-likely sources. Shay scoring any goal would have been a stunner, but for him to get two, including one direct from a corner, bordered on the downright miraculous. The side was bolstered by two emergency sign-ings, wing-half Stan Crowther from Aston Villa and tiny inside-forward Ernie Taylor from Blackpool, while the likes of Ian Greaves, Freddie Goodwin, Ronnie Cope and Colin Webster already knew the United ropes. The remaining two places were filled by Alex Dawson, a rookie centre-forward who had already filled in for Tommy Taylor with some success, and 18-year-old debutant Mark Pearson, an inside-forward.

After that, not surprisingly, our League results were poor, but against all the odds Jimmy led his patchwork side on an emotion-charged rollercoaster ride all the way to the FA Cup Final at Wembley. Some might think sympathetic opponents gave United an easy passage because of the air crash, but don't you believe it. Oh, there *was* sympathy, genuine sympathy, but it was strictly limited to before and after the games. In the heat of the action, all gentle thoughts went out of the window, and we wouldn't have had it any different.

Having got over the initial hurdle of Sheffield Wednesday, Jimmy looked round for further reinforcements, and many names were mentioned, including our old team-mate Jeff Whitefoot, Bolton full-back Tommy Banks, and there was even a whisper that the great Hungarian goal machine, Ferenc Puskas, might be on his way to Old Trafford. In the event, other clubs didn't want to let their good players go and there were no more signings that season, which placed an awesome burden on the reserves and youngsters. The way they rose to the challenge – bolstered soon by the return to action of Bobby Charlton and, towards the end of the campaign, of Dennis Viollet – was utterly magnificent.

As for me, I was desperate to regain fitness as quickly as possible to do my bit for the cause. After my operation in February I was out of hospital in time to watch the FA Cup quarter-final replay against West Bromwich Albion on March 5 and I made my first-team comeback in a 2-1 win at Sunderland on April 7. I had been sidelined for only five weeks, representing a record return from a cartilage operation in those days, the usual time being ten to 14 weeks. Unfortunately I came back too soon and, with the benefit of hindsight, I must admit it was rash. But

A night of incredible emotion: Bill Foulkes leads out United for their first match after the Munich disaster, an FA Cup tie against Sheffield Wednesday at Old Trafford.

United beat Wednesday 3-0, but there is only emptiness in the eyes of crash survivors Harry Gregg (second left) and Bill Foulkes (third left). Also in shot (left to right) are Ronnie Cope, trainer Jack Crompton, Ian Greaves, Freddie Goodwin and two-goal Shay Brennan.

I felt I was needed and there was no way I was going to let United down. I didn't cruise through games – that was never in my nature – but gave it everything, so after every outing my knee was horribly swollen. Inevitably that would mean missing the next match, then I would be back again, out again and so on. In this crazy fashion I managed four appearances, all the while striving to prove to Jimmy that I would be fit enough to face Bolton Wanderers at Wembley. Alas, it wasn't to be. I gave it my best shot right up until the final week, but I had to sit out the last League game at Chelsea, after which the constant application of kaolin poultices failed to reduce the size of my ailing joint to anything like playable proportions. I can accept now that I'd have had a better chance of making the big match if I'd taken things more steadily, but that's simply not the way I'm made. I guess I've paid for it in later years, when my knee has caused me further problems, but I've no regrets about that. It was all about trying to win the battle, and even though I lost in the end I could say I'd tried my very best. I would have felt elated if I'd made it, but didn't feel devastated because I'd failed. I just thought: 'That's life!'

Meanwhile United had captured the imagination of the entire sporting world with their astonishing progress in the FA Cup. It took replays to overcome West Brom in the last eight and Fulham in the semi-final with Harry Gregg at the absolute top of his game throughout the run. The big Irishman was brave, brilliant and an inspiration to his teammates, and he carried that fabulous form into that summer's World Cup Finals in Sweden, in which he was voted the tournament's best 'keeper. Bobby was fantastic, too, especially in the second clash with Albion, when he made the late winner for Webster, and I must mention Alex Dawson, who banged in a hat-trick in the Highbury rematch against Fulham. After all that, it was a shame that things didn't go well in the final, but the lads weren't at their best – understandably in view of all the club had been through – and Bolton deserved to win. Having acknowledged that, they were gifted the first of their two goals by Stan Crowther being slow to come out, thus playing Nat Lofthouse onside, and Nat's second, for which he charged Harry into the net, was a sick joke. Some called it a foul, but it was more like an assault. We were badly served by the referee when McParland butted Ray Wood a year earlier, and this was equally blatant, but there's no point in complaining, certainly not after all this time. These days, when I bump into Nat, I'll just have a joke about it.

Every neutral wanted United to win the trophy, not least because of the Busby factor. Even before Munich he was one of the most popular figures in the game, and since then people had willed him to recover from his awful injuries, then rejoiced when he left hospital. He came to the final hobbling on sticks, but it seemed to those close to him that his pain was psychological as well as physical. According to his son, Sandy, still a friend of mine, Matt was on the verge of quitting the game at that point. That's what was in his heart and in his mind, but first he wanted to win that cup, maybe to do it for the players who had died. In the end I think he was talked out of retiring by his family, especially his wife, who said that the lads would have wanted him to carry on, to try and rebuild what had been shattered.

Everybody at the club was glad that eventually he decided to fight on. The accident wasn't down to Matt Busby. It was easy afterwards to say there had been three attempts at take-off and surely he should have intervened. But he was a football man, not an expert on air travel; he was in the hands of the professionals and, quite rightly, accepted their guidance.

Still, it was easy to understand that he might have had enough. He had been in charge of his boys and so many of them had died. Even though he couldn't logically be blamed, he felt a certain responsibility. We must remember, too, that alongside all that anguish, he suffered a huge amount of physical pain. In the immediate aftermath of the crash he was so perilously close to death that he received the last rites several times and spent days in an oxygen tent. When his wife paid her first visit to the hospital she walked straight past his bed without recognising him, so ravaged was he by his ordeal. As to how he must have felt as he began to recover, only to find out which of his young charges had gone, I cannot begin to imagine the trauma. It must have been sheer agony, and to come through it as he did bears testimony to a truly remarkable spirit.

Matt's players had to reveal deep reserves of character, too, none more so than Harry Gregg, who had distinguished himself at the scene of the disaster by returning to the burning wreckage to rescue a baby. I was a fan of Ray Wood, who was honest, loyal and terrific at reaction saves, but there is no doubt that Harry represented a radical improvement as our last line of defence. Certainly the newcomer cut a contrasting figure to his slim predecessor; indeed, with his imposing frame, his shirt stretched taut across his muscular chest, he might have been Superman as he strode into our dressing room for the first time. My initial impression was of a tough, confident, charismatic athlete and I never had cause to revise it. Unlike Ray, Harry was anything but a line 'keeper. It shocked me at first when he charged outside the penalty box to intercept, to clear or sometimes even to make a tackle, but we came to realise that nothing, but nothing, was going to stand in his way. If necessary, he would run through his own defenders as well as opposing forwards. Inevitably, given that swashbuckling style, he was bound to suffer injuries, and it might be argued that in the end he was too courageous for his own good. His method cost him many appearances, and medals, too, and he was monstrously unlucky to leave Old Trafford without a solitary club honour to his name.

Harry was strong in other ways. He knew tragedy in his personal life, losing his first wife to cancer when she was very young, then having to bring up two children, but he battled through all his difficulties. It's true that he was a volcanic personality and sometimes I'd have to turn away because he was being so outrageous in his opinions. Yet when he said something you had to listen; you were drawn in irresistibly. He would put his points on players, games, anything under the sun, with immense force and he relished an argument. If he got upset he'd chase you, grab you, do his best to throttle you, and he frightened a few in his time. Of course, stories always grow in the telling, and there is one in this category which has Harry pursuing Johnny Giles and smashing down a hotel door to get to him. This happened, allegedly, during a tour and so outraged Matt that he said if he found out who the culprit was he'd send him home. Harry always denied it, but a lot of people thought he was responsible.

Bill Foulkes, too, was a tower of strength as Manchester United tried to pick up the threads of playing football again, and he accepted the captaincy, even though it was a position he never coveted. But I'd have to say the single most influential contributor on the pitch during this hideously difficult period for the club was Bobby Charlton. We all knew he was prodigiously talented, and I'm certain that he would have gone on to become one of the game's greats even if Munich had never happened. But before the accident, so classy were the men around him that he could concentrate wholly on his role as an inside-forward, knowing that everything else was in reliable hands. But now it was as though he had matured almost instantly to take on massive extra responsibilty for the team. His game developed extra dimensions and he ranged to all areas of the pitch, working like a demon and lifting everybody by his supreme example. Not that he was alone in making a mammoth effort; for example, Dennis Viollet was still Dennis Viollet, a fine player who had terrific games, but it was Bobby who took on the mantle of greatness. He was a bit good, was Bobby; a bit special.

The rest of the side, too, played their parts, many of them nobly in the closing months of that uniquely taxing campaign, climaxing with the FA Cup Final. Big Ian Greaves and Bill Foulkes were bulwarks at full-back, while Ronnie Cope was steady at centre-half. Ronnie was a really nice person who wouldn't hurt anybody in the world – certainly he didn't have a ruthless streak like Bill – and some would say that's not the best qualification for a central defender. But he could play beautifully, invariably opting to pass the ball out of defence rather than hoof it into Row Z. After Munich he had plenty of opportunity to cement his place, and he made more than a century of appearances, but somehow he never quite nailed it. After all his experience with United I expected him to thrive elsewhere, but sometimes it doesn't happen, as it didn't for Ronnie. That was a shame but he has remained a friend and I catch up with him regularly at meetings of our Former Players Association.

Our wing-halves were contrasting types. On the right was Freddie Goodwin, a 6ft 5ins beanpole who played about a dozen games of county cricket for Lancashire as a fast bowler. He had grown up with United and was a thoughtful performer who could pass the ball nicely, but who hadn't looked likely to get past Eddie Colman before the crash. The left-half was Stan Crowther, a craggy ball-winner who had played for Villa in the 1957 final. He was hard, but without being unkind I'm not sure that he had the necessary quality. I don't believe he was the United type and, in all modesty, I don't believe he would have been signed if I hadn't been injured.

Orchestrating the attack was another newcomer, the vastly experienced little inside-forward Ernie Taylor, who offered invaluable advice

The brave smiles say one thing, but the black ties tell another story. The scene at the Salford home of Eddie Colman after his funeral. At the back, left to right, are a family friend, Grandad Dick Colman, Bobby Charlton, and Eddie's mother Liz. At the front are Eddie's pal Derek Kevan (the West Bromwich Albion centre-forward), a young member of the Colman family, myself, Brian Stone (another friend), and Dick Colman, Eddie's father.

Murphy's miracle: Jimmy (second left) leads United out at Wembley for the 1958 FA Cup final, followed by skipper Bill Foulkes and new signing Stan Crowther. Bill Ridding is the Bolton boss, with captain Nat Lofthouse on his heels.

to me and to the rest of the youngsters. He was exactly what we needed after the crash and was an inspired signing by Jimmy. One of Ernie's sayings was 'It's not about how many games you play in the season, but how many seasons you play in the game.' Although he had done just about everything during his time with Sunderland and Blackpool, he wasn't a know-all, but shared his knowledge about training and looking after yourself in an unassuming way. I thought that if I listened to his words of wisdom then I could look forward to many years in the First Division. Alas, that wasn't to be, but that didn't alter the fact that he did a marvellous job for United, even though he was only at the club for a short time during the twilight of his own career.

A huge problem for Jimmy was deciding which of the Munich survivors were ready to return to the fray. Bobby Charlton did so with distinction, Albert Scanlon was out for the rest of the season and Dennis Viollet turned out at Wembley but, with the benefit of hindsight, he didn't look ready for it. That left Kenny Morgans, the teenaged right winger who had been flying so high before the tragedy that he had unseated no less a thoroughbred than Johnny Berry. Kenny was a gem of a lad who had always been chirpy, and unquestionably he had the ability to become a top player. But although he wasn't badly injured in the crash, he was never the same afterwards. It was as though all his confidence and self-belief had evaporated, and when Jimmy stuck him in for half a dozen games ahead of the final he just didn't do himself justice. Not too long afterwards he went home to Wales, playing for Swansea and then Newport but never fulfilling all that scintillating potential. It was a crying shame.

Our shortage of wingers meant that sometimes Colin Webster was played wide, though usually he was asked to lead the line in Tommy Taylor's place and did a workmanlike job. Also there were opportunities in various forward positions for youngsters Alex Dawson and Mark Pearson, two hugely promising footballers who I feel suffered by being asked to shoulder massive burdens too early in their careers. Not that I'm blaming Jimmy Murphy, who was just doing the best he could in unspeakable circumstances and had no choice but to pitch them in. Alex was a bull-like centre-forward who had already made his mark with three goals in as many games when Tommy was injured towards the end of the previous term. He would battle for lost causes, make bad balls into good ones, was wonderful in the air for a lad who wasn't the tallest and he found the net on a regular basis. Had he enjoyed the luxury of being introduced to the side gradually, and alongside great players, he might have carved a long-term niche for himself at Old Trafford. As it was he let nobody down with 54 goals in 93 appearances, the sort of ratio most managers would kill for. But Matt Busby was a wonderful judge of a player and, in time, he identified David Herd as his preferred spearhead, meaning that Alex was surplus to requirements. That was hard, but Alex went on to become a hero with Preston, where they called him 'The Black Prince of Deepdale', and at least he was picked for the 1958 final.

Inside-forward Mark Pearson wasn't so lucky. After playing in all the other post-Munich FA Cup games, he had to step aside for Dennis Viollet at Wembley, an understandable decision in view of Dennis' class and experience but one which backfired as the older man was nowhere near being back to his best. Mark was very small but what a big heart he had! If someone tried to hurt him he would stand up for himself fearlessly, and he had skill to burn. In the wake of the disaster he had to play because United were so short of footballers, but I'm convinced it sacrificed his career in the long term. He needed at least another 12 months in the junior ranks before mixing it with the big boys. When you're thrown in at the deep end prematurely you either get away with it and become a hero, or it knocks you back. Unfortunately it knocked Mark back, and he never quite regained the momentum of his early years.

Of course, in the prevailing circumstances, Alex and Mark were only too glad to do their bit, and would never refer to themselves as victims. The real victims were the ones who died, and those who were maimed; those supremely talented boys who, but for Munich, would have flowered beyond the scope of everyday imagination to become the best team in the history of British football.

Chapter 8

A SEASON IN THE SUN

THE MUNICH air disaster opened up Manchester United to the world. It's a fact, albeit a rather macabre one, that a lot of people from all over England, indeed all over the globe, began to support the Red Devils because of the tragedy. Afterwards nothing was ever the same again. The club's image was magnified, so that everything connected with it was hot news – and that makes it curious, by my reckoning, that our feat in finishing as First Division runners-up in 1958/59, the first season after being robbed of ten top-quality footballers by the accident, has tended to be overlooked when Matt Busby's achievements are reviewed.

As we approached the new term, we knew we weren't the worst of sides, despite the grievous loss of so many of our comrades. After all, we had not been disgraced in the semi-final of the European Cup the previous May, somehow managing to beat AC Milan 2-1 at Old Trafford before succumbing, bravely but inevitably, to the tune of 4-0 in the San Siro. In fact, United might even have pushed the Italian giants even harder, but for an incredibly insensitive, some might say callous, decision by the Football Association to insist that our best player, Bobby Charlton, should miss both matches so that he could join the England party for some friendlies ahead of the World Cup Finals. It wouldn't have been so bad, but after weakening our team so cruelly, they didn't even pick Bobby for any of their four games in Sweden. Imagine a modern equivalent, which would be the FA telling Sir Alex Ferguson that he couldn't have Wayne Rooney for a European Cup semi-final! Of course, Matt was convalescing at the time and could hardly be expected to do battle with the authorities. Also it should be remembered

Spurs centre-forward Bobby Smith can run, but he can't hide, as I prepare to launch myself into a tackle at Old Trafford.

The Manchester United side which defied logic by finishing as title runners-up in the first full season after Munich. Back row, left to right: Freddie Goodwin, Bill Foulkes, Harry Gregg, Ian Greaves, Joe Carolan. Front row: Warren Bradley, Albert Quixall, Dennis Viollet, Bobby Charlton, Albert Scanlon, myself.

Harry Gregg was voted the best goalkeeper in
the world at the 1958 World Cup finals, and I
wouldn't argue with that. Here he parries a
close-range effort from Everton's Jimmy Harris,
while I wait to tidy up the rebound.

Now that's what I call true fame! The front cover
of Charles Buchan's Football Monthly in
February 1959.

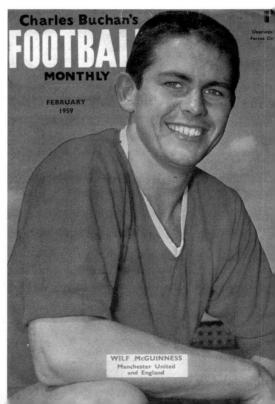

Charles Buchan's

FOOTBALL

MONTHLY

FEBRUARY
1959

Overseas
Forces Ov

WILF McGUINNESS
Manchester United
and England

that attitudes were different in those days, when the selection committee's word was law.

But let me dismount from that particular hobby-horse and return to 1958/59, which was to prove the most successful season of my life. Not only was I a regular member of the team, playing 39 times as we finished a comfortable second in the First Division – six points behind champions Wolves, five ahead of third-placed Arsenal – but also I completed my set of England honours by making my full international debut.

The season began as positively as was possible in the circumstances, with the players' spirits lifted by Matt's decision, after much private agonising, to battle on. We started with an exhilarating 5-2 home win over Chelsea which featured a hat-trick by Bobby Charlton, and that set the tone for the next eight months. In the opening games Ernie Taylor was still pulling the strings in midfield, but he had reached the veteran stage so Matt broke the British transfer record by paying Sheffield Wednesday £45,000 for the signature of Albert Quixall, who had a reputation as the golden boy of English football. He was blond, he had bags of flair, and he was an eye-catcher who was remarkably skilful with either foot. It's fair to say, though, that while he was a delight to play with when we had possession, when we lost it the fellow playing behind him had two opponents to mark. Albert didn't do enough in those situations and sometimes he had to be reminded of his responsibilities quite forcibly. As a character he was very quick witted and was a wicked practical joker, though sometimes his sense of humour didn't accord with other people's. I won't be drawn on details in case impressionable youngsters are reading this!

For all Albert's exceptional natural ability, he took some time to settle, but by late autumn he had bedded into a free-flowing forward line which was to notch more than a century of goals in that First Division campaign and was the basis of our success. The other newcomer was Warren Bradley on the right wing, who was enlisted from the leading non-League side Bishop Auckland and proved to be a surprise packet, staggering the majority of critics by leaping from amateur international to full England status virtually in the space of a season. He was quick and tricky, carried a goal threat and was a feisty little fellow who could never be knocked out of the game. It was a pity that Warren didn't last longer in professional football, but he had his sights on a teaching career,

A transfer coup for Bolton? Not really, it's an England gathering at Burnden Park in 1958 ahead of the game with Northern Ireland in which I won my first full cap. Left to right are the Trotters' Tommy Banks, myself, skipper Billy Wright and Bobby Charlton.

The programme for the match reveals that there was no shortage of illustrious names on show.

Thumb Nail Sketches of England..

By
SAM LEITCH
Sports Columnist
"Daily Herald"
London

COLIN McDONALD (Burnley). England's star player of the World Cup. This will be his home international debut. Stylish, safe and an automatic choice since debut in Lenin Stadium, Moscow, last May. Aged 25. League debut 1954-55, five previous "caps." 6ft. 12st.

DON HOWE (West Bromwich Albion). Safest right-back in Britain. Only 23, this will be 12th "cap" after graduating through Young England ranks. Rarely wastes a ball. Born in Wolverhampton. 5ft. 11ins. and 10st. 13lb.

TOMMY BANKS (Bolton). Identical international record as McDonald. Five previous "caps," but this will be home international debut. Eleven years a Bolton player. Sturdy, tough, fearless tackler; 28 years of age. Dressing-room comic. 5ft. 9ins., 12st.

RONNIE CLAYTON (Blackburn). This will be his 22nd "cap" and only 23 years of age. Strong, resourceful wing-half. International baptism against Ireland in 1955. 5ft. 10ins. and 11st. 4lb.

BILLY WRIGHT (Wolves). His 97th "cap" to-day. "Fantastic consistency," says England team manager Walter Winterbottom. Skipper of England in 1950, '54 and '58 World Cups. At 34 he has won every honour in game. Should make fabulous 100 "cap" record this season. 5ft. 9ins., 12st. 3lb.

WILF McGUINNESS (Manchester United). Twenty-year brilliant "Busby Babe" making his international debut to-day. Now takes over the left-half berth from late Duncan Edwards, both in United and England sides. League debut at 17. 5ft. 8ins., 10st 8lb.

PETER BRABROOK (Chelsea). Ted Drake signed him six years ago despite opposition from Arsenal, Spurs, Wolves and West Ham. Made League debut eight days after 17th birthday. Now 21, he is making home international debut. 5ft. 9ins., 10st. 3½lb.

PETER BROADBENT (Wolves). Another home international debutant. Skilful inside-forward at 25. Signed from Brentford for £9,000 eight years ago. Previous international experience—one "cap" against Russia. Born in Dover. 5ft. 9ins., 11st. 4lb.

BOBBY CHARLTON (Manchester United). With only three "caps"—at inside right—behind him, the most discussed footballer in England. Hardest shot in both feet in the country. Twenty years of age; Munich crash survivor. Last capped against Yugoslavia. 5ft. 9ins., 11st.

JOHNNY HAYNES (Fulham). Master planner of the attack. His 13 goals already this season have shot Fulham to top of Fulham's Second Division. Twenty-fifth "cap" to-day and 23. Undoubtedly finest passer of ball in English football. 5ft. 11ins. and 12st. 13lb.

TOM FINNEY (Preston). At 36 the oldest player in the England side. This will be his 74th "cap." Outspoken critic this season of England selectors for World Cup policy and selection methods. Ball playing genius and the only man to have been awarded "Footballer of Year" trophy twice.

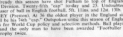

Pen Portraits of Irish Team

By
W. H. McClatch
"Ralph the Rove"
of the
"Belfast Telegra

HARRY GREGG (Manchester United). Acclaimed by Swedish public as best World Cup goalkeeper. Perhaps his greatest performance was against England at Wembley last season. Previous clubs—Coleraine, Doncaster Rovers. Statistics—aged 24, height 6ft. 1½ins., weight 12st. 10lb. International appearances 14.

DICK KEITH (Newcastle United). One of the most polished full-backs in Britain. Made impressive start on nerve-shattering Wembley last season. Previous club—Linfield. 24, 6ft., 11st. 8lb., 8 "caps."

LEN GRAHAM (Doncaster Rovers). Left-back; originally a reserve inside-forward with Linfield Swifts, was converted into a full-back with Brantwood, who transferred him to Rovers. Has played at both right and left-back for his country. Deputises for unavailable Alfie McMichael. 30, 5ft. 9½ins., 11st. 4lb., 13 "caps."

DANNY BLANCHFLOWER (Tottenham Hotspur). Rated amongst the top tacticians and captains in world soccer. A delightfully constructive wing-half, too. Previous clubs—Glentoran, Barnsley and Aston Villa. 31, 5ft. 10ins., 11st. 11lb., 35 "caps."

WILLIE CUNNINGHAM (Leicester City). Has never let Ireland down in either full-back berth. More recently occupied centre-half role as deputy for injured Jackie Blanchflower—a Munich air crash survivor. Previous club—St. Mirren. 28, 5ft. 10ins., 11st. 6lb., 21 "caps."

BERTIE PEACOCK (Glasgow Celtic). There are few who can get through the wing-half job more efficiently—or unobtrusively—than Bertie. Brilliant in defence and attack, and amongst best wing-halves in World Cup. Previous clubs—Coleraine and Glentoran. 28, 5ft. 6¼ins., 10st. 10lb., 19 "caps."

BILLY BINGHAM (Luton Town). Acme of consistency in the Irish team and still seems to be improving if his form in Sweden can be taken as criterion. Previous clubs—Glenavon and Sunderland. 26, 5ft. 7ins., 10st. 2lb., 33 "caps."

BILLY CUSH (Leeds United). A little man who does big things on the field. Teak-tough inside-forward, he is the most popular player at Elland Road. Gets married on Monday. Previous club—Glenavon. 29, 5ft. 4ins., 11st., 16 "caps."

TOMMY CASEY (Portsmouth). Can play wing-half, inside, or even centre-forward with considerable success. Does a confident and competent job. 27, 5ft. 9ins., 11st. 7lb. 10 "caps."

JIMMY McILROY (Burnley). Links up particularly well with Peacock and McParland. Amongst country's best inside forwards; has played for British side against Europe. Previous club—Glentoran. 26, 5ft. 9ins., 11st., 31 "caps."

PETER McPARLAND (Aston Villa). For long time was unable to find form; then came resurgence in Sweden where he was amongst top-scorers. Controversial hero of Villa's F.A. Cup Final win over Manchester United two seasons ago. 24, 5ft. 11ins., 11st. 7lb., 19 "caps."

and he went on to become a successful headmaster and schools inspector. Still, he will always be remembered as a key component of that marvellous attack which read: Bradley, Quixall, Viollet, Charlton and Scanlon. Bobby, who was world-class by then, top-scored with 29 goals. Dennis, also magnificent, contributed 21; Albert Scanlon, who was rewarded with an England under-23 call-up, chipped in with an invaluable 16, easily the best tally of his career; Warren added 12 in just 24 appearances and Quickie, who played much deeper, hit the target four times.

Of course, no team excels without a decent defence, and we had one of those, too, with Harry Gregg at his brilliant best, and the rest of the lads gelling more effectively than many people had expected. We employed the old 'W' formation, with full-backs Bill Foulkes and Joe Carolan covering centre-half Ronnie Cope, and the wing-halves, Freddie Goodwin and myself, working on a swivel basis rather than one hanging back and the other going forward. I built up a terrific understanding with Joe, who lined up behind me on the left. His style was to slide into tackles to nick the ball with his long legs, which meant that opposing wingers had to knock the ball a long way from their feet if they wanted to get past. Anticipation was one of my strengths, so many was the time a Carolan challenge enabled me to pounce. We became a well-oiled double-act – Joe would plunge in and I would cover. He made my game easier and I think the team benefited. One of my most vivid recollections of our genial Irish left-back was the day Stanley Matthews was booed off at Old Trafford for taking a dive against Joe and gaining a penalty. There's nothing new under the sun!

A personal highlight for me came at West Ham in September, when we lost 3-2 but I knocked in a goal from something like 35 yards. I had strained a thigh muscle and could hardly run, so I was moved to centre-forward, just to shuffle around as nuisance value. The ball came to Noel Cantwell, soon to replace Joe Carolan as United's left-back but at the time captain of the Hammers, and he tried to be clever. Thinking I was practically immobile, he attempted to flick the ball over my head, then run round me to collect it. But I managed to charge it down, then I swung a leg and sent a looping volley over the head of their 'keeper Ernie Gregory. I didn't get many goals – in fact, that was the second and last of my senior career – which is probably why I remember it in such detail.

I missed the next game, but that was one of only two absences in the whole season as I began to put my game together with some consistency. In all modesty, having been handed the opportunity of an extended run in the team for the first time – albeit in the most tragic of circumstances, with poor Duncan gone – I was fit and confident, and felt I was playing pretty well. Certainly I think Matt and Jimmy were satisfied with my input, and somebody else must have agreed with them because in early autumn I was picked for the Football League against the Irish League at Anfield. I played a blinder, too – my passing and tackling had never been better. Then, on October 4 at Windsor Park, Belfast, came the moment I had been waiting for ever since I first kicked a ball in earnest – I ran out to play for the full England team.

My selection – ahead of more regular performers like the Wolves pair, Ron Flowers and Bill Slater – didn't come as a complete shock. I had played a few times at under-23 level and there had been some speculation in the press that I might get the nod, but that did nothing to lessen the thrill. I was still a kid at heart – still am now, some would say, and I'm in my 70th year at the time of writing! – but one look at our teamsheet was enough to have me pinching myself to make sure I wasn't dreaming. I was at left-half, alongside skipper Billy Wright at centre-half, with Johnny Haynes and Tom Finney ahead of me at inside-left and outside-left, and my mate Bobby wearing number nine as a centre-forward with a roving brief. Pretty rarefied company, and as if that wasn't enough I was facing the classy likes of our own Harry Gregg, Spurs captain Danny Blanchflower, the gifted Burnley schemer Jimmy McIlroy and two potentially destructive wingers in Billy Bingham of Luton and our old friend Peter McParland, the villain of the 1957 FA Cup Final; all men who had shown up impressively on their way to the last eight of the recent World Cup tournament.

It was England's first game since their disappointing showing in Sweden, so it was a chance for me to be in on the ground floor as the coach, Walter Winterbottom, began to build for the future. As I stood to attention for the national anthem, a stirring prelude to the action, I thought deeply about Duncan, and how he should have been wearing England's number-six shirt that day. By God, I was determined that I wasn't going to let him down on my international debut, and I don't believe I did. I was reasonably contented with my display in a 3-3 draw

In close combat with Peter McParland, dubbed the villain of the 1957 FA Cup final by United fans upset by his reckless charge which seriously injured our goalkeeper, Ray Wood.

Albert Quixall (left) and I show off our ball skills – and yes, I did have some! – to a group of schoolchildren in 1959.

Working up a sweat during a pre-season training session in Germany in 1958. The front five are, left to right, Ray Wood, Bill Foulkes, myself, Bobby Charlton and Colin Webster.

in which Northern Ireland took the lead three times, but were pegged back by two magnificent long-range efforts from Bobby, who also set one up for Tom Finney. It was the 30th strike of the Preston Plumber's international carreer, emphasising what a truly phenomenal performer he was. The star of the show, though, was undoubtedly Bobby, who well and truly rubbed in the misguidedness of not picking him for the World Cup. I have always wondered just how far England might have gone in 1958 if Munich hadn't happened and if they had picked Bobby. Byrne, Edwards, Taylor, Charlton, maybe Colman ... we might even have challenged the Brazillians and their young genius, Pele.

Even though Slater, and then Flowers, were recalled for subsequent internationals, I felt that at least now I was on the right road, I was part of the set-up. Proof that I remained in Walter Winterbottom's thoughts arrived with selection for the under-23s in France, a game in which Maurice Setters of West Bromwich Albion – destined soon to join Manchester United – was cautioned because of a foul I had committed. I flattened a Frenchman, the referee blew up and Maurice protested so vehemently that he was booked. I thought: 'Bloody hell! It's usually me opening my mouth and putting my foot in it!'

Overall I was pretty satisfied with my form for both club and country, and when the season ended I was given a place on the tour of South America, during which I won my second full cap, against Mexico. It was not the most successful trip, with early defeats by Brazil and Peru, although the second of those encounters was memorable for a debut goal by a chirpy young lad called Jimmy Greaves, who went on to become one of the most deadly goal-scorers in the history of the game. My chance came along in the third match, but I'm afraid I didn't make the most of it. We played at high altitude in Mexico City, so Walter Winterbottom told us to take it steady, to pace ourselves so we wouldn't run out of energy. I tried to follow his advice but that wasn't my game at all. My natural approach was to throw everything into it, high-octane stuff from start to finish, so when I attempted to hold myself back I just didn't do myself justice. My best moment was delivering a long throw to Bobby – in that thin atmosphere it must have travelled all of 35 yards – which put him through on goal when the score was 0-0, but he missed. Soon after that we took the lead through a header from big Derek Kevan of West Bromwich Albion, but then they won a corner and I was detailed to mark Cardenas, who towered above me by nearly a full foot. Our goalkeeper, Eddie Hopkinson of Bolton, wasn't the biggest and he didn't come for the cross; I was outjumped by the Mexican giant, who nodded the equaliser. A few minutes later, with only half an hour gone, I was hooked off by the management, who thought I was knackered, and they sent on Ron Flowers. It felt particularly rotten because substitutes were rarely used during that era, but I wasn't on my own as the winger Dougie Holden was also replaced, by my new clubmate Warren Bradley. We lost that game 2-1, then completed the tour with an 8-1 victory over the USA in Los Angeles, which was marked by Bobby's first full international hat-trick and Billy Wright's final England outing, his 105th.

Football-wise I have to admit that it was all rather anti-climactic for me, but it's not sour grapes when I say that Walter Winterbottom wasn't everybody's cup of tea as a coach. Sometimes he came across like the schoolteacher he had once been, speaking in a donnish manner that might have alienated one or two of the lads. I'd worked under the likes of Billy Nicholson and Ron Greenwood at under-23 and youth level and enjoyed that, although Walter was often around and I could sense his influence.

Overall, though, it had been an expedition I wouldn't have missed for the world. Visiting such exotic places represented an unbelievable

Bursting with pride as I show Mum my messages of congratulation following my England call-up.

Practically my last act as a full England international, twisting in a desperate but unsuccessful attempt to prevent Cardenas from scoring in Mexico City.

adventure for a young lad from north Manchester, not too long out of Mount Carmel school. I shall never forget seeing the statue of Christ in Rio de Janeiro, visiting the posh British embassies and the swanky bowls and polo clubs. At the other end of the spectrum it was a real eye-opener to witness the appalling poverty in parts of Peru, and to mingle with the seething masses of Mexico City. Then there was the thrill of swimming at Copacabana beach, although that almost ended in disaster for myself and Bobby Charlton. One minute we were messing about in the surf near the shore, then the next we were swept some 200 yards out to sea. It was a tricky situation and I was very close to panicking, but I calmed down and we struggled back to safety.

On the plane journey home I reflected that things hadn't gone my way, but I wasn't despondent. After all, I was still only 21 years old, I had just completed a tremendous domestic campaign, I was playing for a club which I loved and which had finished as runners-up in the First Division. I had every reason to be confident that 1959/60 would be the season in which my career would kick on to the next level. Fortunately for my peace of mind that summer, I had no idea what was just around the corner ...

Chapter 9
BROKEN DREAMS

IT WOULD be a grotesque understatement to say that 1959/60 didn't work out quite the way I had hoped. After United's strong showing during the previous campaign and my elevation to the England side, I had visions of a genuine title challenge as Matt Busby continued with his reconstruction job in the aftermath of Munich, alongside a concerted personal bid to consolidate my place in the international reckoning. But after a useful pre-season tour of Germany, my grand scheme started to go awry. Despite fielding most of the same players who had finished second to Wolves in 1958/59, we lost half of our first ten games, dropping 12 of the first 20 points available. We just couldn't find any consistency, particularly in defence, where Matt soon shuffled his pack. He had started with Ian Greaves at right-back and Bill Foulkes at centre-half, but pretty quickly he restored Ronnie Cope as pivot, returned Bill to right-back and dropped Ian, while trying Shay Brennan at right-half instead of Freddie Goodwin. Still the side didn't quite gel, which was hugely frustrating because we knew we were capable of playing exhilarating, free-flowing football.

Around late October, early November, I was hit by another worry as I was beginning to feel excruciating pain around the area of my right shin. I could train or play as normal, but when I stopped it ached like mad. I had it X-rayed but that showed nothing, so I thought it was safe to carry on. For about four weeks I got into the routine of having treatment through the week, then turning out on Saturday, but all the time I wasn't performing at my best and the team's form continued to be variable. Clearly Matt needed to change something and in early December, after a particularly tepid display as we lost 2-1 at Everton, he acted boldly, leaving out four internationals, Bobby Charlton, Harry Gregg, Warren Bradley and myself for the home game with Blackpool, bringing in Mark Pearson, young 'keeper David Gaskell, Alex Dawson and Shay Brennan. None of us could complain – and nor did we – as we had been well below our best, although time would show that I had a reasonable excuse. What I didn't know at this point was that I had played my last game of first-team football not long after my 22nd birthday.

I was desperate to regain my place as soon as possible, maybe not least because it had gone to Shay, one of my closest mates, who I didn't think was a patch on me as a left-half, although later he would develop into a highly polished full-back. I was still in pain so the medics gave me another thorough going-over but still could find nothing wrong so I turned out for the reserves against Aston Villa, finishing the game with a throbbing shin. Another week on and I remained as eager as ever, especially as now I was being told my injury must be muscular, and that I could have injections to deaden the pain. Duly, on the Saturday morning of 12 December, I went to St Joseph's Hospital at Whalley Range where the orthopaedic surgeon directing the needle was Mr Sidney Rose, who was also a director of Manchester City.

Thus protected by medical science, or so I fondly believed, I ran out to face Stoke City reserves at Old Trafford that afternoon, and played normally for some 20 minutes before going into a routine tackle with Peter Bullock, an 18-year-old England youth international inside-forward. I heard a sharp crack and felt a sudden, searing pain as I went down in a heap. Later other players told me they were startled by the horrible snapping noise which resounded across the pitch. I was stretched out on the ground and as I attempted to lift my right leg the bottom half stayed flat – that's when I knew I was in serious trouble.

My father was at the game and he went with me in an ambulance to the hospital, where I was given morphine but had to sit it out for three or four hours while waiting for a specialist. It was bloody agony. When the eminent expert did arrive, he confirmed what I already feared, that both my tibia and fibula had gone. The bones were set, the leg was encased in plaster and I realised that my season was over, though I did not contemplate the end of my career at that point. People did recover

Taking on Arsenal's David Herd (right) at Highbury in February 1959. He scored a goal in their 3-2 victory – I liked him much better when he joined United a couple of years later.

My expression is grim as United physio Ted Dalton examines my broken leg. At this point I was beginning to fear for my footballing future.

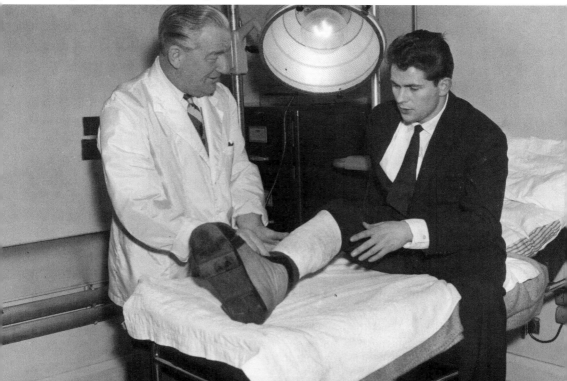

Making the best of a bad job in hospital, with my mother, my fiancée Beryl and my dad.

With the possibility of a players' strike in the air, I check out the local labour exchange with Dennis Viollet. I wasn't looking for sympathy – I really needed those crutches!

from broken legs, after all, so I was optimistic about a comeback in the fullness of time. However, I was warned that it was a particularly horrendous injury, with the edges of the fractures overlapping, which would make it difficult to mend.

Now I had ample time to contemplate the circumstances leading up to the incident which, I must stress, was a complete accident, with Bullock totally blameless. But in retrospect it seems abundantly clear to me that when I had experienced the discomfort a month or so earlier, I was already suffering from a stress fracture. However, there was not the same awareness about that condition in those days as there is today, so it wasn't picked up and, unwittingly, I did the worst possible thing – I carried on playing football.

I left hospital after ten days with a cumbersome cast all the way to the top of my leg. Right from the start I called at the ground most days, just to keep in touch with everybody because there was nothing I could do at that stage to improve my situation. After about a month I started upper-body training, which at least gave me something to do, but then gradually I began to realise that I was facing a truly daunting challenge, and at that stage I might have become depressed if it hadn't been for Matt Busby. He could not have been more thoughtful when I was at my lowest ebb, reassuring me that I was still in his plans and urging me to remain strong, always finding the time to give me an encouraging word.

By September 1960, though, it had become clear that the fractures were not healing neatly and it was decided that I should have a bone graft from my hip to make the broken places stronger. Still, though, the doctors did not reckon the bones were uniting as they should and when my umpteenth plaster came off around New Year 1961 one leg was an inch shorter than the other. I made attempts to train, but it just didn't feel right. After some 14 months of fighting to regain fitness with every fibre of my being, it looked as if my life in professional football was over, and I was utterly devastated by the prospect. The possibility had been hanging over me like a black cloud for some months, but now it seemed a miserable exit from Old Trafford was inevitable. There I was, engaged to be married to Beryl in the summer of 1961, and I presumed I was facing the prospect of imminent unemployment. In fact, salvation was at hand in the shape of Matt Busby and the blessed offer of a coaching job at Manchester United, but before embarking on that hitherto unexpected but deeply fulfilling stage of my life story, there are one or two detours I'd like to make.

Viewed from a distance of nearly five decades, the first one seems like an uproarious giggle, but I can assure you that it had me wracked with worry at the time. It was during the period after I had broken my leg but was still hoping to make a comeback. Though I was hobbling around on crutches I would still join the other players at Davyhulme golf club after training on Mondays. If the weather was good they'd play golf, if not it would be snooker or cards. Then there would be a meal before going into town to the cinema on our free passes. That was the ritual throughout the season.

Of course, I couldn't drive in my condition – although by then I was the proud owner of a Morris Minor, snapped up at an auction for £400 – so I hitched a lift with Shay, along with Johnny Giles and Jimmy Shiels, and we headed from Old Trafford towards Davyhulme. That morning the two Irish lads had brought a couple of water pistols with them and had been larking about in the dressing room, peeping round corners and shooting – daft pranks but great fun for a load of young guys together. As we were driving along we spied a group of girls on the other side of the road and Johnny shouted: 'Stop the car, Shay. I want a word with these young ladies.' So we pulled up at the kerb, John wound down his window and stuttered: 'C-c-c-can you t-t-t-tell me where Ch-Ch-Ch-Church Street is, please?' Not surprisingly, they didn't quite catch what he said and leaned closer – at which point he doused them with his water pistol. Then the cry was: 'Off you go, Shay', and we drove away chortling our heads off. Some of the girls were laughing, too, shouting things like 'You swine', but certainly they didn't seem too upset.

I must emphasise that there was nothing malicious involved, that it was just a bit of fun on a bright sunny day, but it did occur to me that one or two of our 'victims' might not have enjoyed it, and I said as much to the lads. All I got in return was: 'Don't worry about it, Wilf' and soon we came upon another bunch of girls, who received the same treatment. Then we went through the same routine with an older guy wobbling along on a stick, and a bunch of women in their thirties and forties. By now I was getting anxious. I couldn't believe what the boys were doing, and I told them we could easily get into trouble over this escapade. But they just told me not to be a coward. As the Irish lads put it: 'In Dublin we do it with ink, not water! What's the matter with you? It's your turn next.' Thus goaded, in the end even I had a squirt, soaking yet another group of girls. There were five or six incidents all told as the four intrepid sharpshooters left a trail of soggy victims in their wake before fetching up at Davyhulme.

We had lunch, then Shay, Johnny and Jimmy played golf while I waited for them. Come the early evening the two Irish lads were going to the cinema, so Shay said he'd drop them off at a bus stop before taking me home to Blackley. After leaving Johnny and Jimmy, who might well have been planning to wreak havoc on Manchester's public transport system with their carefully concealed weapons, we called at Shay's house in Ryebank Road, Stretford, to tell his wife, June, where he was going. We were dumbfounded by her greeting: 'Thank God you've got your car back!' 'What on earth do you mean?' gasped Shay, open-mouthed. Then June explained that the police had been round to say that his car had been stolen by a gang and the thieves had been terrorising Urmston and Stretford with water pistols. I thought: 'Oh dear! We need help.'

Now, I wasn't the senior of the four culprits by age, but I was in terms of football experience, so I took it on myself to ring Matt Busby. Imagine how I felt, calling the Boss to say: 'The police are looking for four of your players!' My hands were shaking as I dialled his home number, and as I broke the news to him there was a disbelieving silence at the other end of the phone. Then he ordered: 'You get up here right away.' So Shay and I drove round to his house in King's Road, Chorlton, our hearts in our mouths. When he answered the door his face was like thunder, and he growled at us. We knew we were in trouble because the Boss was always so calm, he wasn't a natural growler. 'What the hell have you been doing?' was the gist of his enquiry, though it was spiced with one or two uncharacteristically colourful adjectives. So, rather haltingly, we blurted out our story, then he gave us that much of a dressing-down that his wife, Jean, felt she had to interrupt. 'Come on, Matt, be fair to the boys. Remember the days when you used to tie milk bottles to door knockers before tapping and running away?' But he wasn't impressed. 'Don't talk about that,' he said. 'It happened in totally different circumstances.'

Eventually he called the Chief Constable while we sat there quaking, and came back with the instruction that we were to make an official statement, then forget about the incident unless we heard anything else. Anxious though I was at my own predicament, I recall being impressed that our manager had instant access to such an important person, a reflection of his own important status in the Manchester community. In due course the four of us went round to Stretford police station and, rather shamefacedly, gave our version of events. Then, as Matt had told us to do, we put it out of our minds. Unfortunately, that wasn't the end of our brush with the law. A few weeks later we were summoned to appear before the magistrates, an outing rendered all the more intimidating because the court was situated at Strangeways prison.

Naturally, the press got hold of it and they were out in force as we turned up together in Shay's car. We were some way away from the court when I first glimpsed the heaving gaggle of reporters and photographers, so I told Shay to pull up and park. I said to the lads: 'They'll get enough pictures anyway, but let's not give them a nice shot of us climbing out of the car. Let's walk up in single file and make it awkward for them.' Not that I was experienced in frustrating the press at court cases, you understand, it was just a spur-of-the-moment thought. So that's what we did, and Shay, Johnny and I walked straight past the journalists and through the court door. But Jimmy, for some daft reason known only to himself, covered his face with his jacket. What a picture! It looked like somebody on a murder charge, somebody who had something to hide, exactly what the photographers wanted. That was the first ricket we dropped that day, but it wasn't the last.

We pleaded guilty – we could hardly do otherwise – which meant that the witnesses' statements were read out rather than our victims having to appear in person. It all assumed ominous proportions as one of them mentioned an acid-like liquid, which might have been implying urine or even something more sinister, but that was totally wrong. We might have been stupid but we weren't that stupid. We were larking, not being filthy or dangerous, and none of us would have dreamed of using anything other than clean water.

Overall it was a rotten experience because we were made to feel like real hooligans, even though we were guilty of nothing more than an innocent prank without the slightest hint of nastiness. But even then,

Of course you can coach, there's nothing to it! That might have been the message from trainer Jack Crompton (centre) as I limped into Old Trafford. I have to say that centre-half Ronnie Cope looks a mite doubtful.

when we were up against it, we couldn't quite stop pranking – and that was our next mistake. There were three magistrates, including quite a large lady, and I whispered to Shay to smile at her, thinking he could charm her just like he did the girls. But as he began to grin disarmingly, the chairman of the bench jumped in with: 'This is no laughing matter!' They carried on in that vein, treating us as though we had done something truly despicable. I feel they went way over the top, and I can only think that was because we were Manchester United footballers. It seemed they were determined to make an example of us, just for having a harmless laugh. To be fair, though, as it was pointed out to us afterwards, if somebody calls you over to a car window and then pulls what looks like a gun, it could be enough to give some people a heart attack. I have to admit that we hadn't considered that angle, which was a perfectly valid one.

Disgusting trick' United stars' told

28 FEB 1961

EVENING NEWS REPORTER

SEVEN times four Manchester United footballers pulled up in a black saloon car belonging to 23-year-old full-back Shay Brennan and squirted water at pedestrians with water pistols.

And at Manchester county magistrates court to-day they were told by chairman, Mr William McGrail:

"This is a disgusting and despicable action for young men to take and I hope it will be the last offence of this sort each of you will ever commit."

Seamus (Shay) Brennan, of Eyebank Road, Stretford, James M. Sheils, aged 22, and John M Giles, aged 20, both of Gorse Crescent, Stretford, and Wilfred McGuinness, aged 23, of West Lee street, Blackley, Manchester, were bound over for 12 months

In the end we were bound over to keep the peace for a year and fined the sum of five shillings and sixpence each, the equivalent of around 27 pence in today's money. We were extremely embarrassed, feeling that we might have let the club down a little bit, but deep down we wouldn't have minded squirting the chairman of magistrates for being so pompous. Okay, we'd stepped out of line, but our offence hadn't been that serious in the great scheme of things. When ticking us off he knew the press was hanging on his every word, and he addressed us as though we were hardened criminals. Even now, when I'm older than he was at the time of our sentence, I can't quite accept that he needed to be quite so draconian in his approach, but I guess it takes all sorts.

A much weightier matter which occupied much of my attention while my future remained in the balance was the Professional Footballers Association's battle with the League to establish fair levels of pay and terms of employment. I had followed in the eminent footsteps of John Doherty and Jackie Blanchflower as United's PFA representative and by 1961 the freedom of contract issue was coming to a head. The situation as it stood was so grossly unfair, with one-sided contracts weighted so heavily towards the clubs that we didn't believe they should be legally binding. Once a player had signed, he couldn't join another club even when the term of the agreement had run out, yet the club could retain him or free him at will. At the time the maximum wage was £20, which admittedly compared favourably to the national average pay of £12, but the clubs were pulling in enormous attendances every week and we couldn't help but wonder where all the money was going. There were all sorts of rumours, including one that some clubs had special turnstiles which collected cash which was never declared, though I never saw any hard evidence of that. Whatever, the clubs were awash with money and not much of it trickled down to the players, without whom there would have been no football.

I was never a polished committee man, more of a rough diamond willing to voice my own opinion and that of my fellow professionals at Old Trafford. But I relished my work with the PFA, partly because I believed so passionately in the justice of our cause, but also because it was a pleasure to operate alongside two such able and committed people as the chairman, Jimmy Hill, and a lovely Welshman named Cliff Lloyd, who was the secretary. A lot of people have a go at Jimmy Hill, but not me. He was an inspirational leader and today's handsomely rewarded footballers owe him a huge debt. Jimmy had never been a great player, and had never claimed to be; rather he was a hard-working bustler for Fulham, powerful and honest, but limited. But he will go down in history for his magnificent work with the PFA, after which he became a visionary chairman with Coventry City, then a hugely successful broadcaster. Because he has never been afraid to voice controversial opinions, and maybe a little bit because of that famously prominent chin, sometimes he is portrayed as a buffoon. But take it from me, nothing could be further from the truth.

Back in 1961, there came a point when we were considering strike action, and my job was to make sure the United players were aware of all the facts and that they went along to the meetings. There was one enormous gathering at the Grand Hotel in Manchester at which the Bolton left-back Tommy Banks, a famously blunt, outspoken individual, stood up and asked if he could put a question to Brother Matthews. It was a remark which produced a massive roar of laughter because we were never a political organisation, rather a group of workers campaigning for our rights. When Stan climbed to his feet and declared that he would support his fellow players to the hilt, it was a brilliant moment because at that time he was the biggest name of all. Everyone leapt to their feet and cheered him to the rafters, then there was a unanimous vote to strike if necessary. It was generous of Stan to back us because he could have earned ten times his weekly wage at Blackpool for a single exhibition match, or picked up even more by accepting offers from abroad.

I believe the solidarity of our stand showed that the Football League was in the wrong morally. It was a battle we had to win and we won it because our opponents had no leg to stand on. Quite simply, we highlighted the truth that they had been coining money off the players' backs for far too long. It was downright wicked and I was delighted by the lifting of the maximum wage in 1961, and by George Eastham's victory in his 1963 court case against Newcastle, which finally scuppered the iniquitous 'retain and transfer' system. Mind, I think the League played their cards wrong in trying to knock us back completely on both wages and freedom of contract. If they had accepted a compromise then the pace of change might have been slower, though it would have come to the same in the end.

The result of our efforts was a gigantic jump in the standard of living for leading performers. Most famously Johnny Haynes, the marvellously talented Fulham and England midfield general, became Britain's first £100-a-week footballer, while I believe United's leading earners were getting somewhere between £60 and £80. It didn't make a lot of difference to my personal circumstances because I was about to finish as a player, but I was proud to have played my small part in achieving social justice, and in opening the door for high-quality footballers to earn what their skills deserved. Still, though, there was no question of riches beyond our wildest dreams. Players didn't think of becoming multi-millionaires in my day. For the majority, if they could get enough money together to run a business, maybe a newsagent's shop, when they had laid aside their boots, then it was enough.

While that unforgettable PFA campaign was gathering momentum, then reaching its tumultuous climax, and I was engaged in my ultimately doomed struggle to rescue my career, Matt Busby was marshalling his forces and beginning to rebuild his ravaged team. Shortly after my injury in December 1959 he brought in the combative Maurice Setters from West Bromwich Albion, ostensibly to replace the gentler Freddie Goodwin at right-half. But actually the newcomer fulfilled my role in the team and I don't believe he would have been recruited if I had remained fit. The most remarkable feat by a United man that season, in which we finished seventh in the First Division, was that of Dennis Viollet in scoring 32 League goals, still a club record at the time of writing, although Cristiano Ronaldo pushed him close in 2007/08. It was nothing short of a scandal that Dennis wasn't capped before the air crash, and it did little to mitigate the selectors' blind incompetence that they finally gave him his chance at the end of his most prolific term. Indeed, the fact that they discarded him after only two appearances merely emphasised their lack of judgement.

In 1960/61, reconstruction gathered pace with the arrival of the eloquent Irishman, Noel Cantwell, to take over from his countryman Joe Carolan at left-back. It seemed hard on Joe, but Noel was vastly experienced, the Republic of Ireland captain and a born leader. He was always going to get the nod and it would be only a matter of time before he took over as United skipper. As a player he oozed class and loved to play the ball out of trouble, though occasionally he would be caught out when he tried something a little too flashy. Like Bill Foulkes, who finally settled in his best position of centre-half in the September, he commanded enormous respect and the two of them played integral roles in another seventh-place finish, commendable enough in the circumstances. The Boss viewed both men as dependable bulwarks as he steadily assembled the building blocks of what would become his third great team. Meanwhile, though my own playing career was in ruins, my future also lay in the benevolent hands of Matt Busby.

Chapter 10
A FRESH START

DESPERATE THOUGH I was to fight back from my broken leg and reclaim my place in the Manchester United team, during 1960/61 there had been a gradual dawning of realisation that I might not make it. One of my early targets had been to recover sufficiently to claim a place on the close-season tour of the United States and Canada only six months after suffering the injury, but that proved entirely unrealistic. I wasn't happy to be left at home but, as I still harboured dreams of a top-level return at this point, I was ready to work like a demon to regain fitness. Even after that tour in the May and June of 1960 I couldn't train with the others because I couldn't kick a ball properly, and my leg was far too weak to withstand a tackle. So I went through my paces on my own in the afternoons, running with a limp and pushing myself as hard as I could to get the rest of my body in the best possible condition for when the limb finally knitted together satisafactorily.

As Matt and Jimmy witnessed my feverish efforts, they must have drawn two conclusions. The first would have been that I wasn't going to be much use to them as a player, which is why the club claimed insurance money to cover the loss of my services towards the end of 1960/61. But the second would have been far more positive from my point of view. They could see that my passion for both the game and the club was undiluted by my mishap, and they could identify a niche for me at Old Trafford as they continued their own mammoth task of rebuilding in the wake of Munich.

It so happened that Bill Inglis was due to retire as assistant trainer to Jack Crompton in the spring of 1961, and Matt put it to me that I might

The first day of the rest of my life: I gather up the footballs and set off for the training pitch.

take Bill's place. He was very diplomatic and didn't write off my playing future out of hand, although he stressed that, having discussed my case with a wide variety of doctors and bone specialists, my chances of a playing return were mighty slim. He knew me very well and probably understood that, deep inside me, there still burned a tiny spark of ambition that I might yet complete my comeback against all the odds. In the real world, meanwhile, if I accepted his offer I could continue to work on my fitness while earning a wage – £20 per week, the same as the maximum pay for a first-teamer at the time – and widening my experience enormously.

This was fantastic news, not only because it removed the creeping fear that I might be forced to leave the United 'family', but also because Beryl and I were getting married in July 1961 and I had to make a living. In fact, the club proved to be generous beyond my wildest expectation as they bought a house for us, 5 Moss Lane in Timperley, just down the road from where we live now, and rented it to us for £1 a week

No employer could have treated me better, or made it more abundantly clear how much they valued me, and now I wanted to respond in kind. So, without entirely jettisoning my private hopes of a miracle, I lost as little time as possible in gaining the necessary coaching and medical qualifications and I was ready to start my second career with Manchester United in July 1961, the day after getting back from our honeymoon.

The wedding took place at St Aidan's Church, Wythenshawe, with Shay Brennan as my best man and lots of guests from the club. Beryl had laid down only two conditions when we set the date: one was that my leg was out of plaster, so that I didn't have to hop down the aisle; the other was that there were to be no water pistols at the church or the reception. No problem, I was a mature 23-year-old now!

After our two weeks in Majorca, I was ready to throw myself into my new life with every bit of enthusiasm and determination I could muster, and that was quite a bit. Indeed, it wasn't long before some of my new charges, who also happened to be my old pals, were beginning to think I might be taking my job a little *too* seriously. Pre-season training is always very tough – it has to be if it's going to do the players any good – and I was eager to take the United squad's fitness to a new level. At that early point of our preparation all the age-groups worked together,

One of those rare days in my life when football took a back seat. Best man Shay Brennan looks less nervous than me outside the church; Matt Busby steals a kiss from Beryl, my lovely bride; I still look a tad tense in this group comprising, left to right, United fan Harold Hodgkinson, Dennis Viollet, Bill Foulkes, Bobby English, Maurice Setters, Shay, Matt, the happy couple, friend Ronnie Curran, Bobby Charlton and Gordon Clayton.

and I drove them so mercilessly that Dennis Viollet jokingly christened me 'Adolf Eichmann.' At least, I like to think he was joking!

On a serious note, maybe 18 months of utter frustration had found an outlet. At last I could release the pressure induced by my enforced inactivity, and use my boundless energy for the good of the club. I found that even with my dodgy leg I could run at the front of the group, and I saw no reason why the rest of the lads shouldn't keep up with me, at the very least. In truth, despite Dennis likening me to the notorious Nazi war criminal, I felt the senior players reacted brilliantly to my new regime, though I couldn't say the same for some of the youngsters. For instance, there was Eamon Dunphy, the sharp-witted, distinctly lippy little Dubliner who was destined to become an award-winning writer – though not an award-winning footballer, despite some decent achievements for Millwall and the Republic. Once he upset me so much with his moaning that I dragged him out of the dressing room to remonstrate with him in private. He begged me not to take him to Matt Busby, so I bundled him into the ball boy's room and gave him a couple of slaps in an attempt to knock some sense into him. That wasn't the end of it, though. The next day his big pal Barry Fry – a useful player and a cocky Londoner who talked even more than me (he still does!) – clattered into me with a couple of late tackles in a five-a-side, then told me I wouldn't be taking him to the ball boys' room as I had Eamon. I told Barry I had no quarrel with him, but he continued to rant, insisting that we went to the back of the Stretford End to sort out our differences. By then I was so incensed that, unwisely, I agreed and pretty soon we launched into a tremendous punch-up – which I was winning comfortably, let me add – when we were interrupted by senior trainer Jack Crompton. Understandably Jack went potty at the sight of his assistant lacing into one of the young players, who had blood streaming from his nose and my arm round his neck in a headlock. I could have been for the high jump, I might even have lost my job, but for Barry's quick thinking. 'It's all right Jack,' he said. 'Wilf was just showing me one or two wrestling holds.' Jack swallowed the explanation, though whether he believed it was another matter. I was forever grateful to Barry, firstly for not bearing a grudge, secondly for having his wits about him, though probably I had him running even harder in training the next day.

Working under Jack was a privilege. He was an old-fashioned trainer rather than a tactical coach, a tough taskmaster who knew how to get footballers fit, a straight shooter with no frills about him. While I didn't agree with everything he did – in some things I was more adventurous, being a young man with fresh ideas – I held him in total respect. Jack was a phenomenally hard grafter who demanded the highest of standards from everyone around him, but sometimes he was so zealous that he kept us at the training ground when, in most people's eyes, there was no need. Much of our work wasn't in the slightest bit glamorous. We had to dig dirt, do our share of skivvying, but that wasn't a problem for either of us. There were no specialist kit-men in those days, so we had to get everything ready, pack it in skips and then hump them to whatever form of transport we were using.

Overall, my transformation from footballer to trainer was an exercise in growing up, in stepping into the real world. For instance, no more were there long afternoons off to play golf or snooker. Before I broke my leg my golf handicap was on its way down towards single figures, not quite on a par with Bobby, Shay and Johnny Giles, but I think I might have equalled them if I'd had the time. However, my new responsibilities meant there was no time to practise and my handicap shot up. Instead of pacing the fairways I might be at a reserve or schoolboy game, or preparing new training routines, or even collecting smelly piles of filthy shirts, shorts and socks for the laundry. The evenings weren't free, either, what with the never-ending procession of matches at different levels, and sessions for the juniors and amateurs at The Cliff on Tuesdays and Thursdays. Not that I was complaining. To use the modern idiom, you might say that I lived the game 24/7, but it was a way of life that I relished. There was an uplifting feeling that I was doing my bit towards the reconstruction of the club, helping to bring through talented young-sters such as Ian Moir, Phil Chisnall and Sammy McMillan, then David Sadler, Bobby Noble, Willie Anderson, John Fitzpatrick and a certain George Best.

True, it was exhausting and overwhelmingly time-consuming, but being a trainer at Old Trafford was also exciting and fantastically enlightening. It revealed to me the inside of the game, how it really ticked, what it meant to make decisions while looking at the big picture as it affected the whole club, rather than concentrating on the comparatively narrow concerns which naturally pre-occupy you as a player.

Sundays were very special. In an era before games were played on the sabbath, the routine was to assemble at the ground in the morning to assess any injuries suffered the day before. Then, around midday, there would be a meeting in the boardroom, presided over by Matt, with Jimmy, Jack, coach John Aston, club doctor Francis McHugh, physio Ted Dalton and myself all in attendance. There would be a bottle of best malt whisky in circulation, with maybe a drop of water or dry ginger, and I would absorb wisdom from all sides as we talked football, chewed the fat about every aspect of the game in general and United in particular. We would review the previous day's game, plan what was happening the following week, examine tactics and put all our footballers under the microscope: how they could be improved, where best to deploy them, which ones might be struggling, which needed an arm round their shoulder and which might need a boot up the backside.

Then there was the question of the youth players, only a tiny handful of whom would be good enough for Manchester United in the long term. Perhaps the most painful process in the game is telling a young hopeful with stars in his eyes that he is not going to make the grade at the club he worships. I always tried to be gentle with them but also realistic, pointing out that the world was a big place and that there would be somewhere in it for them to achieve something worthwhile, even though it hadn't worked out for them at Old Trafford. Above all, I told them to believe in themselves and urged them not to accept being on the scrapheap in their teens. These principles were espoused by everyone on the United coaching staff from Matt Busby downwards. They were part of the club's family ethos, to which I keep returning and which was always in evidence at those Sunday get-togethers. Everybody around that boardroom table really cared about the people in their charge, and I was proud to be associated with them.

I suppose I was in a rather unusual position at the time. Having been a Busby Babe so recently and being still in my early twenties, I was a close friend of many of the players, and that might have proved awkward in my new, responsible role. But I set myself a strict code of behaviour and I adhered to it rigidly. I would never pass on to the management what was said by the players in my presence, and vice versa. The way I saw it was simple: I'm United, they're United, so where's the problem? Certainly I don't believe the players saw me as a potential snitch and we had some terrific times together. Of course, we had differences of opinion and plenty of spirited discussions over a pint or two, often in the Quadrant pub in Stretford after a game or on a Sunday lunchtime. Newcomers such as Noel Cantwell and Maurice Setters loved to talk exhaustively, and sometimes their views, particularly on modern coaching methods, would contrast radically with mine, which had been inculcated through growing up at Old Trafford. But that was all part of the fun. They knew I wasn't going to go running to the manager with what they had said. Anyway, Matt was well aware that Maurice, in particular, could be something of a barrack-room lawyer, as he demonstrated with a sharp rebuke after one match with West Ham in which not everything had gone according to plan. 'It seems to me, Maurice, that yours is the only voice I hear when I come into this dressing-room. Well, I don't want to hear it again.' Such was the force of the Busby personality, that the voluble Setters said no more.

A good friend of mine was, and remains, Matt's son, Sandy Busby, and he was in a similar situation to me, hearing two sides of everything. But he was always totally discreet when he was with the players, and I'm absolutely sure he didn't tell tales out of school to his father. Sandy is a charming individual, who reminds me strongly of both his parents and is great company. There was a time when he had hopes of a football career, but spells at Blackburn, Oldham and United all came to nothing. There were similar experiences for Jimmy Murphy's boy, Nick, and my own son, Paul, who both found that it's extremely difficult to follow a father who has done a bit in the game.

As I continued to bed in to my coaching responsibilities, so Matt pushed on with the painstaking process of shaping his new team, and while I felt we were always moving in the right direction, results were not always encouraging. In 1961/62, for instance, we slipped to 15th in the table, which didn't reflect the quality in the squad. By now young men such as Johnny Giles, Jimmy Nicholson, Tony Dunne and the two Norberts, Stiles and Lawton, were beginning to pile up the appearances, but it remained to be seen whether they could become established in the long term. Meanwhile Matt surprised many observers by changing his centre-forward, selling Dennis Viollet, who had been such a key component of the side and part of the fabric of Old Trafford since before Munich, and bringing in the Arsenal man, David Herd.

Although he took time to settle, there was no argument about David's quality, and he wasn't exactly an unknown quantity to the Boss. Matt had played with Herdy's dad, Alex, at Manchester City and had known the lad all his life. Although David was a Scottish international, he had grown up in Manchester and, ironically, had been a school chum of Dennis Viollet. In fact, he had come close to joining United from his first club, Stockport County, as a teenager before ending up at Highbury, where he had been superbly successful and won his five caps. David packed an explosive shot and he never stopped working, but he wasn't a flashy performer. At the end of many a match it might be mentioned that he'd had a quiet game, but it was a fair bet that his name would be found on the scoresheet.

So I could see the attraction of David Herd, but it was much harder to understand why such a thoroughbred as Dennis Viollet was allowed to depart for Stoke City when he was still only 28 and in his free-scoring prime. The only answer which springs readily to mind is that maybe Matt was already working on the incoming transfer of Denis Law, who would arrive in the summer of 1962, and may have been under pressure to balance the books financially. After all, it's a fact that our manager was always a bit careful with money – I would never have called him tight myself, though I knew a few people who did!

As 1962/63 kicked off, with the incomparable Law having been recruited from Torino for a British record fee of £115,000, I was even more convinced that Manchester United were on their way back to becoming a major force in the game. In fact, we were in for a traumatic season of transition, most of which was spent disturbingly close to the wrong end of the First Division table. At one point there were even mutterings in the press about Matt Busby being sacked. To me, and to the players, this was unthinkable and we viewed the mere suggestion as an outrage. Even now I find it hard to believe that it was ever a serious option for the board to dispense with the services of the man who had built the modern Manchester United, and who had suffered so much in the service of the club. Fortunately Harold Hardman, a fellow of sound judgement, was the chairman and sane counsels prevailed. Honestly, I was shocked that the words 'Busby' and 'sack' could even be mentioned in the same sentence, but nothing should ever shock you in the crazy world of football and I suppose there were parallels with Stan Cullis being dismissed by Wolves after winning three championships and the FA Cup. Stan was a father figure at Molineux in exactly the same way Matt was at Old Trafford, though he was a somewhat wilder figure than the United boss. As we walked up the tunnel after beating his boys 1-0 in the second leg of the 1954 FA Youth Cup Final, I recall him aiming a kick at the backside of one of his players for conceding the penalty, converted by David Pegg, which secured the trophy for us. Never in a year of Sundays could I imagine our manager doing such a thing. Jimmy maybe, but certainly not Matt!

During that Arctic winter of 1962/63, it was not only the possibility of relegation that occupied our minds, but also the difficulties in keeping the players fit during the big freeze, which dictated that we didn't play a League game between Boxing Day and the end of February. The surface at The Cliff was rock hard, and my duties extended to digging holes in an attempt to get rid of the water under the ice. With Jack as my taskmaster, there was no question of shirking, and many's the day I headed for home with an aching back.

When the blessed thaw finally set in, United had a new arrival to parade in the shape of Paddy Crerand, the sweet-passing Scottish international wing-half who had been signed from Celtic. He wasn't an instant success – indeed, the fear of demotion intensified as he finished on the winning side only once in his first ten League outings – but in the long term he was to exert a gigantic influence for the good. As it was, Paddy improved steadily as the season wore on, and after the spectre of the drop was eventually banished with only one game to play, he emerged as a shining star as United concluded a difficult campaign on the highest of notes by lifting the FA Cup.

The final against Leicester, who were hot favourites after finishing near the top of the First Division table, was the turning point in the development of our new team. It was a sunny day at Wembley and we played football to match, winning 3-1 thanks to a goal from Denis Law and two from David Herd. True, we were helped by some uncharacteristic errors from the City goalkeeper Gordon Banks, our old Youth Cup adversary in his Chesterfield days, but we fully deserved to win and that performance sent a surge of renewed belief through the club.

Not everybody at Old Trafford was happy, though. Johnny Giles was being played on the right wing, which didn't suit him, and I'm certain that contributed to his departure to join Leeds in the following August. I don't know all the details, but I believe he and the manager had a bust-up about where he was being played from which there was no going back. I was disappointed at the prospect of waving goodbye to such a good pal and tremendous player, and shortly before the move went though I said to him: 'Let me have a word with Matt, He might change his mind.' The mega-talented little Irishman's reply was typical: 'He might change his mind, but I'm not changing mine.'

John was thoughtful, deeply intelligent and an extremely strong character. He always told me that I was too much of a romantic, and I dare say there were other people who agreed with him. Certainly I was a romantic in comparison to John, who was very much a hard-nosed realist. I cared deeply for Matt, the club and its tradition, and that outlook tended to dictate many of my actions. Apart from my personal regard for John, I didn't want United to lose a man who, I was convinced, could play an enormous part in the reconstruction of the team. He was such a clever footballer, both skilful and strong – it was difficult to get anywhere near him on the training pitch. John went on to do a magnificent job as a midfield play-maker for Don Revie at Elland Road, and my mind boggles to contemplate what he might have achieved alongside Best, Law and Charlton. Maybe it would have been hard to accommodate the lot of them, but it's essential for every successful club to have a squad of top-quality players and I'm positive that Matt Busby could have deployed them all successfully.

For most people when they leave Old Trafford, the only way is down, but John was unusual in that he went on to scale lofty peaks elsewhere. It was a different story for two of his contemporaries, Nobby Lawton and Jimmy Nicholson, both of whom had made promising starts at United but never quite made the step-up to become first-team regulars, and left the club while still in their early twenties. Though the pair of them went on to enjoy long and extremely worthy careers – Nobby captained Preston in an FA Cup Final and Jimmy became a stalwart for Huddersfield and Northern Ireland – neither of them quite lived up to their early potential. Nobby, who could play at inside-forward but was most effective as a wing-half, was a decent, correct individual and that's

The United reserve side which Matt Busby entrusted to my tender loving care. Back row, left to right: Mike Lorimer, Frank Haydock, Nobby Lawton, David Gaskell, Ronnie Briggs, Ian Moir, Alex Dawson, coach Wilf McGuinness. Front row: Alan Atherton (father of former England cricket captain Mike Atherton), Ernie Ackerley, Sammy McMillan, Phil Chisnall, Bobby Smith, Tony Dunne, Jimmy Nicholson, Willie Donaldson.

how he played the game. He was a cultured passer adept at switching the play, he was dutiful in supporting team-mates on the ball and picking up opposition runners when we lost possession, and he was willing to put himself about physically. Add all that up and he sounds like an ideal United footballer, but somehow he proved slightly below the level Matt was looking for and was allowed to go. Jimmy was another talented wing-half and I really thought he had the makings. The fans loved him, both for his football and his film-star looks, but he was saddled from an early age with the most ridiculous tag of all. People called him the new Duncan Edwards, and that was way over the top. In the end he didn't make it in Manchester, enduring poor luck with injuries but also, perhaps, there was too much competition from the likes of Paddy Crerand, Maurice Setters and one of my favourite people, Nobby Stiles. I'll spend some time talking about my pal from Collyhurst in a later chapter.

Chapter 11

THREE VISIONS OF GREATNESS (AND THE REST WEREN'T BAD, EITHER!)

THE 1960S WERE fabulous years for me – what a shame 1970 had to happen! True, I had missed out on what should have been my footballing prime, in my hometown, with the greatest club in all the world. But, my goodness, there were compensations. Although I was denied the opportunity to play in the same breathtaking Manchester United team as George Best, Denis Law and Bobby Charlton, I had the privilege and the sheer joy of joining them on the training pitch, helping to prepare them for the magnificent conquests they were destined to make, and relishing every last kick and scuffle of the five-a-sides we shared.

No British side has ever been blessed with three such superb performers at the same time, three European Footballers of the Year. People often ask me who was the best of that incomparable trio, and it's impossible to offer a definitive answer. Each of them painted a picture for me in my head – they offered three contrasting visions of greatness.

My abiding image of George is one of this wiry little figure twisting and turning like an eel, perfectly balanced under the most extreme of pressure. It was almost impossible to knock him down and on the rare occasions when he was flattened he would bounce back up in the blink of an eye, like one of those children's toys which always return to the vertical no matter how hard they're smacked.

Look at those muscles – and Bobby's are pretty impressive, too! On holiday in the early 1960s with a Real Madrid fan, who is holding my daughter, Anna.

Law and, er, Charlton. Heston, that is, as United visit the set of the epic film 55 Days In Peking during a summer tour.

Then there was the phenomenon that was Denis, rising like some jet-propelled salmon to propel a bullet header towards the goal, seeming to hold himself in the air against all the known laws of physics. What a fantastic sight for United fans, though he was enough to scare the pants off everybody else, because nobody was spikier than Denis on the football pitch.

Finally there was Bobby, who was like a thoroughbred racehorse, all grace and style. When he was surging forward, drifting past helpless opponents, you might have been watching ballet. Where George was quicker and jinkier, and Denis sharper and more aggressive in his movement, Bobby flowed like a river on its way to the estuary, and his estuary was the goal. He was what so many people wanted their football to look like – beautifully smooth but with an explosion at the end.

In training George had the ball so much that we had to change our techniques, otherwise nobody else would have got a kick. In the short-sided games he held possession so long that we made it two-touch, then one-touch, but he even got round that by knocking it against his opponent's legs and getting it back. He didn't have Bobby's awesome power, or Denis's predatory instinct around the box, but he had genius in his feet. Not that he was a show pony in any way. For all his dribbling and selling dummies that left defenders on the floor, he had a shrewd football brain. George was particularly adept at using his team-mates, pretending to pass to them, then heading off in the opposite direction. This didn't always go down brilliantly with other players who might have made 50-yard runs to receive the ball, but they didn't mind when he scored a sensational goal from a seemingly impossible position – and he did it all the time.

Yet for all his celebrated artistry, and the unrivalled delicacy with which he manoeuvred a football, he was as tough as teak, too. I think it should be a requirement for all modern youngsters to watch videos of George Best being kicked, hacked, pushed, but refusing to go down. He would have scorned the very idea of diving, opting always to stay on his feet and try for a goal. That was his answer to all the abuse – I'm NOT going down. A perfect illustration came against Chelsea at Old Trafford in the League Cup in October 1970, towards the end of my time as manager. George danced past the fearsome Ron Harris, who did his best to live up to his famous nickname of 'Chopper' by attempting to boot our little Irish fella to Kingdom Come. But George rode that horrendous tackle – if that's what you want to call it – and knocked in a memorable goal. It was as though he was indestructible and he was telling opponents: 'Come on, do your worst, it won't stop me.' And it didn't.

I was learning my trade as a coach at the time he arrived, and I got to know him well during his time in the youth team, a period of his life when he was as good as gold. It would be fantastic for me to be able to say that I nurtured George's gifts and directed him on his pathway to stardom. But that would be a load of rubbish. George didn't scale the heights of the game because he was nurtured, it was because he was a once-in-a-lifetime talent and Manchester United were lucky that he landed in their lap.

Matt realised that from the outset and nursed him a little because he was only a wisp of a lad when he crossed the Irish Sea and he might have been clogged all over the shop had he turned out regularly for the reserves. Of course, he was a fixture in the first team some five months before his 18th birthday, but never was there a hint of conceit about him. At that stage, off the pitch, he was just like all the other teenagers at Old Trafford, enjoying ten-pin bowling and trips to the cinema – there wasn't the slightest hint of the problems that were to beset him later in his career.

The story has often been told of his early homesickness, and he did return to Belfast after his initial arrival, but that state of mind didn't last long and for all that little bit of uncertainty, I think he was always confident in his ability. How else do you explain the way he made a mug out of Harry Gregg in one of his first training sessions? Harry, don't forget, was a larger-than-life personality, a fiery individual who had no truck with nonsense and a fellow Ulsterman held up as a national hero in their homeland. But when George met him on the training ground for the first time, he made absolute mincemeat of our international goalkeeper. With his delicious, unreadable swerves and feints, George sent him plunging so many different ways that Harry ended up in a heap in the mud, like some circus contortionist whose act had run hopelessly out of control. Not surprisingly, it made Greggy mad: 'Don't ever do that to me again, son,' was the gist of what he said, though the language might have been a tad more industrial. George wasn't bothered. With ability like that, why should he care? And yes, he did repeat his trick on his famous countryman, and without any unpleasant consequences. For all his natural embarrassment that first time, Harry was a true footballing man at heart and appreciated quality as much as the rest of us when it stared him in the face. As for the rest of us, we had a laugh – in fact, Shay and I use to fantasise jokingly about becoming George's manager and agent, which was just about the only way we were going to be able to retire as relatively young men!

As he developed so rapidly and spectacularly, the demands on his stamina, as well as his extravagant natural gifts, became ever more intense, and for quite a few years he took them all in his increasingly confident stride. There was one insanely hectic week which started with George helping the first team to beat Nottingham Forest at Old Trafford on the Saturday, then travelling down to Swindon for the first leg of the FA Youth Cup Final on the Monday. After scoring in a 1-1 draw with Don Rogers and company – what a truly terrific prospect that boy was – George flew to Belfast on the Tuesday ready to face Uruguay in his second full international a day later. On the Thursday morning I collected him at Manchester airport, then whisked him away for an afternoon of rest before he was off again for that evening's second-leg youth encounter with Swindon, which we won comfortably, courtesy of a David Sadler hat-trick – and all David's goals were set up by George! It all added up to four important games in six days and he came through that formidable sequence in fine, bright-eyed fettle. Of course, no player would be allowed to entertain such a schedule today, and quite right too, but it just goes to emphasise what a phenomenal athlete he was.

Obviously George was the shining light of that successful youth side, but there were some other tremendous contributors, too. Jimmy Rimmer was in goal, Alan Duff and Bobby Noble were the full-backs, the half-back line comprised Peter McBride, John Farrar and John Fitzpatrick, and there was a swashbuckling attack made up of Willie Anderson, George, David Sadler, Albert Kinsey and John Aston junior. Only Duff, McBride and Farrar didn't go on to make at least one appearance in the first team, and six of the boys became regulars, at least for a time. The older John Aston was their chief coach, with Jimmy Murphy in overall charge, but I was involved, too, and I found the work profoundly satisfying. I have always had a soft spot for the FA Youth Cup, having picked up a hat-trick of winner's medals in the 1950s, but there was also a sense of helping to put a few bricks in the wall of the new post-Munich Manchester United.

Returning to George, despite the trauma of his later years and a few problems he caused me in my management days, which I'll discuss later, I'll always maintain that he was a terrific human being, a well-mannered lad 99 per-cent of the time. It was only natural that as his talent came to the fore he acquired a certain self-assurance, but for all his fantastic achievements and colourful exploits, he was essentially a genuinely modest person.

So was Denis Law, whose passion for privacy exceeded that of any other player I have known. He had five children and a lovely wife, and all he wanted to do after training was go home to them. Not that he was a killjoy. He always had – and still has – an irrepressibly bubbly sense of humour and he would enjoy terrific fun with the lads, but when his work was done, then he was off. Denis was no townie.

But what a player he was! Absolutely electrifying. There was a sense of the dramatic about everything Denis did on the pitch, whether it was climbing to prodigious heights to reach a header, scoring with a seemingly impossible bicycle kick or conducting an explosive rant at whoever happened to be near him when something had not gone according to plan. Denis played with a remarkable intensity of feeling. He was a study in aggression, a born winner, and even in training you had to be careful to avoid his flailing elbows.

I recall one game against Burnley, it must have been in the late 1960s, when young Michael Docherty, the son of Tommy, got under Denis' skin. There was no allowance for inexperience as the Lawman jabbed his tormentor savagely with his elbow, and Michael went down flat on the floor as if he had been pole-axed. First on the scene was Paddy Crerand, not exactly a shrinking violet but even he was startled and he demanded of his fellow Scot: 'Why did you do that? He's only a boy.' The growled reply from Denis summed up his fierce, single-minded attitude to his work: 'If he's only a boy then he should be at school!'

But although raw aggression and superb athleticism were integral parts of his footballing make-up, there was far more to his game. He had sensational natural ability, which was obvious from his early days at Manchester City when he would collect the ball in deep positions before taking it past opponent after opponent. It wasn't often we saw him do that for United because Matt employed him as a striker, but there was one example of his quicksilver dribbling skills that I will never forget. It happened at Old Trafford in a fabulously entertaining Charity Shield encounter with Spurs, which finished 3-3 and in which the Tottenham 'keeper Pat Jennings embarrassed Alex Stepney by scoring with a towering drop-kick which caught the wind. But even Pat's unforgettable freak wasn't the goal of the game. That was laid on by Denis, who picked the ball up in the left-back position on the edge of his own box, then linked up with Brian Kidd and weaved past three tackles before setting up Bobby, who almost burst the net with a 25-yard thunderbolt that was spectacular even by his exalted standards.

As for Bobby himself, his colossal achievements and his personal closeness to me run through this story like a constant thread. He was an all-time great in terms of both talent and sportsmanship, and he went on to become arguably the finest ambassador that British sport has ever known.

It must have been intimidating for any group of players to be faced by three of the finest footballers ever to walk the planet, but one man who did his utmost to turn that challenge to his own side's advantage was Bill Shankly, the inspirational manager of Liverpool in the 1960s and a close friend of Matt Busby. It's a story that has done the rounds, but bears repeating because it sums up both the astronomical regard in which George, Denis and Bobby were held, and the unique motivational powers of the man who transformed the Anfield club from serial underachievers into an enduringly successful force.

As he was giving his team talk before sending out his lads to meet Matt's men, he ran through the United side individually, and it went something like this: Stepney, he can't catch; Brennan, he's slow; Dunne, can't play, couldn't make a pass to save his life; Crerand, oh he's deceptive, slower than he looks ... and so on, until he had made verbal mincemeat of eight members of our team. Then he stopped, and one of the Liverpool boys piped up: 'That sounds great, Boss, but what about Best and Law and Charlton?' The great motivator's reply, in that familiar rasping voice, was a show-stopper: 'Och well, son, they can play a bit, to be sure, but if you can't beat a team with only three men then you shouldn't be wearing a Liverpool shirt in the first place!'

Of course, when he made his assessment of United's line-up, Bill's tongue was very firmly in his cheek, as I know he had the utmost respect for them all – and so he should, because quite a few of them were international stars in their own right. They were mates of mine, too, and none more so than Nobby Stiles, who had been baptised at the same Collyhurst church as me and reminded me a lot of myself – although I was far better looking, of course!

Nobby, four and a half years my junior, began making an impact at Old Trafford after I'd broken my leg and moved into coaching. I always felt tremendous empathy with him, partly because our roots were in the same place, but also because of his never-say-die attitude and his chirpy personality. His family was smashing, too – his dad was an undertaker, he'd be the last man to let you down!

As a teenager Nobby had shown extreme promise as an inside-forward, but he went on to make his name for both Manchester United and England as an indestructible ball-winner, most successfully in the centre of defence for his club and in midfield for his country. Invariably he was characterised as a destroyer, and I'd be the last to deny that when Nobby tackled an opponent, then he stayed tackled. But there was far more to his input than blood-curdling challenges. He was a creator and a thinker, who read the game magnificently, moved into spaces and often embarked on clever runs. Sometimes it was as though Nobby was watching a film of the game, and so sharp was his sense of anticipation that he appeared to see the action several frames ahead of everybody else. He could sniff out danger before it materialised and often he didn't have to tackle because he had made a cunning interception.

Had it not been for my accident, we might have been rivals for the same role, but I was out of the picture by the time he broke through, and the man blocking his path was Maurice Setters. But Nobby was a better all-round player and it wasn't long before he pushed Maurice out, settling into a marvellously efficient partnership with Bill Foulkes in the middle of the back four. They complemented each other perfectly, with Bill usually going for the first challenge and Nobby mopping up. Nobby liked playing with Foulkesy because he knew exactly what the big fella would do in any given situation. He much preferred that to partnering someone who tried to be flashy. Nobby didn't have any time for that, and he would give such people the mother and father of all rollickings.

Mind, he would do that to Jack Charlton occasionally when they linked up for England, and nobody could accuse Big Jack of being a Flash Harry. In one of their earlier games together, Jack did something that Nobby thought was sloppy and the little man started ripping him apart. Now Jack was not a man to turn the other cheek when abuse was being handed out, and he strode over to sort out the little upstart. But when he reached him there was Nobby practically frothing at the mouth and spitting nails, so Jack decided to let it lie. That was Nobby's fire, and in the heat of the action it was all-consuming, but there were two things which made it acceptable. One was that he was such a lovely person away from the pitch, and the other was that he knew the game so well. Invariably when he was ranting and raving at somebody, they realised, deep down, that he was right, and so they put up with it.

As a character, he was one of the most popular at the club, always up for some fun, even though the laugh was often on him. Nobby was incurably clumsy and one of his nicknames was Clouseau, after the inept French detective portrayed by Peter Sellers. If there was wine or soup on the tablecloth, usually it could be traced to Nobby, who always used the excuse of having contact lenses. Sometimes the short-sightedness line could backfire on him, though, never more hilariously than the day a referee tried to book him for kicking someone at Burnley. Nobby came over all innocent, apologised profusely and said his mistimed challenge was due entirely to the fact that he could barely see his hand in front of his face because he was getting used to his new contacts. But then he spoiled the effect, rather, by glaring at the referee's notebook and pointing out: 'By the way, you spell Stiles with an "I", not a "y"!' Nobby was absolutely priceless. Sometimes in the 1960s I would give him a lift to Old Trafford and he was always brilliant company.

As a footballer, I believe he was far more influential than most outsiders understood as Matt Busby's beautifully rebuilt team went from strength to strength in the mid-1960s, winning the League Championship in 1964/65, reaching the semi-finals of the European Cup in 1965/66 and claiming another First Division title in 1966/67.

Another key performer and larger-than-life individual in that side was Paddy Crerand. The first time I saw him in action following his arrival from Celtic in February 1963 he took my breath away with a sumptuous drag-back in front of the south stand at Old Trafford. His marker fell

Toasting Manchester United's League title triumph in 1965, our first since Munich. Left to right are physio Ted Dalton, Matt Busby, a certain chuffed-to-bits reserve team coach, Jimmy Murphy and trainer Jack Crompton.

for the move and I marvelled at his skill. The next moment he unloosed a raking crossfield pass, the type that would become a Crerand trademark, and I thought to myself: 'This is just the sort of player United need.' And I was right. He kept the ball moving and he created countless goals for the likes of Herd, Law, Best, Charlton and John Connelly, the England winger signed from Burnley. Sometimes Paddy's distribution was over-ambitious, but that's bound to happen if you're trying to open up tight defences, and it's fair to say that the majority of his dispatches found their targets.

No matter what the company, it was impossible to miss Paddy because he always wanted the ball. If things weren't going well for the team, he would never hide. Our 'keeper could throw the ball to the right wing and there would be Paddy, ready to receive it and start an attack. Arguably he shouldn't have been out there; maybe he ought to have been helping his defence by chasing down Billy Bremner or whoever. But he was always positive. That's the way he played the game and that's why the supporters loved him, even if he could be a bit of a luxury when we didn't have possession.

Temperamentally he was inclined to be fiery, and he still is! He grew up in a hard school in the Gorbals district of Glasgow and he was not a man you wanted to upset. To say he was able to look after himself was a feeble understatement, and I was always thankful for the fact that I was too small to hit! I've seen him crack a few and his timing of a punch was fantastic. Once I saw him hit a foreign goalkeeper for pushing Matt Busby. Paddy happened to be standing behind the Boss, but he didn't stand on ceremony. One smack and the fellow was on the floor, crawling through people's legs to escape from the angry Scotsman. Later, when he ran The Park, a pub in Altrincham, he was in trouble for breaking one miscreant's nose in three places – in the bar, in the lounge and on the pavement! Okay, maybe I'm taking a bit of artistic licence there, but you get the drift.

In his playing days he was always late for the team coach, and actually got into more trouble for his timekeeping that he did on the field. He always had extremely strong opinions, quite outrageous ones at times, and was virtually impossible to argue with because he would never yield an inch. It's much the same now in his job as an MUTV pundit. I know I'm biased towards United, but he's even worse than me.

Having said all that, though, he has always had the good of United at heart, and he's held in enormously warm regard by pretty well everyone connected with the club. Paddy Crerand was a tremendous footballer and a terrific personality who brings much-needed colour to the game.

A hugely underrated figure in Matt's new team was John Connelly, who proved to be the final piece in the title-winning jigsaw after arriving from Turf Moor. I had a lot of time for John, both as a person – I'd got to know him when his wife, Sandra, was in the same maternity ward as Beryl – and as a footballer. In 1964/65, his first season at Old Trafford, he scored 20 goals from the right flank, including five in Europe, as the lads picked up our first League Championship since Munich. That was a phenomenal contribution in itself, but he also helped to create bags of chances for Charlton, Herd, Law and Best, all of whom hit double figures. He never stopped working up and down his line, he wasn't afraid to dig into a tackle, he was intelligent and he was equally effective on either wing. What more could anyone want?

Matt usually bought proven players and John was no exception, having won the championship with Burnley five years earlier and turned out in plenty of internationals. The only pity was that he didn't stay longer, but he went to Blackburn in the autumn of 1966, apparently after having some sort of barney with the manager. Clearly he was still at the top of his game because he'd played in the first match of that summer's World Cup finals, but John was always a fellow to stand up for himself, as even that renowned disciplinarian Alf Ramsey discovered. During the squad's get-together at Lilleshall before the tournament, John went out for a pint with Nobby Stiles and Alan Ball and didn't observe the strict curfew which had been imposed. When he discovered that, Alf said to trainer Les Cocker and myself that if the three of them didn't apologise in the morning he would send them home. I've got a feeling that when the manager took that line he believed I would warn them of the danger they were in, which, naturally enough, I did. Duly, when they were hauled before Alf the next day, Alan and Nobby were full of suitable regret, but John was not so meek, telling the England boss: 'I think you're overdoing it, Alf.' Les and I could hardly believe his temerity, but fortunately Alf chose to be lenient, perhaps taking the winger's words as something of an apology anyway. Be that as it may, it was absolutely clear there was no way John Connelly was going to be trodden on by anybody. What passed between him and Matt I have no idea, but I'm not surprised that neither of them would back down. Of course, in such a situation there is only going to be one winner, and that isn't the player. So he was sold to Blackburn, where he did well, but I'm convinced he could have made a further invaluable contribution to the Old Trafford cause if he'd stayed.

At that time, everywhere you looked in the United side you saw excellence. Of course, the star-studded forward line tended to collect most of the credit, and that was understandable. The half-backs were pretty well recognised, too, but I've always believed that the full-back partnership of my old pal Shay Brennan and the ultra-efficient little Irishman Tony Dunne deserved far more credit than it received.

Shay was a Mancunian whose parents were Irish so he was eligible for both England and the Republic at international level, and there was a time when it looked like he might opt for the country of his birth. In fact, Walter Winterbottom picked him in his preliminary squad of 40 for the 1962 World Cup finals in Chile, but he was behind the experienced Jimmy Armfield of Blackpool in the pecking order and then Fulham's George Cohen came on strongly, so in the end Shay chose Ireland. But whoever he played for, Shay was a supremely polished performer. When he walked out for a game he was always immaculate, with spotless white shorts, perfectly pressed red shirt, not a hair on his handsome head out of place. Then when he returned to the dressing room after a hard-fought game on a muddy pitch, his shorts would be spotless, his shirt perfectly pressed ... at least, that was the joke. Of course, I'm exaggerating, but only up to a point. The fact was that Shay rarely tackled so he didn't get his kit dirty. He didn't need to because he was very quick and the epitome of cool, preferring to usher his winger away from the danger area rather than diving in. If he did decide to make a challenge, or was hurried into an emergency clearance, then invariably he would end up just touching the ball over the line instead of whacking it over the stand. Sometimes his approach used to infuriate dear old Jimmy Murphy, who relished the physical side of the game, rather like me, but the Brennan style was much smoother – and it worked.

Alongside him was the dark-haired little Dubliner Tony Dunne, who might have been even pacier than Shay. He knew the game inside out, reading situations so superbly that he always seemed to be in the right place at the right time and was brilliant at covering his fellow defenders when they were stretched. Often it would seem that an opposing forward was clean through and you would think a goal was inevitable, but then Tony would materialise as if from nowhere to save the day. He embarked on regular overlaps, too, but sometimes he was so fast that he would reach the attacking area before anyone was there to receive a pass. Sometimes his final ball was a trifle erratic, but that's only a minor criticism of one of the finest full-backs I've ever seen.

Tony was a smashing, easy-going lad, typically Irish, and it's sad that we don't see much of him these days because he has decided to cast off the United connection. I know he was hurt by the way he was tossed aside during the Tommy Docherty era when he still had so much more to offer, as he proved so comprehensively afterwards with his splendid service to Bolton, but it all happened such a long time ago. I, too, was deeply hurt by the way I left Old Trafford after my spell as manager, but I don't see the point of carrying on with the grievance forever. I'm proud of most things I did during my time at United, which left me with so many rich memories, and I'm sure that, deep down, Tony feels the same way. He was one of our great footballers, we all love him dearly and our Former Players Association would like nothing better than to welcome him back into the fold.

A telling illustration of the need for everyone to make the most of life's blessings while they can is to be found in the tragic experiences of another United full-back, who arrived on the Old Trafford scene in the mid-1960s and was so exceptional that he forced Shay out of the side. I coached Bobby Noble at youth level and I have no hesitation in declaring that he had the potential to have developed into the best flank defender in the country. He was so sharp and aggressive in the tackle that he made any opponent jump, and his timing was supreme. The moment the ball arrived at the winger's feet, Bobby would be on him, never giving him an inch in which to move. In some ways he was similar to Gabriel Heinze, who did so well for Sir Alex before suffering serious injury, but he was smaller and a bit more precise in his challenges than the Argentinian, who can be a bit of a mauler.

Such was the excellence of the young Mancunian that during 1966/67, with United in the process of lifting their second title in three seasons, he was slotted in at left-back with Tony moving to the right

Another year, another championship. This time it's 1966/67 and that's trainer Jack Crompton with his hand on the trophy. Looking on is coach and former United player John Aston (centre), and me clutching a glass of bubbly.

The men who brought the title back to Old Trafford in 1965. Back row, left to right: trainer Jack Crompton, Bill Foulkes, David Sadler, Pat Dunne, Shay Brennan, Graham Moore, Paddy Crerand, Noel Cantwell, Matt Busby. Front row: John Connelly, Nobby Stiles, Bobby Charlton, Denis Law, Tony Dunne, David Herd, George Best.

and Shay making way. But then, one Saturday night on his way home following a game at Sunderland and with the championship almost in the bag, he suffered serious head injuries in a car accident on Washway Road at Sale. He spent days in a coma in Altrincham hospital and for some time we feared for his life. Eventually he recovered, but not enough to play football again despite courageous efforts at a comeback. His eyesight and co-ordination were badly affected, and watching him trying to do the simplest of things, like trapping a ball, was extremely harrowing. Bobby was an honest, straightforward lad and it was monstrous that such a promising career should go down in flames at such an early stage. Even worse, he suffered family tragedies in later years, and life has not been easy for him. Of course, it pales into insignificance compared to his personal loss, but Bobby's injury was a body blow to United, too. But for his horrific mishap, I'm positive that he would have been a fixture in the side for at least a decade, which would have raised the collective quality immeasurably.

Just as the club was well served for full-backs in the 1960s, so we had some gifted goalkeepers, too, though nobody quite managed to monopolise the position until Alex Stepney made it his own after arriving from Chelsea in 1966, and even then there were periods when he gave way to Jimmy Rimmer. But for his rotten luck with injuries I dare say Harry Gregg would have dominated, certainly until mid-decade, and there were those who thought very highly of his younger challenger David Gaskell. The two were rather similar in style, frighteningly brave and occasionally even reckless in their disregard for their own physical safety, but I never felt that David ever quite matched the big Irishman. He was immensely confident in his own abilities, some would say excessively so. In his early days, after making his debut as a 16-year-old substitute for the injured Ray Wood in the 1956 Charity Shield, he would run out to claim a cross while shouting shouting 'Cherries!', intimating that it was as easy as plucking fruit off a tree. But that sort of flamboyant antic put some people's backs up. When he was going through a spell of indifferent form a little later, and allowed a few shots and centres to skid through his hands, he didn't mention cherries any more but reckoned the ball was like glass. Not surprisingly, perhaps, there wasn't too much sympathy going for him then.

Like Harry, probably as a result of his neck-or-nothing style, David also suffered horribly from injuries, which afforded an opening in 1964/65 for Pat Dunne, an extremely jovial Irishman and a pretty decent 'keeper who made the most of his chance and pocketed a title medal that term before fading from the scene when Greggy regained fitness in time for 1965/66. It was ironic that Pat should play just the one complete season and earn that honour, while poor Harry, in all honesty a far more accomplished performer, served the club faithfully for nine years without winning anything.

But mention of Pat Dunne always reminds me of the one incident in my time at Old Trafford when I experienced something akin to blind panic. It was in November 1964, we were facing Borussia Dortmund in Germany in the old Inter-Cities Fairs Cup, and for the first time I was standing in as first-team trainer, because Jack Crompton was ill. That meant it was my responsibility to treat injuries and when Pat got a bang on the head I tore on to the field at top speed, clutching my medical bag. When I reached him he was all over the place, as groggy as hell, and he could hardly see. My mind was racing and I was so anxious to do the right thing as I reached for an ammonia capsule for him to sniff to clear his head. Feeling as if the eyes of everyone were on me, I found myself rushing and, instead of snapping the top off the capsule a safe distance away from my patient, I did it right in front of his face. As a result the raw ammonia squirted into poor Pat's eyes and he squealed: 'God, Wilf, now I can't see at all.' To such an inexperienced medical practitioner as me, this would have been a crisis at any time, but what made it worse was that the referee had just blown for a corner – and I had just blinded our goalkeeper!

By now I'm practically frantic and thinking: 'Oh no, what have I done? This'll be the end of my career.' All I could do was seize my sponge and splash water into his face until he could see a little, by which time the referee was hurrying me on, which added to the pressure. But even then, I hadn't finished with my bumbling Frank Spencer impression. Having done my best for Pat, I started sprinting for the nearest touchline and as I ran my bag burst open so that scissors, bandages, ointments and everything else exploded all over the six-yard box. There was nothing for it but to grub around in the mud on my hands and knees, trying to make sure I picked everything up – I wouldn't have been very popular if a player had impaled himself on a stray pair of scissors – while the referee stood over me with his hands on his hips. It was a real Inspector Clouseau effort, and my only comfort as I slunk away with my tail between my legs was that Pat, despite my disastrous ministrations, managed somehow to keep the corner out.

In fact, fair play to a lad who had his share of critics, sometimes he looked wonderful when dealing with crosses, the ball seeming to stick to his hands like iron filings to a magnet. On other occasions things didn't go quite so well for him, but he was brilliant for most of that season and thoroughly deserved his medal. And, I'm happy and relieved to report, there *was* a happy ending to my humiliating Rhineland evening, as we beat Borussia 6-1 with Bobby Charlton scoring a hat-trick.

Mulling over the United men with whom I worked as a coach in the 1960s prompts me to mention the efforts of another Busby Babe who had genuine hopes of sharing in their serial successes but never quite made it – me!

In the early part of 1966/67, a campaign which United were to finish as champions, I was feeling extremely fit. After all, I was fresh from training with England's World Cup winners, and also I had worked with the United players, often taking part in extremely physical small-sided practice games, for five years. Still only 29, I believed sincerely that I still had it in me to play again in the First Division, and I knew that if I didn't give it a go then I would regret it for the rest of my life. I had a chat about it with Matt Busby, told him that I thought I wasn't far short, and he understood why I needed to try. There were a few medical and insurance formalities to be sorted out, but Matt and club secretary Les Olive attended to that, and it was a truly wonderful day for me when I signed on as a Manchester United player for the second time.

I knew perfectly well that I wasn't going to walk into any of United's teams after such a long time out of the reckoning, so I threw myself into extra training sessions in the afternoons, pushing myself as hard as was humanly possible. I had a bit of a limp and was getting a bit of arthritic pain, but I wasn't going to let that stand in my way and I was pleased with my early progress. My first big test came along in September, in a reserve derby with Manchester City at Maine Road. That had been my target for some time, but there was some unexpected glitch over insurance and clearance did not arrive until two hours before kick-off. That was good enough for me, and I arranged for Jack to take over my training duties for the evening. Then, when poor Carlo Sartori arrived at the ground expecting to play, I had to break the news to him: 'Sorry Carlo, you're not needed. I'm the number-four tonight.' Not surprisingly, at first he thought I was kidding, but accepted the decision with good grace when he realised I was serious. He was always a good lad, Carlo.

That night, as I ran out behind skipper Noel Cantwell and alongside a fellow Collyhurst product, the young Brian Kidd, I was the most excited footballer in England. Whatever else you might do, there's nothing like playing, and after all the heartache of being invalided out of the game in my early twenties, this was a fantasy come true. At one point in the match I went down writhing with pain and everybody thought 'Oh dear, he's broken down, he should never have gone out there in the first place.' But it was nothing but cramp and soon I was on my feet, completing that game and looking forward to the next one.

Ever the optimist, I thought I had done really well and made a decent contribution to our smashing 4-1 victory. Now visions of pushing Nobby and Paddy for their first-team places swam tantalisingly before my eyes. Of course, I was indulging in a flight of fancy at that stage, and although Matt and Jimmy were really pleased for me, they stressed that it would be a month or two before they could gauge whether I had the genuine potential to make a senior comeback. That was all the encouragement I needed so I redoubled my efforts in training, continued to turn out for the reserves and hoped against hope for my big opportunity. Later in the autumn a first-team injury crisis gave me a whiff of a chance, but apparently there were still insurance complications and the call never came. In the end the nearest I got was a place on the substitutes' bench – remember that only one sub was allowed in those days, and then only in the event of injury – for the visit to Leicester in November. At one point Paddy looked to be struggling and I was squirming with excitement, thinking to myself: 'Get off, Paddy!' But he played on, we won 2-1 with goals from Denis and George, and soon after that I had a heart-to-heart with Matt, who told me both the club and myself had a massive decision to make.

I really believed, and prayed, that I could make it back to the first team, but it wasn't to be. Still, I enjoyed my 30-odd games with the reserves. Here I lead out goalkeeper Jimmy Rimmer and striker Brian Kidd at Old Trafford.

If I wanted to persist with my full-scale comeback attempt, then United would have to fork out £25,000 to the insurance company, and they would have to be absolutely certain that I was a viable proposition fitness-wise. Matt cautioned me, too, that even if I went ahead, I would be battling for a place with feisty young rivals such as John Fitzpatrick, which wouldn't be easy. But the clincher was the fact that I would have to be replaced as a coach, as Matt was adamant that I couldn't hold down both jobs. That really was a sobering thought, because I was still deliriously happy at the club and, for all my dreams of a Roy-of-the-Rovers return to the top level, I wasn't ready to risk what I saw as a long-term future at Old Trafford.

When I stood back and reviewed my situation objectively, there was only one sane thing to do – bite the bullet and withdraw gracefully. After all, I'd given it a decent go and, in my heart, while I still believed I could compete as a player, I knew that there was something missing from my game. Of course, that was inevitable after an absence of nearly eight years, and even if I had managed, by some miracle, to return to the first-team reckoning, how long could I have expected to last as a half-crippled 30-year-old? Against that, there was no reason why I couldn't carry on coaching for the rest of my working life.

Mac's back

Wing-half W i l f Mc-Guiness, who broke a leg seven years ago, made a shock come-back last night for Manchester United reserves against City reserves. McGuiness, now 29, who last played in December, 1959 is United's assistant trainer. But he has been anxious to play again.

So it was agreed that I should stop playing even for the reserves, of which I had become captain. It was a particular wrench to give up that responsibility, which I had relished and through which I like to think I had been of some use to the youngsters in the team. When the news came out, everyone at the club was very kind to me. Most people had been surprised that I'd made the attempt but, without exception, they had encouraged me wholeheartedly. In the end I had no regrets. It simply wouldn't have been in my make-up not to try, even if I'd been hopping on to the pitch on one leg! Oh, it would have been wonderful if I'd managed to play in just one First Division game, but it wasn't to be and I have no complaints about that. Life was still very, very good, and there were plenty of challenges around the corner.

Chapter 12
TWIN PEAKS

M Y ULTIMATE football ambitions, of winning trophies and experiencing glory as a player with Manchester United and England, had been pushed beyond my reach by my broken leg, but pretty soon I found there were handsome compensations to be found in my new life as a coach. I have always been an optimistic soul, and rather than be consumed by despair or envy at watching old pals such as Bobby Charlton, Nobby Stiles and Shay Brennan fulfilling themselves in Matt Busby's latest great team, I resolved to enjoy every second of my own involvement with the United renaissance.

With all due modesty, I believe my enthusiastic attitude paid off, not only through my steadily increasing status at Old Trafford – which culminated eventually in my taking over the reins of the first team from Matt – but also in re-establishing contact with the international scene, something that hadn't entered my thoughts as I had taken my first steps in coaching back in 1961.

I guess I was lucky in that the FA chose The Cliff, United's training ground, for one of their youth trials in 1963, and that when they asked the club for a trainer, Matt sent me. Right from the off I threw myself into the role, determined to make the most of a delightfully unexpected opportunity. I knew the local set-up, so I checked out their hotel, made sure everything was all right and moved in myself to be on hand to help in any way that was needed. Maybe my background of captaining England sides at various levels stood me in good stead, but they must have been pleased with my latest efforts, too, because they asked if they could have my services on a part-time basis for a couple of midweek days, whenever there was an England youth trial. Matt was pleased that I was wanted for the coaching team set up by new England boss Alf

Ramsey, and he must have felt that the fantastic experience I would gain working with the best young players in the country would help to improve my contribution to the club.

Certainly I found it stimulating to bounce ideas off different people instead of spending my entire time cocooned in the United bubble. Apart from advancing my personal development, it also enabled me to monitor other clubs' promising players, which meant I could offer advice on their strengths and weaknesses when United faced them. Also I picked up on the latest training techniques and innovative free-kick routines, which were then introduced at Old Trafford. One that paid off big-time involved Denis Law running up as if to take the kick, then sprinting over the ball and past the defensive wall; the ball was then slipped sideways to a team-mate standing a few yards wider, and he played it into space for the still-charging Denis, who scored. When that went in – and I only wish I could remember the opposition – I felt just as satisfied as if I had stuck the ball in the net myself. It was a fabulous sensation, and it offered tangible evidence to everyone else that I was making a significant contribution.

As for the England youth games themselves, things could hardly have gone any better. Though Alf Ramsey was in overall charge, on a day-to-day basis I was working with the England youth manager Pat Welton, a former goalkeeper with Leyton Orient and a natural teacher. We gelled immediately and I learned a great deal from Pat, as did the marvellous collection of young players in our charge. Those lads included Johnny Sissons (West Ham), Jon Sammels (Arsenal), George Jones (Bury), Tommy Smith (Liverpool), Ron Harris (Chelsea), Lew Chatterley (Aston Villa), Len Badger and Bernard Shaw (both Sheffield United), an immensely talented group, and it didn't surprise me when we won the so-called Little World Cup (even though it included only European teams) at Wembley. We retained it a year later in Holland, too, by which time the side included United's David Sadler (who had been part of the squad 12 months earlier without playing in the final), Howard Kendall (Preston), John Hollins (Chelsea), Peter Knowles (Wolves), Harry Redknapp (West Ham) and Mick Wright (Aston Villa) among others, all lads with whom it was a privilege to work. I pushed them hard physically, but I got a positive reaction from them, and it was tremendous to see them all progress so successfully in their subsequent careers.

The sweet taste of success with England. Youth team skipper Howard Kendall is chaired aloft with the European Junior Cup after victory in the Amsterdam tournament in 1964. Crouching at the front is United's David Sadler; the other England boys are, left to right, Alf Wood, Mick Wright, John Hollins, Harry Redknapp and Peter Knowles.

A football coach's life doesn't get much better than this. Lining up with the England squad at Lilleshall ahead of the 1966 World Cup finals. Back row, left to right: Martin Peters, Geoff Hurst, Bobby Tambling, Keith Newton, Peter Bonetti, Jack Charlton, Norman Hunter, Ron Flowers, Johnny Byrne, John Connelly, Nobby Stiles, Terry Paine. Middle row: coach Les Cocker, trainer Harold Shepherdson, Gordon Banks, Bobby Moore, George Cohen, manager Alf Ramsey, myself. Front row: Jimmy Armfield, Jimmy Greaves, Alan Ball, Ron Springett, Gordon Milne, Ian Callaghan, Roger Hunt, Gerry Byrne, George Eastham, Peter Thompson, Ray Wilson, Bobby Charlton.

Laying down the law at an England youth training session, while the extravagantly talented Peter Osgood looks on with a grin.

Importantly to me, Pat allowed me a say in how they played, too, which helped me to develop new tactical ideas, an opportunity I relished.

At this point, with Matt's latest team on the rise and my international experience growing, I could hardly have been happier – well, only if I'd been captain of both Manchester United and England, and even my eternal optimism didn't stretch that far, given all that had happened to me! But in the spring of 1965, when Alf Ramsey was pondering on his line-up to face Scotland, I was lifted still further when the England manager demonstrated enough faith in me to seek my advice about his team selection. He asked me whether I thought Nobby Stiles, uncapped at the time, would play his usual hard game against clubmate Denis Law if he was picked for the crunch Wembley meeting, or would he go easy? That was the simplest question I ever had to answer. Nobby would have put Mother Teresa over the touchline if she was playing for the opposition, so there was no way Denis would get preferential treatment.

I was delighted to give Nobby a boost, which he richly deserved and fully justified by the brilliant way in which he went on to serve his country. I've joked with him since that if it hadn't been for me he might never have played, and therefore the nation would never have been treated to the astonishing spectacle of the delirous little fellow from Collyhurst dancing a jig around Wembley while waving the World Cup above his head. Of course, I didn't really claim the credit, but it was too glorious an opportunity for pulling his leg to let it pass.

More seriously, I was enormously proud that Alf, who wouldn't ring Matt because he was Scottish and therefore might have divided loyalties on this occasion, had sought out my opinion on such a crucially important matter. It proved to me that I had been accepted fully into the national set-up, and that I was genuinely valued, which sent my confidence – admittedly never of the fragile variety – soaring into the stratosphere.

From the outset of my involvement with the England youth team, sanctioned readily by Matt, I had got on famously with the future Sir Alf. He had travelled with us on several trips and we had chatted extensively, really got to know one another and seemed to share quite a few ideas about football. Even so, it came as a bombshell when, a few weeks before the 1966 World Cup Finals on home soil, he invited me to work with his squad. Would I come down to Lilleshall? *Would* I come

down? His request made me feel ten feet tall. Here were England about
to embark on the adventure of a lifetime and I was going to be part of
it. So down I went and trained with the players for just over two weeks
before they set off on a warm-up tour of Scandinavia. The FA being the
FA, not exactly renowned for their generosity even when it might have
helped the team to have an extra coach to assist Harold Shepherdson
and Les Cocker, I wasn't invited on that trip; they didn't even allow one
of the two team doctors to go. But as they departed from Lilleshall, Alf
pulled me to one side and said: 'If we get to the final – and we *are* going
to get to the final – you'll be there.'

By now I felt such a part of the England effort that when I went on
holiday to Spain, I took time off from the family to watch Uruguay, our
first opponents of the tournament, playing in a friendly, then sent an
unsolicited report on them to Alf. I don't know whether it proved useful
to him, but he thanked me in his usual gracious way and I felt I had
contributed something.

I was home by the time the finals got under way and watched some
terrific games involving Brazil, Portugal, Hungary and Bulgaria in the
north-west qualifying group at Goodison Park and Old Trafford. I loved
every minute of that, trying to soak up every bit of knowledge available
while feeding odd pieces of information back to the England camp.
Meanwhile I cheered the lads all the way through the goalless draw in
the opener against Uruguay, the 2-0 wins over Mexico and France in
the other group games and the tempestuous 1-0 victory over the immensely talented but fractious Argentinians in the quarter-final. Best of
all, I celebrated my old friend Bobby Charlton's two-goal match-winning
performance against Portugal in the semi-final.

That was a classically entertaining contest full of terrific football from
both sides, but it was emphatically not, no matter what popular folklore
might decree to the contrary, the game which spawned one of the most
repeated of all Nobby Stiles yarns. The story goes that in the dressing
room before kick-off Alf had ordered his most tenacious marker to put
the Portuguese star, Eusebio, out of the game, and Nobby is supposed
to have replied, in a deadpan voice: 'What, just for tonight, Alf, or for
f***ing life?' In fact, he didn't come out with anything of the kind,
although perhaps he wishes he had. It's just a tall tale put about by ...
me! It came to me one night in the mid-1980s when I was the trainer at

Bury and our manager, Martin Dobson, was addressing his troops before they ran out to face Preston. Martin was a bit worried about their left winger, who was a bit of a flier, so he told our right-back, Trevor Ross, to put him out of the game – and it was Trevor who came out with the immortal line: 'Just for tonight, Boss, or for life?' His timing was perfect and the whole dressing room erupted in laughter. By then I was already doing a spot of after-dinner speaking, and jotted it down as a piece of prime material. However, when I thought about it, with all due respect to Trevor Ross I didn't think it would achieve maximum impact if I mentioned his name – so I substituted Nobby's. Since then it has been pirated by all sorts of speakers, all of whom swear it to be true, but I can now reveal that they're all telling porky pies!

But, neither for the first nor the last time in this book, I digress. Back in July 1966, having almost lost my voice shouting for England as they overcame Portugal, I was looking forward to the final without giving a thought to Alf's promise that I would be with his team if they won through to the final. Then, somewhere around midnight, still buzzing with thoughts of that evening's semi, I was sitting at home when my phone rang and it was Alf. He said: 'Wilf, I would like you and your wife to come to London on Friday. I want you to be with the players' wives as the FA representative when they go to a show in the evening. On Saturday morning they'll be taken care of, so I want you to join us at Hendon Hall for breakfast with the players, then come to Wembley on the team bus, join us in the dressing room, then be with us when we've won the World Cup.

I could hardly believe my ears. I must have been like a schoolboy who had won the football pools. Certainly I needed no second bidding, and Beryl and I joined the ladies in time for a West End showing of *Charley's Aunt*, which turned out to be the dampest of squibs. It wasn't funny at all, though Beryl managed a laugh – just the one – but that was hardly going to spoil my weekend! The next morning you can be sure I was at Hendon Hall in good time for the toast and cornflakes, and I found the players in a relaxed frame of mind, with Alf radiating calmness. By this time I knew them all pretty well, and to me they looked genuinely confident of accomplishing the task in front of them.

As we arrived at Wembley we were greeted by fans with huge banners proclaiming 'Nobby Stiles for prime minister'. That gave everyone a huge laugh, though I reckoned he might have been a decent choice. He'd have sorted out Collyhurst, anyway!

In the dressing room Alf ensured that everybody kept to their normal routine, and he moved from player to player having a quiet word with everyone. Bobby Moore was quiet and self-possessed, Alan Ball was noisy and busy, Jack Charlton was shouting the odds as ever, while brother Bobby was characteristically matter-of-fact. The manager had declared repeatedly to the media that 'England *will* win the World Cup' and there is no doubt that he believed that utterly. More importantly, he made his players believe it, and when they took to the pitch they felt they were going to do a job that was well within their compass. So it proved, but not without a few alarms and excursions along the way to an unforgettable 4-2 victory over the West Germans at the end of extra time.

My impressions of the game might not be seen as entirely unbiased, but I felt that we deserved to win after giving away a soft early goal. I think we were unlucky to concede the free-kick from which the Germans equalised at the death in normal time, but I have to admit that our third goal might have been a bit dodgy. From my seat in the stand it did look as though Geoff Hurst's shot had crossed the line after bouncing down from the crossbar, but enhanced TV evidence does suggest that maybe it should have been disallowed. But that's football.

After the game there was so much happiness and it was a privilege for me to be invited into the dressing room to witness this moment of English sporting history. The trophy was passed from hand to hand by the ectatic players, but anyone hoping to see Alf perform a jig like Nobby's during the lap of honour was sorely disappointed. He remained cool and self-contained, a man content to have done his job but not ready to indulge in outward displays of extravagant emotion.

The bus journey to the Royal Garden hotel, the venue for the celebration function, was unforgettable, with car drivers honking their horns, the streets bedecked in red, white and blue, and huge grins on every face. It seems a bit archaic in these politically correct times, but when we arrived the wives were ushered to a separate room to have their meal, then the players all moved off to find their places in the main hall. For me, though, an anti-climax was awaiting. No place had been set aside for me, and I was preparing to withdraw gracefully when Alf noticed that I had been left out and called the head-waiter. 'Make a place here for Wilf McGuinness,' he commanded, indicating the space at his right-hand side. The chap looked aghast and I was a bit embarrassed because Harold Shepherdson and Les Cocker, who had done far more than me for the team effort, were in less prominent positions. So I said: 'Don't worry, Alf, I'll be fine.' But he refused to take 'no' for an answer, insisting that I joined him, and I ended up as the special guest of the manager who had just lifted the World Cup. Even on the greatest day of his life he was thinking about someone who had helped him along the way, and that was the mark of the man. During the meal he was quiet, without a hint of triumphalism. It was as though the outcome was just what he expected; indeed, exactly what he had been telling us all along. The only time during the whole tournament when he had offered a glimpse of passionate feeling was when he stepped between George Cohen and the Argentinian Alberto Gonzalez to prevent the Fulham full-back from swapping shirts after the stormy quarter-final. In that emotional moment, after the South Americans had attempted unsuccessfully to kick his team out of the competition, he let himself go as far as to dismiss them as 'animals', which amounted to a seismic eruption from the usually ice-cool Alf. Thereafter, though, he returned to character and never let his public mask slip again for as long as I knew him.

After the celebratory meal, the party split up, with some of the lads going to Danny La Rue's club, while Beryl and I joined Bobby and Tina Moore, Bobby and Norma Charlton and one or two others at the Playboy Club in Park Lane. My old chum was consumed with happiness at what he had helped to achieve, but he has never been one to brag and this was no exception. He was as modest as ever, for all the world like he had spent the afternoon having a kick-around with friends in the park. The down-to-earth feel continued the next day as Bobby, Norma, Beryl and myself were driven back to Manchester by Alan Ball, another of the Wembley heroes, who had played the game of his young life. His wife-to-be, Lesley, was also with us in the car. Picture how different the scene would be today if Capello's team pulled off a similar triumph – and although it's early days for Fabio, it does require a bit of a stretch of the imagination. The players would be feted beyond belief, their every need catered for, rather than being left to make their own way home across country. But the modern way of going over the top only amounts to window dressing. All that really mattered was the astronomical feat pulled off by Alf Ramsey and his wonderful team, and I felt truly privileged to have played even the tiniest part in England's greatest footballing glory.

To most followers of the game, it might seem impossible to credit that any other victory could mean more to me than England winning the World Cup on home soil in 1966. Indeed, as a passionate patriot I can understand exactly where they are coming from. But, hand on heart, I have to admit that when Manchester United lifted the European crown two years later, it topped the lot. When we beat Benfica on that sweltering night at Wembley in May 1968, we had reached the end of a long, hard, cruel road. There had been so much toil and heartache along the way, and when Matt Busby finally reached out and claimed his equivalent of the Holy Grail, ten years after the calamity of Munich, to me and to everyone associated with United, it represented the ultimate achievement.

In fact, Matt's third great team should have reached that goal two years earlier in 1965/66, when it was at its peak. We reached the semi-final, and were favourites to go on and capture the prize, but lost unexpectedly to Partizan Belgrade. At that time George Best, Denis Law and Bill Foulkes were all carrying injuries, continually playing when they were nowhere near fully fit, and you can only get away with that for so long. George, in particular, was struggling physically in the first leg when we went down 2-0 in Yugoslavia but even he, so tough and resilient as well as being a genius, had to bow to his body and miss the second leg. He was replaced by his fellow Youth Cup winner Willie Anderson, a bright and breezy Merseysider who had been more powerful and direct than George in his teens and who had pipped the Irishman to a senior debut, but whose later development could not keep pace. He tried his hardest and we managed a 1-0 victory at Old Trafford, but despite mounting wave after wave of attacks, we couldn't force an aggregate equaliser.

That had been a sickener and there was no shortage of pundits who reckoned United had missed their best chance of lifting the trophy they coveted above all others. But we qualified again by winning the championship in 1966/67, then disposed of Hibernians of Malta, Sarajevo and Gornik Zabrze to reach another semi-final, where we were

In the presence of Manchester United's Holy Grail. I felt a genuine sense of awe to be pictured with the European Cup in 1968, perhaps because it was in pursuit of the trophy that so many of my friends lost their lives.

No need for words. Bill Foulkes puts an arm around Bobby Charlton as the two Munich survivors leave the pitch after winning the European Cup in 1968. That's me in the background, hurrying to catch up with them.

faced by our old nemesis, the mighty Real Madrid. Inspired by George, we beat them 1-0 at Old Trafford, but when we were 3-1 down at the Bernabeu with only 20 minutes left it looked as though we were going to fall again at the penultimate hurdle. But then David Sadler bundled in a scrappy goal, which put us level on aggegate, and that most unlikely marksman Bill Foulkes slid home an unbelievable winner. That night my reserve-team duties had decreed that I remain in Manchester, where I was listening on the radio, kicking every ball in my mind and dying a thousand deaths, but still my feelings when the final whistle went were indescribable. It felt as though we had pulled off something not far short of a miracle. Surely, this time, the name of Manchester United was going to be inscribed on that lovely big trophy.

But soon an unexpected cloud appeared on my horizon. On the Wednesday of the final against Benfica at Wembley, I was due to be in Hungary, helping Spurs manager Bill Nicholson to prepare the England under-23s for a game on the Thursday. When I realised that there was a clash of dates I was aghast, and although United agreed to fly me back to watch the final, they didn't have the last word. That lay with Alf Ramsey who, when I asked him for permission to go on what amounted to compassionate leave, to be there for the biggest night in United's history, stopped me in my tracks with a devastating single-word response. 'No!'

However, he added that as he was not in charge of the under-23s, in the end it was up to Bill Nicholson. I didn't quite discern a twinkle in the Ramsey eye, but there might well have been one, and I like to think that perhaps he was having a bit of a joke with me. As it was Bill gave me the nod straight away. I'd known him for a long time and he knew what this meant to me. He was a lovely person, charming, calm and a gentleman, and his character was reflected in his teams. He loved good, flowing, push-and-run football, the sort of entertainment served up regularly by the Tottenham team in which he had played for so long alongside Alf Ramsey.

Thus reprieved, I made my way to Wembley and was waiting for Jack Crompton when he arrived in the dressing room to lay out the kit. I always helped Jack if there was no reserve game because I relished the atmosphere, particularly on a big occasion, and there were none bigger than this. It turned out to be a very tense game, goalless at half-time, then Bobby put us in front early in the second period, only for Benfica to snatch a late equaliser. Throughout the drama I was on the bench, occasionally leaping to my feet and shouting at the top of my voice. I couldn't help it, I just couldn't keep my emotions to myself, and the people on the Benfica bench didn't like it, motioning angrily for me to belt up. From the looks on their faces it was probably just as well that I didn't understand Portuguese! Matt and the lads were used to me. They knew I could be as excitable as Jimmy Murphy and invariably indulged me, which they did on this occasion, too. If I had been irritating him he would have told me in no uncertain manner, but he didn't so I carried on my merry way.

At the end of normal time, as the players slumped to the turf and Matt passed among them with wise words of encouragement, I went on to the pitch and massaged Nobby's legs. When the 90 minutes were nearly up he had lost touch with the brilliant Eusebio, who had burst through on goal and looked certain to slot in the winner. Happily the great man had opted for power and crashed the ball straight into the waiting arms of our 'keeper Alex Stepney, and the danger was past for the moment. But I was determined that Nobby would be in the best possible shape to deal with 'The Black Panther' in extra time. I couldn't be out there to tackle Eusebio myself, so the next best thing was to help the man who could.

As it turned out, the Portuguese star never threatened again as United ran away with the match in the first 15 minutes of added time, our skill and fitness coming together when the chips were down. There were goals from George Best, Brian Kidd – what a way to celebrate his 19th birthday! – and a second from the skipper, Bobby Charlton. The one which really turned the contest irrevocably in our favour was the spellbinding effort from George, involving a mesmeric swerve around the Benfica 'keeper, which put us 2-1 in front, and I could hardly believe my ears in the dressing room afterwards when Shay Brennan claimed a lion's share of the credit. 'You have to remember that it was me who created that goal,' he declared, but I wasn't having any of that. 'Come on, Shay. It was Brian who flicked it on and George who got himself in the clear,' I pointed out. But he persisted: 'That's all very well, but it was me who passed it back for Alex (Stepney) to whack it downfield, which allowed Kiddo to flick it on!' Put like that I couldn't fault the Irish logic, and dear Shay would stick to his story for the rest of his life. But I'm getting ahead of myself here. I mustn't miss out some of the most magical, memorable moments in my own life.

When the final whistle blew, I just stood and clapped Matt. It was ten years since the crash and his new team had won the trophy for the boys who had died while blazing the trail into Europe. We were all overcome with emotion and empathised totally with our manager, our leader, the man we had come to love. We understood the heartache he had suffered, losing so many of his fine young men, and although nothing could ever bring them back, this triumph stood as a fitting tribute to their memories. It wasn't that he had been vindicated for his courageous decision to enter the European Cup, so long ago now that it seemed like a different lifetime; nothing as base as that. It was just that something noble which he had started had come finally to glorious fruition.

There were special feelings, too, for Bobby Charlton and Bill Foulkes, who had lived through the catastrophe, then picked up the threads of their lives and their careers, and continued valiantly to carry the standard of Manchester United until they planted it exactly where it belonged – at the pinnacle of European football. I was so proud for everyone who had been involved along the way. My mind leapt back to all my pals who had died or been injured, and to their families. This had been more than a football match, more than a cup final, more than any sporting contest I could imagine.

Until it was all over I hadn't quite realised how much it meant, but one look at Bobby put me straight on that. He was exhausted, totally drained, so much so that he missed most of the celebration banquet later that night, just nipping down from his room for a few minutes towards the end, maybe in time to hear Matt singing *I Belong To Glasgow*. When everyone else was tucked up safely in bed, I left to catch my early-morning flight back to Hungary. I was back on under-23 duty in plenty of time for the match that evening, which England won. At the end of it all, Bill Nick told me I'd have to buy champagne, so I did. I was happy to do that.

Chapter 13
CLUB AT THE CROSSROADS

AFTER REACHING the end of our rainbow to win the European Cup, and also pushing Manchester City to the last day of the season in the 1967/68 title race, the following campaign proved to be a classic case of 'After the Lord Mayor's Show.' The big trophy slipped out of our grasp, we lost a stormy World Club Championship clash against violent Argentinian opposition and we finished only halfway in the First Division table. There was talk of change in the air, some people called it a crisis, and yet as that fateful term had kicked off I was perfectly content with my lot, particularly as I had just been promoted to be take charge of the England youth set-up, following the departure of Pat Welton. Certainly at that stage, the thought hadn't entered my head that, come the spring, I would be taking over from the newly knighted Sir Matt Busby at the helm of the Manchester United first team.

It's all too easy after the event, but in the light of the club's mixed fortunes over the next few years, it has often been stated that Matt should have stepped down in 1968 at the moment of his defining glory. He was nearly 60 years old, he had been to hell and back on behalf of United, and then he had ascended to the mountaintop with his third fantastic side. What more was there to prove? Surely, especially with some of his key players having seen their best days, the only way was down? That was the theory, but it's not one to which I would necessarily subscribe. I can understand why he wanted to go on, to lift that European crown for a second time, and he must have felt the boys had it in them. Why wouldn't he? After all, as he scanned his resources in the summer of 1968, he would have concluded that his three geniuses still had something in the tank. Okay, Bobby Charlton had entered his thirties but, like those old geezers Ryan Giggs, Paul Scholes and Gary Neville in modern times, he remained supremely fit and his loyalty couldn't be questioned. Denis Law was only 28, and although he was still battling with the knee problems that cheated him of a European Cup winner's medal, there was every prospect that he would recover. Meanwhile George Best was a mere 22, with the footballing world at his feet. For Matt to turn his back on what that young man might have achieved would be like Sir Alex Ferguson signing Wayne Rooney and Cristiano Ronaldo, then walking away to spend his Saturday afternoons pushing a trolley at Tesco. Would that make any sort of sense to a man who had given his life to the game?

Looking around the rest of his squad, goalkeeper Alex Stepney was 23, striker Brian Kidd was 19, defender-cum-midfielder David Sadler was 22 and winger John Aston junior, man of the match in the Wembley defeat of Benfica, was 21, so there was no age issue regarding any of them. Left-back Tony Dunne was in his prime at 27 and Nobby Stiles was a year younger, although he was carrying a debilitating injury which meant he would never he quite as effective again. That said, Matt wasn't to know that Nobby wouldn't make a full recovery, especially given the little fella's gargantuan appetite for the fray.

Admittedly Paddy Crerand, our midfield creator alongside Bobby, was almost 30, but he had never relied on speed and was showing no obvious sign of decline, which leaves only centre-half Bill Foulkes and Shay Brennan, the right-back. Now Bill was 36 with a dodgy knee so he was entitled to be creaking a bit, and although he was still mightily strong it was obvious that he would have to be replaced in the near future. It seems Matt believed that young Steve James could do the job, and he gave him a fair go, but it turned out that although the lad was neat and tidy, he lacked the crucial bit of devil which Foulkesy had in spades.

Meanwhile Shay was five years younger than Bill, but showing signs of wear, and I have to admit that in his position there wasn't youthful back-up of sufficient quality within the club. Probably John Fitzpatrick was the pick of the kids coming through and he was versatile enough to play at full-back or in midfield, but he was plagued by injuries and wasn't able to realise his full potential. Then there was another full-back, Francis Burns, who was reliable and knew the game but wasn't the quickest, while others like defender Paul Edwards and midfielder Carlo

Sartori were decent players and good lads but not quite of the required calibre. It would have been perfect timing if there had been another wave of exceptional youngsters, but they don't arrive to order, there is no conveyor belt guaranteeing a steady supply. After the Babes in the 1950s, there was nothing remotely comparable until Scholes, Beckham and company in the early 1990s.

Yet while it's fair to say there were some question-marks over certain areas of the 1968 squad, there was no tangible indication of imminent decline. It wasn't as if Manchester United were in meltdown and Matt, hardly a stranger to reconstructing football teams, had sound reasons to believe that his foundations remained firm.

Against that, most neutral observers might have concluded that we needed one or two or even three high-quality defenders, so what did we do? We signed Willie Morgan from Burnley, a magnificently gifted winger who later did well as a conventional midfielder, but I'm not sure how many people would have identified him as a priority at the time. Of course, anyone who studied Matt's transfer policy down the years won't have been surprised at the lack of activity. He was always careful with the club's money – that might just be the understatement of the century – and while he was willing to fork out for an individual he really needed, such as Tommy Taylor or Denis Law, there was never likely to be a mass purchase.

In retrospect, the most pressing question was this: did the Boss seem up to carrying on? Only he could have supplied the definitive answer, and I must admit that I respected him so much that, in the immediate aftermath of the European Cup win, the possibility that he might step down never even crossed my mind. Elated beyond belief after that balmy night at Wembley, I wanted him to stay forever, in much the same way as most United fans feel about Sir Alex today. It can be argued that it would have been the perfect moment to go, having scaled the ultimate pinnacle, and maybe if he'd been thinking in purely selfish terms he would have stepped aside. But I'm certain he would have been thinking of protecting his staff, the likes of Jimmy Murphy, Jack Crompton, John Aston senior and myself, knowing that if a new big-name manager was brought in then we might have been swept away.

Whatever his reasoning, he led us boldly into 1968/69 and, in fairness, the season was hardly an unmitigated disaster. Having qualified to re-enter the European Cup as holders, we made a creditable fist of defending it, reaching the last four and then going out 2-1 on aggregate to AC Milan in wildly controversial circumstances, the referee disallowing a 'goal' by Denis Law in the second leg at Old Trafford even though the ball appeared to have crossed the line. In addition, we were involved in a tempestuous home-and-away World Club Championship encounter with Estudiantes de la Plata, some of whose players conducted themselves with such outrageous savagery that in the end it barely seemed to matter that we were beaten 2-1 over the two legs. I'm afraid the team from Buenos Aires really dragged football through the gutter, and there is no place for such behaviour at any level of sport. In domestic competition there was no disguising the truth that we were mediocre by our own lofty standards, and by the turn of the year speculation was rife that Manchester United were on the verge of changing their manager for the first time in nearly quarter of a century.

'IT'S A TREMENDOUS HONOUR FOR ME'

McGuinness a Babe born to be boss

JOE ARMSTRONG

Naturally, the newspapers started bandying the names of possible replacements, with the early favourites being two of the biggest names in the game, Jock Stein of Celtic and Leeds United's Don Revie. I wasn't even on the radar at first, though plenty of members of the United family were mentioned. First among these was the Boss's faithful lieutenant, Jimmy Murphy, but I'm sure he wasn't looking for the job. He'd had his career standing shoulder to shoulder with Matt, as well as guiding the fortunes of Wales, and wasn't looking for such a massive challenge at his

Matt and his boys with the greatest prize of all. Back row, left to right: Bill Foulkes, John Aston, Jimmy Rimmer, Alex Stepney, Alan Gowling, David Herd. Middle row: David Sadler, Fred Owen from the United office, Tony Dunne, Shay Brennan, Paddy Crerand, George Best, Francis Burns, scout Joe Armstrong, trainer Jack Crompton. Front row: Jim Ryan, Nobby Stiles, Denis Law, Matt Busby, Bobby Charlton, Brian Kidd, John Fitzpatrick.

time of life. Noel Cantwell was mentioned, having done well at Coventry since leaving Old Trafford, and some pundits threw in the likes of Bill Foulkes and Bobby Charlton, though I would have been staggered if either of them had ended up in the post. While Bill might have seemed a canny call as he was already earmarked to join the United coaching staff, I don't think he would have fancied the idea of sitting behind a desk, and I can't imagine that Bobby would even have contemplated such a momentous job-switch. For one thing he was still playing at the top level, readying himself for another tilt at the World Cup in Mexico in 1970.

I realised that if a Stein or a Revie took over, they would probably bring in their own people and therefore elbow me out, but I didn't dwell on that possibility for a single second. I've always been a very positive person, and I don't think bad thoughts or fear the worst. Of course, sometimes it happens to you anyway, and then it can hurt all the more because you haven't even considered the possibility. But in the early part of 1969, when every man and his dog had a theory about who would take over from Sir Matt, I wasn't feeling in the slightest bit insecure. That came later …

Chapter 14
MEET THE MANAGER

I<small>T WAS</small> only the day before I got the job that I let myself believe for the first time that the footballing fortunes of Manchester United were going to be placed in my hands. True, there had been endless conjecture about who would replace Sir Matt as the inevitability of his imminent retirement took hold, and my name had been mentioned along with countless others, but it was not until the spring of 1969 that my odds appeared to shorten dramatically.

Suddenly the press photographers were buzzing round me at a reserve game and I began to feel they might know something that I didn't. Then I heard a whisper from one of our longest-serving scouts, Billy Behan from the Republic of Ireland, who was a close confidant of Matt. He pulled me to one side and said: 'You're in with a shout, Wilf.' That's when I really began to take my chances seriously, though it wasn't until the day before the official announcement that Matt gave me the slightest inkling that anything was afoot.

Even then he kept his cards pretty close to his chest. After finding me in the Old Trafford dressing rooms, all he said was: 'Wilf, tomorrow I would like you to come in looking smart, wearing a collar and tie.' That's all – not a word about taking over one of the biggest jobs in the sporting world! I knew better than to question Matt, so I just said: 'Oh, right.' I wasn't going to press him because, while I was certain what was coming by now, I knew that he would tell me only when he wanted to tell me. Apart from that, I didn't want to give him the chance to change his mind!

Finally, the next morning, he called me into his office and said simply: 'Wilf, I want you to be the next manager of Manchester United.' Those were words which the little lad from Collyhurst, whose love affair with football had been comsummated so passionately with the help of a brick wall down the road in Blackley, could have imagined hearing only in his wildest dreams. It was a truly fantastic moment, and I felt like roaring my joy to the heavens. But that wouldn't have been the reaction Matt expected of his successor in the Old Trafford hot seat, so I remained outwardly calm.

He went on to explain that I wouldn't be known as the manager straight away because the title would add unnecessary extra pressure, so I would be referred to as chief coach. I would be responsible for fitness and tactics, and I would pick the team. Meanwhile Matt would remain in charge of discipline, transfers and wages and continue as the club's spokesman. Basically, I was team manager and he was general manager, an arrangement that suited me down to the ground.

I was overjoyed that Matt, someone I had revered for so long, was showing so much faith in me. I believe my appointment was basically his own decision, with the directors having very little to do with it, and that was a colossal honour in itself. All I could think was: 'Matt Busby's chosen *me* to be the next Matt Busby!'

On the threshold of the Theatre of Dreams.

Put it there, Boss. I shake hands with Matt Busby, the patriarch of Old Trafford and a man I had come to love as well as respect, on the day I am unveiled as his successor.

Later people asked me if I was nervous at the prospect of being handed the reins of a world-famous institution but, in all honesty, I wasn't. Not even a tiny bit. I was only 31, the youngest team boss in United's history, so maybe I was experiencing the false confidence of youth, but it seemed to me that the situation couldn't have been better. I had just been given the ultimate job in football, and now had the opportunity to grow into it under the guidance of the man whom I honoured above all others in the game.

All this flashed through my mind as Matt made a few more encouraging remarks, then we went downstairs to the directors' lounge in the south stand where I was confronted by the massed ranks of the press. I knew a lot of them already and I felt perfectly at my ease as they quizzed me on the task that lay ahead. In fact, I was ready to have a bit of fun. Pretty early in the proceedings the chairman, Louis Edwards, announced that he had received more than 30 applications for the post, and I piped up with: 'Yes, and I wrote all of them.'

In those days the press process was a lot more civilised than it is now; it wasn't a case of tabloid hacks seeking to bury a stiletto between your shoulder-blades at the first opportunity. They asked the obvious questions: Was I too young for such a mammoth responsibility? Did I have enough coaching experience? Was it a problem that I had grown up alongside some of the players who would now be in my charge? I was able to point out that I had been a United coach for almost a decade, that I had contributed to England's preparation for the 1966 World Cup and that I got on well with the players, both personally and professionally. Of course, I had close pals at the club, but although I realised I would have to treat some of them with a bit more detachment than in the past – certainly I could not be seen to have favourites in my new position – I saw the friendly relationships as a positive. They all wanted me to do well – and why wouldn't they? After all, my success would be their success, too. As for the lads themselves, I thought they were delighted for me, happy that one of their own had got the big job. Some of them might have been surprised, but they didn't say so to my face, and I had no doubt that they would show me the same loyalty and industry that they had shown to Matt.

Similarly, I had the enthusiastic support of Jimmy Murphy, who seemed as pleased as punch that one of his proteges had done so well, and his encouragement meant so much to me as he had always exercised such an enormous benevolent influence on my life. Although Jimmy was getting close to retirement, it was important to me that he stayed at Old Trafford. He didn't fill a specific role, but he was always on hand, imparting his wisdom, talking to the scouts, giving his opinions on young players, generally helping to make sure that things ran smoothly. Yet somehow – and this is peculiar, given the depth of my regard for the feisty little Welshman who had forgotten more about football than most people would ever know – I didn't consult him as much as I ought to have done. I suppose I was so incredibly busy, and tied up in my own thoughts, that sometimes I forgot that he was there. Looking back now, I'm sure that if I had spoken to him more he would have helped me avoid certain mistakes. My failure to do that remains one of my few regrets.

As 1969/70 got under way, I was genuinely optimistic. The players had given their all to Jack Crompton in pre-season training, then looked in super form during comprehensive friendly victories over a Danish Select team and FC Zurich. Yet for all my eager anticipation as I travelled to London on the Friday for the next day's First Division opener against newly promoted Crystal Palace at Selhurst Park, I couldn't help wishing that the League's fixtures secretary had given us a home start. In the early hours of that morning Beryl had given birth to our second daughter, Clare, and I'd have loved to have spent some time with her immediately, but at least I knew that both mother and baby were in rude health so I could approach the game with a glad heart.

Though bursting with characteristic confidence, I must admit to having a few butterflies in my stomach before kick-off, but unlike most new bosses I knew all the lads well and was comfortable with them. The side I named that day was Jimmy Rimmer in goal, Tony Dunne and Francis Burns at full-back, Bill Foulkes and David Sadler in central defence, Paddy Crerand and Bobby Charlton in the centre of midfield, Willie Morgan on the right wing with George Best roaming everywhere from a starting position on the left, and a front pair of Denis Law and Brian Kidd. Now that was a fair old combination by anybody's standards, complete with three European Footballers of the Year, so I fully expected to win and therefore was disappointed to come away with a 2-2 draw.

In fact, we had needed a second-half equaliser from Willie Morgan to escape with a point which wasn't what I'd had in mind at all, but the situation was destined to deteriorate before it improved. Our second game brought a 2-0 home defeat by Everton, who would go on to lift the championship. They dominated proceedings courtesy of their magnificent midfield trio of Alan Ball, Colin Harvey and Howard Kendall, who outnumbered and hustled Bobby and Paddy. It was clear to me that when we faced them in the Goodison rematch a mere six days later we would have to offer stiffer opposition, though the radical changes I made were to backfire on me dramatically.

Before then, though, there was another calamity to endure, a 4-1 Old Trafford drubbing by Southampton in which the Welsh international centre-forward Ron Davies gave poor Bill Foulkes the runaround to score all four, and my old mate Shay Brennan, restored at right-back because of injury to Tony Dunne, was turned inside out by the Saints' elusive left winger John Sydenham. In all fairness I must explain that Bill was nearly 38 at the time and doing the club a favour by playing at all. By then he was wanting to concentrate on his coaching and had been conscripted back into the first team because a couple of the youngsters we had groomed as possible replacements, Steve James and Paul Edwards, had not developed as positively as we had hoped. He was labouring horribly with a knee injury which would continue to give him hell for the next 35 years, and now it was clear to all concerned that he shouldn't be expected to play again. In retrospect I'm sad that such a stalwart servant to the United cause should bow out in such distressing circumstances, but that did nothing to detract from his long-term achievements. Only Bobby Charlton and, now, Ryan Giggs has made more appearances for United than Bill, and he will always occupy a unique niche in the club's history.

Of course, at the time I had rather more pressing concerns. We were off to Goodison shortly and it was clear that a shake-up was needed. So what did I do? The history books say that I dropped Denis Law and Bobby Charlton, but when I announced my team it was more like I'd dropped the atom bomb. Some wag even said that I'd have axed George Best, too, if I could have found him!

Strictly speaking, no matter what the spin adopted by the media, Denis had not been dropped. He had been struggling with a groin problem, and although often during his career the courageous Scot had performed brilliantly while carrying injuries, I felt it was wrong to push him into what was certain to be a gruelling physical battle against formidably tough opponents.

As for Bobby, he *was* dropped for tactical reasons, and looking back I have to admit that it was rather a rash decision, especially as Denis was going to be absent. Losing one world-class footballer might be construed as careless, but losing two ... well, it doesn't bear thinking about! My reasoning was that we had been hopelessly outrun in midfield by Everton in the first match. The centre of the pitch had been a pretty frantic place, very crowded and with everything moving at 100 miles an hour, and I felt that Bobby had been bypassed. I wanted something different for the rematch and went for a completely new formation. This involved the young Irishman Don Givens as an out-and-out spearhead, with Brian Kidd playing just behind him, and a midfield of Morgan, Crerand, Best and Johnny Aston junior, in which the two wingers, Willie and John, played deeper and narrower than usual. I thought it was an energetic and pretty youthful combination which could hold its own against Ball, Harvey and Kendall when the going got hectic.

I revamped the defence, too, which was already deprived of two top men, Tony Dunne and Nobby Stiles, through injury. In the thrashing by Southampton we had proved terribly vulnerable to crosses, so now I left out goalkeeper Jimmy Rimmer, who I had expected to catch everything which came his way but who didn't on that occasion. Also out were Shay, who had failed to stem the flow of deliveries from his winger, and Bill, for reasons already mentioned. In came Alex Stepney between the posts, the vigorous young John Fitzpatrick at right-back and fellow youth team product Paul Edwards at centre-half.

I didn't mention to Matt my intention of changing virtually half the side, and when I did let him have the line-up he made no attempt to interfere. But I had talked it over with my trainers, the highly experienced Jack Crompton and John Aston senior, who agreed that some sort of drastic action was needed. It was all for the good of the team as I saw it. Never for a moment was there the slightest element of me trying to show my top players who was boss, or of attempting to stamp my authority on them with some grand theatrical gesture. If I had been seeking to prove a point, then a bollocking in front of the other players would have done the trick, but I never felt the need to do that. Nothing could have been farther from my mind.

When I broke the news to Denis and Bobby they took it like the true professionals they were. If I was leaving someone, anyone, out of the team I always made a point of speaking to them privately first. Denis was so brave that he would have been willing to play even if he could hardly move, but I think he understood my decision. I guess it must have been particularly hard for Bobby because he was fit and hadn't been dropped for a very long time, but all he said was: 'Fine, if that's what you want.'

In the end, of course, the success or failure of any strategy comes down to results, so there was never any doubt who was going to be the villain of the piece after we lost 3-0 to Harry Catterick's Merseysiders, to make it three defeats in the space of seven days and only one point from my first four games in charge. Maybe I was naïve, but I was dumbfounded by the scale of the reaction in the press and among the fans to the double whammy of getting beaten again and the omission of Law and Charlton. They practically crucified me, and in retrospect I realised that I had made myself a hostage to fortune. I should have tried something less dramatic to achieve a better balance and I should have remembered the old adage: 'If you haven't got anything better, then stick to what you've got.'

Throughout all this, Matt Busby found himself in a truly unenviable position. He had recommended me to the board and now, with things not going well, he wouldn't have wanted to cut the ground from under me by being seen to intervene. Equally I didn't want to run to him with my first problem. Maybe he was waiting for me to come to him, but the opposite was true, too. I had never made any secret of my willingness to draw on his vast knowledge, but there were grey areas in the way our responsibilities dovetailed that never became clear to me.

It was in this atmosphere of uncertainty, just after the second Everton setback, that I was approached, ever so discreetly, by club secretary Les Olive, who said the directors were wondering whether I was in close enough touch with Matt. At first I was a little taken aback by the suggestion that the directors were getting involved with the football side of the club, but on reflection I doubted whether the message had come from them at all. I never knew for certain, but it felt as if maybe Matt had sent Les to encourage me to contact him. That way he might have thought that he could help me, but without appearing to butt in.

Whatever the truth of that, it was clear that we needed to discuss a mounting crisis in the centre of defence and, with Matt in charge of transfers anyway, it was wholly appropriate that he suggested a target. Fine in principle, but I wasn't totally enamoured with his choice of Ian Ure, Arsenal's rugged Scottish international who had had several up-and-downers with his equally fiery countryman Denis Law, one of which had resulted in the pair of them being sent off. During my trips to London on England youth team business I had seen quite a bit of Ian playing for the Gunners and I wasn't sure he was the man to improve our side in the long term. But Matt rated him highly, I respected his judgement and so I went along with him. Accordingly he got on the phone to the Arsenal boss Bertie Mee and we ended up signing him for £80,000.

Pretty soon it seemed that Matt had exercised the wisdom of Solomon as we embarked on an eight-match unbeaten run that turned the season around, and there was no denying that Ure gave us a short-term lift. But still I was becoming ever more convinced that the squad wasn't big enough, solid enough, just plain good enough for Manchester United. We needed an infusion of players who were younger than Ure but with proven ability, but a little later when I came up with the names of potential targets, the money was never made available.

At that point, as I made the best of what I had, what struck me as the thorniest problem facing a manager was the loss of key men to injury. If everyone was in apple-pie order then I could still turn out a tremendous first eleven, but invariably I would lay down careful plans only to lose Denis with a groin problem, Nobby with his knee and so on. In my playing days and beyond, United had been blessed with a vastly experienced physiotherapist in Ted Dalton. He was brilliant at recognising injuries, knowing how long they would take to heal, understanding which ones a footballer could carry into games without doing long-term damage. But he had died by the time I took charge and we had replaced him, first with Laurie Mawson and then with Laurie Brown who were, like me, learning their craft. I'm not saying anything against either of them, clearly they knew their work, but they didn't have the accumulated knowledge of decades to back them up. There has

Pleased as punch on my first day as chief coach of Manchester United.

to be a tight bonding between a manager and his physio and, in our case, that was an area which took time.

Still, as the season continued to stabilise and we moved up the League table, I became ever more optimistic that we were on the right track. Though parts of the side were ageing, the genius of George Best continued to flourish despite his increasing tendency to kick over the traces – more of that later – and several very talented individuals were maturing towards their prime. For instance, there was George's former digs mate David Sadler, who had arrived at Old Trafford as a lean, classy young England amateur international centre-forward. In the end he wasn't going to make it up front, but he proved his versatility both in midfield, where he featured in the 1968 European Cup Final, and as a central defender, which was easily his best position. David was a deliciously cultured performer, a lovely passer and very comfortable in possession, but in my opinion he had one weakness as a stopper at the very top level – quite simply, he was too much of a gentleman.

You could never wish to meet a nicer, more laid-back fellow than David. But while it's a veritable delight to spend time with such an amiable character *off* the field – he's been a hugely popular and efficient secretary of United's Former Players Asssociation for so long, it must be time he put in for a pay rise! – *on* it he was never quite ruthless enough. When you're a defender, winning and losing has got to be a matter of life and death. When the ball comes in, often you have to charge through opponents to head it clear or make your tackle. I'm not saying David couldn't get stuck in or that he wasn't brave; it was just that he never had a nasty bone in his body. Recognising his tremendous all-round talent, I was determined to instil a killer streak during my time as manager, and if I'd been successful I'm convinced he would have won far more than his four England caps. Unfortunately, I wasn't around long enough to find out.

Then there was Willie Morgan, another staggeringly gifted individual, a right winger we signed from Burnley in 1968 and who on his day could practically make the ball talk. That said, he was never up there with George Best, no matter what he thought. That's not just me saying that; it's the opinion of every unbiased observer who watched the pair of them play. You need to know your level, and I'm not sure that Willie did. Still, he played his part in the United story and he enjoyed his most prolific scoring season at the club when I was in charge – but, sadly, he didn't enjoy me. Perhaps because of all the chasing back and harassing of opponents I asked him to do for the team's good, he might have thought I didn't like him, but he was wrong. I did like Willie as a footballer and later, when my successor Frank O'Farrell used him in a midfield role along the lines I had envisaged, he did very well.

Another of my charges with vast ability but who never quite fulfilled his rich potential was Brian Kidd, a lad for whom I always had a soft spot, and not only because he was a fellow product of Collyhurst. In fairness, he did experience that most incredible high of celebrating his 19th birthday with a goal in the European Cup Final, but at that point I thought he would go on and on and become part of the United bedrock. In fact, I believe that if we had strengthened the team significantly during my reign as manager, when he was one of the most promising strikers in the country, he might have progressed to a major international career rather than picking up just two caps. With all due humility, I have a feeling Brian might have fared better if I'd remained as boss, because we shared a history of rising through the Old Trafford youth ranks and I might have got more out of him than either Frank O'Farrell or Tommy Docherty. As it was he ended up travelling from club to club and doing well enough – but it was such a shame he ever left.

Among the other players round about their early twenties, I thought a lot of John Aston junior, who had an unenviable task in following in his father's Old Trafford footsteps. It must have been very hard coming through when John senior was coaching because the boy had to do twice as well as the next player to make his mark, so that no one could call favourites. He overcame the obstacle with the quiet, down-to-earth determination which had always marked his dad, who was a genuine United hero and one of the greatest men to serve the club. He showed further strength of character when he became something of a scapegoat for frustrated so-called fans when things didn't go well for the team, developing a thick skin and battling on regardless to rise above the mindless abuse. Of course, John junior will never be forgotten because of his wonderful performance against Benfica in the European Cup Final. He deserved every ounce of the praise that came his way and I could not have been happier for him. After John Connelly left, he became an important part of the side for his work rate as well as his attacking prowess down the left flank. Perhaps his final ball could have been a tad more reliable, and if it had then I reckon he'd have become an England regular. As it was his career was severely disrupted by a broken leg in August 1968, and although he recovered to play well under me it's fair to say that he was never quite as effective again. Still, I shall always remember both John Astons with immense affection. They were United through and through, and must have been very proud of one another.

Between the posts I had two fine goalkeepers, and although Alex Stepney went on to play more than 500 times for United, there were periods during my time in charge when Jimmy Rimmer had the edge. I had known Jimmy since his successful youth team days and I thought he had a brilliant future. He was a quiet fellow, but at first he was so commanding when he came out for crosses that I thought there was a hint of the great Bert Trautmann about him. But whereas some quiet people have a deep well of self-belief inside them, I'm not sure that Jimmy did and he never progressed to the heights I had predicted for him. The attribute which Alex possessed in abundance, which Jimmy seemed to be missing, was confidence. Alex was a much louder character, and he imposed himself, bossed his box, and that is always good for a defence. He was a thinker, too, and he used the ball well. In the end he won the battle of the Old Trafford 'keepers, but Jimmy enjoyed a decent career afterwards, with Arsenal and Aston Villa. In fact, he collected twice as many European Cup medals as Alex, despite spending only nine minutes on the pitch spread over two finals. In 1968 he was a non-playing substitute for United, then he started the game for Villa against Bayern Munich in 1982 but went off with an injury.

Of course, as I knew only too well through bitter experience, luck with fitness plays a massive part in a footballer's career and one man who enjoyed very little of that commodity was the bubbly little Scot John Fitzpatrick. He could play in midfield or at full-back and there was a bit of Nobby in him, a bit of me. John was what might be called an enthusiastic tackler, a bit wild sometimes, and he was very brave, always ready to play through the pain of his many injuries if it was humanly possible, but they defeated him in the end.

As might be expected of such a fierce competitor, Fitz fell foul of authority at times, but I'm sure there was an element of 'give a dog a bad

The gospel according to Wilf McGuinness: I offer a few thoughts to the first-team squad, with Sir Matt Busby standing at my shoulder …

Nobody can say I didn't win silverware as manager of Manchester United. Here I enlighten the United squad about how we triumphed in the *Daily Express* Five-a-side indoor championship, while proud skipper Bobby Charlton clutches the precious prize.

name' about some of his punishments. I once accompanied him to a hearing at FA headquarters, where we were faced by the chairman of the disciplinary committee, who also happened to be on the board of Leeds. I spoke for Fitz, admitting that the timing of his tackle had been poor, but adding that I had been a wing-half and since the incident had been coaching him hard. We had to leave the room while the verdict was considered, and on our return the chairman said: 'Well, Mr McGuinness, because of what you said we're inclined to be lenient, so we're sentencing Fitzpatrick to only four weeks' suspension.' Four weeks! Call that lenient? I was furious, and my state of mind wasn't helped by the fact that the punishment had been handed out by a man who represented one of our closest rivals. How could that be fair? It was utterly ridiculous.

Fitz's fellow Scot Francis Burns was another whose promising impetus was hit by injuries. He was a steady young full-back who read the game well, and if he lacked a little bit of pace for the top level, what he needed most was more luck. After playing throughout most of United's triumphant European campaign in 1968, he lost his place to Shay Brennan for the second leg of the semi-final against Real Madrid because Matt felt Shay would have a better chance of keeping up with the lightning-quick Francisco Gento. Of course, Shay did well and kept his place for the final, which must have been a colossal blow to Franny. He coped well with his disappointment, though, and fought back to earn a regular place in my side, only to be knocked back by injuries.

Another who had genuine aspirations of a big-time breakthrough in that era was the little midfield buzz-bomb Carlo Sartori, a lovely lad who worked his heart out for me and played some good games but wasn't quite up to stepping into the boots of the greats. Then there was Alan Gowling, a big gangling lad who looked awkward but who I felt had the equipment to have become a very fine striker. Maybe he wasn't the classiest, and perhaps he could have been a bit more assertive in calling for the ball, but he was strong, deceptively quick, pretty good in the air and he could put the ball in the net on a regular basis, which he proved in his subsequent career, especially with Huddersfield and Newcastle. My successor as manager, Frank O'Farrell, tried him in central midfield, but I think that was a mistake. Alan was, and remains, a fascinating character who led a double life as a young footballer, working for his university degree and training in the evenings, which can't have been easy. In later years he has further demonstrated his work ethic by succeeding in business, and he has also done plenty for our Former Players Association.

These days I enjoy reminiscing about the men who strove alongside me to further the cause of Manchester United. It's a pleasurable, leisurely activity, but as I reviewed my resources in the autumn of 1969 the situation was considerably more urgent. It was clear to me, regrettably, that we were not yet strong enough to make a realistic bid for the League title, so I was desperately keen for us to make a big impact in the cups – and so we did.

Chapter 15

SO NEAR AND YET SO FAR

URING MY agonisingly brief sojourn in charge of Manchester United, we reached three major semi-finals spread over seven games in the space of some 12 months. We didn't win one of them, losing each time by a single goal, and I can't help feeling that if we'd had the breaks to reach a final, the rest of my career might never have taken me to the likes of Bootham Crescent, Boothferry Park and Gigg Lane. Not that I didn't relish my time in those much-loved bastions of English football – and I was made gloriously welcome in each of them – but I don't think it will surprise or offend anyone if I declare that my heart never left Old Trafford.

The first of my three semis, in the League Cup in December 1969, could hardly have carried a higher profile. After beating Middlesbrough, Wrexham, Burnley and Derby County, we faced Manchester City over two legs, the first of them at Maine Road. This was in the days when City, run by Joe Mercer and Malcolm Allison, had the best team in their history so we knew it wouldn't be easy. Still, I genuinely believed that we could beat them. Okay, they had Colin Bell, Francis Lee and Mike Summerbee, and plenty of other tremendous players, but we had Best, Law and Charlton, so we weren't going to be overawed. Sure enough, over the two games Denis and Bobby were magnificent, but every little scrap of good fortune went City's way and we lost 4-3 on aggregate.

The Maine Road encounter was particularly frustrating. The game had been pretty even, with Bobby equalising an earlier goal from Bell, and a draw seemed inevitable when, two minutes from the end, Ian Ure stuck out a stray boot which was found by Lee and referee Jack Taylor awarded a penalty. Lee got up to score from the spot – he did that a few times in his career – and then, with the final seconds ticking away, George broke through at the other end. It looked odds on that he was going to level the scores again until he was fouled. I was sure it was a penalty, but Taylor waved play on, leaving George absolutely fuming. The final whistle went almost immediately, but George was too uptight to let things lie, and during an argument with Taylor as they left the pitch, he knocked the ball out of the referee's hands. As a result he was suspended for four weeks, and although our appeal against what we believed to be an unnecessarily harsh sentence meant that he could play in the second leg, we lost him for five games at a crucial part of the season. Obviously what he did was wrong, but there was no violence involved and it was supremely galling for him to receive a more severe suspension for a spot of petulance than if he had injured someone.

We were happy to have him in the side for the rematch at Old Trafford two weeks later, though, and when a brilliant 20-yarder from young Paul Edwards and a typical piece of opportunism from Denis Law put us 2-1 up on the night – that was 3-3 on aggregate – with not long to go, I was confident we would go through. We were all over them at that point, and it seemed that the tide had turned in our favour. But with about eight minutes left Willie Morgan obstructed Ian Bowyer to give away an indirect free-kick. Lee hit it past the defensive wall and Alex Stepney could have let it go past him into the net – it wouldn't have counted. But in the heat of the action Alex tried to catch it, only succeeding in fumbling it to the feet of Summerbee, who knocked it in for the winner. After playing so well it was a monumentally sickening way to go out, especially to City, who went on to win the final against West Bromwich Albion at Wembley.

In the League, meanwhile, we had improved substantially following our dismal start to the season and among our credits was a double over Bill Shankly's Liverpool. A goal by Willie Morgan was enough to win the first game at Old Trafford, but it's the 4-1 victory at Anfield shortly before Christmas that looks so fine in the record books. Of course, the rivalry between United and Liverpool has always been keen – during the mid-1960s we appeared to take it in turns with our north-western rivals to lift the League title – but there was never that bitter edge of something disturbingly close to hatred which a vocal minority of fans from both ends of the East Lancs Road have exhibited in modern times.

Certainly there was no shortage of friendship and respect between the two sets of players and the coaching staff. The Liverpool lot were brilliant people – Shanks, Bob Paisley, Joe Fagan, Reuben Bennett, Ronnie Moran and the young Roy Evans. Whenever I went to Anfield with United reserves, after the game, win, lose or draw, it would be into the famous boot room for a beer, though, to be honest, I wasn't particularly enamoured by their choice of beverage. They would hand round bottles of Export Guinness, which was horrible, like drinking iron, but it wouldn't have been polite to turn it down. The important thing was that they looked after us, and we did the same for them when they came to Old Trafford. It was a terrific relationship and I know that, for all his bluster, Bill Shankly was extremely fond of plenty of United folk. His regard for Matt Busby was well known, but also he had a soft spot for Bobby Charlton. Sometimes when Liverpool were visiting United the Merseysiders would stay at a hotel not far from Bobby's house in Lymm, Cheshire, and Bill was in the habit of knocking on the Charlton door early in the morning for a cup of tea and a natter about football. I used to joke that he was merely trying to put Bobby off ahead of the match, but I always knew that wasn't his motive really. Shanks was head over heels in love with the game, and chewing the fat with a player of Bobby's calibre was an opportunity he just couldn't pass up.

Putting one over on such a great man to the tune of 4-1 in his own backyard was arguably the standout result in my entire tenure in charge of United, yet perversely it served to inflame some critics, who felt that if we could play like that occasionally, then why couldn't we do it on a regular basis? I could see where they were coming from but I thought there were mitigating circumstances. After all, I had not been a boss for long, and I was having to cope with constant injury problems. But we did have our moments – as any team is bound to with Best, Law and Charlton among their number – and such moments reinforced my belief that we were on the verge of getting things right.

Strangely enough, that crushing defeat of Liverpool doesn't remain all that vivid in my memory. I recall that Bobby scored a remarkable goal, which was not exactly a rare occurrence, but the strikes by Willie Morgan and Ian Ure, and the own-goal by Ron Yeats, are shrouded by the mists of time. My explanation is that I was convinced I was looking ahead to many years in the job, and that I was confident there would be

A word in your ear, George. It was a privilege to manage one of the greatest footballers the world has ever seen, but it wasn't always easy.

Manchester United, ready for action at the start of the 1970/71 campaign. I never dreamed that by the New Year I would be gone. Back row, left to right: Steve James, Alan Gowling, Jimmy Rimmer, Alex Stepney, John Connaughton, Brian Kidd, Paul Edwards, Willie Watson. Third row: Tommy O'Neil, Tony Young, Kevin Lewis, Brian Greenhoff, Francis Burns, Ian Donald, Tony Whelan. Second row: John Fitzpatrick, George Best, Eric Young, Bill Fairhurst, David Sadler, Ian Ure, Damien Ferguson, John Aston, Laurie Millerchip. Front row: team manager Wilf McGuinness , Tony Dunne, Denis Law, Willie Morgan, Bobby Charlton, Paddy Crerand, Nobby Stiles, Carlo Sartori, trainer Jack Crompton, general manager Sir Matt Busby.

no shortage of massive occasions to savour. After all, I was still in my early thirties, I knew that Matt Busby had spent a quarter of a century in United's managerial chair and I felt that the club's directors were planning for the long term when they selected me. The way I looked at it, this season was just the start, and wins against the likes of Liverpool were no more than I expected on the way to garnering the biggest prizes the game had to offer.

In fact, there was one trophy in particular on which I had my sights. I wanted to win the Inter-Continental Cup, which would have made us the champions of the world. Of course, to even qualify for that competition we would have had to lift the League title and the European Cup along the way, which was the real ambition. It was the one peak which even Sir Matt Busby had not scaled, and I was desperate to do it, not for my own glory but to take Manchester United to another level. Luckily, I had enough sense not to make this dream public, otherwise I would have been setting myself up for a mighty fall because, in the end, we won nothing while I was manager. Well, we did, we carried off the *Daily Express* Five-a-Side crown, but that wasn't exactly what I had in mind!

Back in the real world, we survived George Best's January absence undefeated, a sequence which included an emphatic 3-0 victory over Manchester City in the fourth round of the FA Cup, which helped more than a little to make up for our controversial League Cup exit at the hands of our neighbours. But it was the fifth round of the professional game's oldest competition which created the most indelible headlines. We were drawn to face Northampton Town on a bit of a mud patch at the County Ground, and George Best was available for selection, having completed his draconian sentence for his spat with Jack Taylor. For some reason which I could never fathom, certain members of the press were extremely forthright in proclaiming that he should not be recalled to face the Cobblers, that I should effectively extend his punishment by leaving him out against the Fourth Division side. Well, they had one word right, and that was Cobblers! I'd never heard such rubbish in my life and there was no way I was going to heed their advice.

George was the type of character who always wanted to prove something to somebody, and I believe he did so that day, scoring six goals as we beat Northampton 8-2. He cut through their defence like a knife through butter, and I'm firmly convinced that he would have done the same no matter what the standard of opposition. Northampton were unlucky to encounter him in that mood, but I don't think even Liverpool would have got off any more lightly. He believed his suspension had been a grave injustice and now he was putting up two fingers – better make that six! – to his critics. George was always keen to play football, but that afternoon he was burning to put on a show, and the outcome was unforgettable.

By now the FA Cup represented our last chance of securing a major honour in my first term, and we moved a step nearer by overcoming Second Division Middlesbrough, who held us to a 1-1 draw at Ayrsome Park before succumbing 2-1 in the Old Trafford replay. But now the going got really tough: in the semi-final we were paired with Don Revie's Leeds, a mighty team which combined fabulous levels of ability with an abrasive physical approach which had made them plenty of enemies. Their players used to hunt in packs. Whenever there was an argument on the pitch there would be a posse of them piling in so it was difficult for the referee to pin down specific trouble-makers. I don't know whether they were acting on instructions from their manager, but I'm certain they knew exactly what they were doing.

But whatever is said about the ugly side of Leeds, there is no question that they could play like a dream. They won some silverware, and thoroughly deserved it, but I believe they would have accumulated so much more if they had been a bit more adventurous. Too often, in my opinion, they would sit on a one-goal lead instead of using their many exceptional players to capitalise on it. For a long time, it seemed that Don Revie restricted them to marking opponents when they might have been expressing themselves, and it was only towards the end of his life that he revealed his regret that he hadn't let them off the leash when his side was in its prime. One of Revie's leading lights was my old friend Johnny Giles, a superb footballer whom I don't believe should ever have left Manchester United. As a Busby Babe he positively oozed class, and he could always look after himself, though he learned far more about that aspect of the game at Elland Road than he did at Old Trafford. Mind, John was only one of many tough nuts at Leeds. Most of them came in hard every time and relished a clash. In fact, I think Eddie Gray was the only one in that team you could rely on not to do you in. He was a beautiful footballer and he wouldn't resort to kicking you. Allan

Clarke was skilful, too, but he could be nasty when he wanted to be, while his partner in the centre of attack, Mick Jones, was all for a touch of rough and tumble. Some say that Jimmy Greenhoff – who later made a name for himself at Stoke before excelling with Manchester United – was allowed to leave Elland Road because he wasn't physical enough for Don Revie. I can't vouch for that, but I do know that Jimmy, who played for me in the England youth set-up, was a thoroughbred performer with limitless all-round talent. He was a great lad, too, and it's a pleasure these days to share corporate hospitality duties with him on match days at Old Trafford.

However, Jimmy had already departed Elland Road by the time we faced them in what was to prove an epic FA Cup semi-final confrontation. Half a decade earlier we had pipped them to the League championship, but after that they often seemed to have the sign over us in tight situations. This time it was to take three meetings before the tie was settled by its only goal, scored by Billy Bremner at Burnden Park. What made our elimination all the more frustrating was that we had played really well in the first game at Hillsborough, and missed a chance or two in the second encounter at Villa Park.

Absorbing though the Leeds marathon was in football terms, it has entered United folklore for rather more lurid reasons concerning the social habits of George Best. It's not exactly an earth-shattering revelation to say that George was chased constantly by beautiful young ladies, and I don't think I'm going to shock anyone by adding that he was an exceedingly willing target. Before the Villa Park instalment of the semi-final trilogy we were based at an hotel in Droitwich, a little south of Birmingham. After lunch on the day of the match the players were relaxing in the television lounge when I noticed that George was missing. Then somebody else pointed out that an extremely attractive girl, who had been spending a lot of time around the communal areas of the hotel, was also nowhere to be seen. Well, I didn't need to be Hercule Poirot for my little grey cells to start buzzing. I was deeply suspicious, to put it mildly.

Time passed with no sign of our handsome Irishman, and when it was time for the lads to go to their bedrooms for some pre-match rest I thought I'd better investigate his continuing absence. I asked the porter if he'd seen George and was told that he'd been spotted chatting with a young lady. So I asked for her room number, invited the porter to accompany me and went upstairs in search of my missing star. When we reached the room I knocked on the door and there was no reply, but I was pretty certain he was in there so I asked the porter to open it with his master key. Sure enough, there was George and, contrary to the colourful stories that circulated later, both of them were fully clothed and looking perfectly innocent.

By now, though, I was fuming, absolutely blazing, because he had taken me for a fool and not opened the door. It seemed to me a blatant breach of club discipline and so, as that was his province according to the agreement when I took the job, I went to find Matt Busby. I explained to Matt that I didn't know exactly what George had been up to – he had been missing for only a few minutes, but who knows? – but it was the day of the game, after all. I left Matt in no doubt that I was furious, and he asked if I still wanted George to face Leeds. Now, some imaginative versions of this torrid tale make out that I demanded that George be sent home immediately, but that was rubbish. We were preparing for an FA Cup semi-final against one of the strongest teams in the land – of course I wanted our best player on the field. So I sent him to Matt, who gave him a severe dressing down and fined him for being in the girl's room when he should have been in his own.

It's impossible to say whether this dalliance had any bearing on the fact that he under-performed in the game. Once, when he was through on goal near the end he stood on the ball and stumbled instead of converting what was a relatively simple scoring opportunity. Had he put that one away, then almost certainly he would have realised one of his lifetime ambitions of playing in an FA Cup Final, and my career path might have been radically altered. But I was never one to wring my hands about what might have been. The fact was that Paul Reaney, the Leeds full-back, did a very fine marking job on George, as he usually did. Afterwards some people joked that the girl in the hotel was a Leeds United plant. One wag even wondered whether she might have been Paul Reaney in drag, but I think George might have twigged that pretty rapidly!

As to the wider picture of what it was like to manage George Best, I feel any adverse effect on my reign has been exaggerated, blown out of all proportion. Of course, I was acutely aware that he wasn't a little angel, but I'm sure that his worst excesses occurred after my departure. I loved him as a player and I had a lot of time for him as a person. He made mistakes, but don't we all?

In the end, the ruination of George Best was down to alcohol, but that never manifested itself as a problem while I was at the helm. As for his other misdemeanours, they didn't exactly cause me to lose much sleep, although I can't deny there many times when the situation worried me.

People are different. For instance, Paddy Crerand was late almost every day of the week. That was his make-up, just the way he was. We all have human weaknesses. Paddy would be disciplined and then we would get on with our jobs. As I saw it, coping with that sort of incident was an essential part of managing a football club, and I viewed George's occasional escapades in the same light. When he went missing for a training session I would send him to see Matt and he would be punished. I don't believe he ever set out with the intention of letting down the team, but sometimes events in his life spiralled out of control. For instance, there was an occasion when he was living in his goldfish bowl of a house in Bramhall, an ultra-modern monstrosity which someone described as bearing a passing resemblance to a public toilet. He told me afterwards that he had gone to bed at 10.30, but he couldn't sleep so he went downstairs and started playing snooker. That became boring and he still wasn't sleepy so, around midnight, he thought: 'Sod it! I'll just whip into town and see who's around. I won't stay long.' In the event he met a gorgeous blonde and they ended up going back to his place at about six in the morning. When explaining himself to me later, he said sheepishly: 'In the circumstances, I don't think you could have expected me to get up and go training, Wilf.' My reaction was: 'Well actually, George, I did. You're disrupting the team and being unfair to everybody else. Now go and tell your story to Sir Matt.'

As I hope I've made abundantly clear, I never held the tiniest shred of personal antipathy towards George Best, but such antics obviously didn't help our club's cause. I'd like to stress, also, that the Irishman was given very many chances, both by myself and by other people at Manchester United.

Still, when the 1969/70 season ended not long after the FA Cup knockout by Leeds, I was neither unhappy about my efforts during my first term in charge nor despondent about our long-term prospects. We had finished in eighth place in the First Division, three places better than had been managed under Sir Matt in 1968/69, and we had reached two semi-finals, both of which had been lost by the narrowest of margins. I thought, too, despite a few scurrilous rumours about dissatisfaction in the ranks, that we were a generally happy crew. Overall, it didn't seem too bad for somebody coping with a monumentally steep learning curve, and I was content that, with two years of my contract left to run, I had plenty of time to prove myself as manager of Manchester United ...

Chapter 16
PROMOTED – AND SACKED

I N THE summer of 1970 I had every reason to believe that my plans for Manchester United were moving in the right direction. Obviously the club and Sir Matt Busby thought so too, because they announced an upgrade in my job description, from chief coach to manager. In terms of my actual duties it didn't make a scrap of difference, but I took it as a signal to the outside world that they were pleased with my work, and ready to support me to the hilt as I embarked on the long haul of restoring United to what I believed passionately was their rightful place in the football world – at the very top of the pile. However, as I reviewed my resources I became convinced that I needed reinforcements on the pitch. Yet despite United remaining one of the biggest clubs in the game, there seemed to be a reluctance to part with any cash.

During the previous spring it had become increasingly clear that we needed an extra top-quality striker, what with Denis Law struggling for fitness and Brian Kidd being best suited, in my opinion, to playing off the main spearhead. The man I had my eye on was Malcolm Macdonald, who had been converted from a rather ordinary full-back to become a rampaging, free-scoring centre-forward for Third Division Luton Town. I checked him out when the Hatters visited Mansfield, slipping into Field Mill incognito and standing on the terrace behind the goal, and I was mightily impressed by his raw power and his evident hunger to put the ball in the net. After my favourable report Matt and Jimmy pulled up their coat collars, muffled their well-known features in scarves and pulled the brims of their trilbies down over their eyes, then stood on the popular side at Kenilworth Road to see if they fancied him, too.

They did, and duly an approach was made to the Luton management team of Alec Stock and Harry Haslam, who gave us first refusal but then wouldn't let Malcolm go because their team was pressing for promotion to the Second Division. This mystified me because that April we allowed four of our players – including first-team squad men Jim Ryan and Don Givens – to join Luton. I don't know why United didn't twist their arm over that package deal by telling them that they could forget signing our quartet unless they sold Macdonald to us. If I'd been a bit more experienced I'd have pushed hard for that, and even to this day I can't understand why Matt didn't go in a bit harder if he truly rated the player, as he assured me he did. Certainly it's fair to suggest that Malcolm Macdonald would have been a sensation in a side that contained the likes of Best, Charlton, Law, Kidd, Morgan and Crerand. How many chances could they have created for such a natural predator? The mind boggles. As it was he spent another prolific season with Luton before banging in plenty for Newcastle and Arsenal which, with all modesty on my part, served only to bear out my initial judgement.

The search for a reliable scorer continued in the summer and at one point Matt told me we were on the verge of signing the magnificent

Welsh international Ron Davies from Southampton. That was fabulous news because Ron was a goal machine at that point of his career, but then I was told the deal had fallen through at the last minute because of a financial problem, whether it was at Southampton's end or United's wasn't specified.

I was gutted by that because our attacking need was so great, and I fared no better in my efforts to bolster our defence. The two men I wanted were the right-back Mick Mills of Ipswich Town, and Colin Todd of Sunderland, who I believed would make an excellent central defensive partner for David Sadler. I'd seen plenty of Todd in the England under-23 set-up and I believed he was a truly exceptional prospect, but my recommendations were not accepted. Of course, Colin went on to become one of the best players of his type in the Football League for the rest of the decade and beyond, and our failure to sign him left me immensely disappointed.

As for Mills, I told Matt he was solid, reliable and with plenty of years ahead of him, just the player we needed at right-back as the long-term replacement for Shay Brennan, who had reached the veteran stage and been released to join the League of Ireland club Waterford. For the first and what turned out to be the only time, I was allowed to get involved in a potential transfer deal. Matt suggested that I offer the Ipswich boss Bobby Robson £80,000, adding that Robson had not been at Portman Road for too long and might be looking for money to finance his own plans. Sadly, Bobby gave me short shrift, telling me there was no chance that he would sell Mills. I could understand his decision because Mick was one of his best players, but it was doubly disappointing for me, partly because I had wanted the right-back so badly and partly because it would have been a feather in my cap to have pulled off the transaction.

However, with Matt the man in charge of the purse-strings, I had no choice but to get on with the new season without my longed-for reinforcements. We started dismally, losing at home to Leeds on the opening day and achieving only three wins in our first dozen First Division outings, but were offered a shot at redemption in the League Cup. After beating Aldershot, Portsmouth, Chelsea – when George Best shrugged off 'Chopper' Harris to score that unforgettable goal– and Crystal Palace, we faced Third Division Aston Villa in the two-legged semi-final and, despite our disappointing League form, we were pretty warm favourites to reach Wembley.

We were drawn to play the away leg first, which offers a slight advantage, but there was a power strike and Villa didn't have a generator for their lights. We did, so the first game was switched to Old Trafford. Of course, losing that edge should not have made the tiniest difference to any Manchester United side facing lower-league opposition, but our poor form persisted against a lively Villa for whom one of our old boys, the winger Willie Anderson, was shining. They held us to a horrible draw, then took us back to Villa Park and beat us 2-1 just two days before Christmas. It was a devastating blow, the media went berserk and, in retrospect, that was the result which sealed my fate.

However, although I was reeling from such a colossal setback and racking my brains for solutions to our problems, I held on to the circumstance that I had a three-year contract and therefore would be given the opportunity to turn the juggernaut around. Call me naïve but, honestly, it never occurred to me that the axe was set to descend on my neck.

Despite training on Christmas morning I made the best of the rest of the day with the family – some things are sacred, even in the pressurised world of professional football – then prepared for our Boxing Day trip to Derby, where Brian Clough was already making steady progress towards a place among football's legends. The team I named for the Baseball Ground was: Stepney, Fitzpatrick, Dunne, Crerand, Ure, Sadler, Morgan, Best, Charlton, Kidd and Law. I don't think anyone would dispute that it contained a fantastic blend of talent and experience, and I list it in full because it was the last I ever picked as manager of Manchester United. Ironically, that was one confrontation we didn't lose. It was a 4-4 thriller with our goals coming from Law (two), Best and Kidd, which earned a valuable point, and immediately afterwards I turned my thoughts to our next encounter, an FA Cup third-round clash with Middlesbrough shortly after New Year.

The next morning, December 27, I went into the Cliff as usual and was surprised when Matt appeared, then asked Jack Crompton to take the players training, and called me into his office. I can remember his words with all-too-vivid clarity. He looked very grave as he said: 'Wilf, the results are not going well. We're halfway through the season and we're near the bottom of the table. The directors have asked me to take over the team again.' I felt as though I had been punched in the stomach. This was grievous news and I just hadn't seen it coming. Still, I didn't just accept it meekly. For about half an hour I fought my corner, arguing my case for being given more time as outlined in my contract, making an impassioned plea to be given the opportunity to see through what I had started. I just couldn't conceive that I was being told to give up my dream. But Matt Busby, although enormously compassionate and understanding the depth of my feeling, was not for turning. The decision had been made and nothing I could say was going to change it.

I left The Cliff to go home at around midday, but first called in at the ground, from where I rang Beryl to break the news. I wandered into the directors' room where I looked for the whisky but couldn't find it, so I grabbed a bottle of sherry. Matt, who knew I was fearfully upset, had evidently asked Jack to follow me back to Old Trafford, and our trainer arrived to find me utterly distraught. To me, at that moment, it was as if the world had ended. I was demoralised, heartbroken, horribly hurt on both a professional and a personal level. I had believed that we were all in it together and that I had three seasons to find success. Now it felt as though I was being singled out while everybody else just sailed on. I'm not ashamed to admit that, in those darkest moments of my career, I literally banged my head against the wall several times and it bloody hurt!

Looking back, it can't have been very pleasant for poor Jack to find me in such a distressed state, but he's a lovely guy and he remained calm. He did his best to console me and to put it all in perspective. I still had my wife and my family, and I was young enough to continue my life in football. Soon I went home to Beryl, and after getting the inevitable tears and recriminations out of the way, I was struck eventually by a positive notion. I remembered all the young players I'd had to disappoint since becoming a manager, the lads who had dreamed of playing for United but who'd had to accept the club's verdict that they weren't going to make the grade. Now it crossed my mind how I'd always told them there was a big world out there and that they had to find their own way to make their mark on it. Suddenly the boot was firmly on the other foot. Now those words applied to me, and it was no earthly good feeling sorry for myself.

It came back to me that, during my fateful interview with Matt Busby, he had told me my old job in charge of the reserves was still there for me. So I was not being sacked by Manchester United and, believe it or not, at that point I still wanted to stay with the club. There was no way I was going to walk out. I had suffered a profound shock but I had too many memories to leave it all behind after one traumatic conversation. Oh, I had said a few hard things in private but still, somehow, I didn't want to hurt the club in public. Quite simply, I loved it too much.

At this point, the afternoon on the day I had been told I was surplus to first-team requirements, the news had still not leaked out and before it did Matt asked me along to that evening's board meeting. Amazingly enough, it was the first, and the last, I ever attended. I had never felt offended by my exclusion. In truth, I had never wanted to go. I imagined that the board talked of weighty financial matters, while all that concerned me was the football. Now, though, I felt I should face my employers and it was an emotional meeting. On a personal level I think I got on well with the directors, and they knew I was United to my very core. As we gathered in the boardroom they were all upset and one, Alan Gibson, a particularly decent man, broke down and cried.

The public announcement was to be made at a press conference the next day, and before that I went to see the players at The Cliff with Matt. He explained the position as humanely as possible, making sure that I maintained my dignity, and told them I would be resuming my old responsibilities with the reserves. The players absorbed the news passively. There was no visible reaction at all, no recrimination, no outpouring of sympathy, nothing. It wasn't until I was leaving the meeting that the silence was broken by Brian Kidd. Turning to his team-mates, most of whom were older than him and many of whom were household names, he shouted something along the lines of: 'It's you lousy bastards that have got Wilf the sack.'

It was a tremendously forthright and courageous utterance from Kiddo, who I believe had a bit of a soft spot for me. Maybe it had something to do with the fact that we both hailed from Collyhurst, but I like to think, too, that it was because I had treated him decently and because he respected me both as a football man and a human being. Whatever, I have never been quite sure exactly what he meant by his outburst, and I have never asked him. Did he mean that they'd cost me my job through not performing well enough? Or was he referring to the rumoured moaning to Matt behind my back? For what it's worth – and, of course, I cannot know for certain – I don't believe I was a victim of any whispering campaign. I think I was axed because of the poor results. If anybody had wanted to criticise me then I hope they would have done it to my face – and nobody ever did. Not a single derogatory word was said to me about the way I did my job, and nobody ever complained to me about being dropped. There might have been a few cross words over a game of cards, but that was it.

It pains me when I see or hear claims that I had a poor relationship with the players. For instance, some time after I left United, I read in a book by Alex Stepney – and I stress that I get on extremely well with Alex these days – that I had ridiculed Bobby Charlton by forcing him to do press-ups on a muddy training pitch while he was wearing a new suit. Well, I do remember the incident, but the spin that was put on it by Alex, and by mischievous people who relished repeating the story, was entirely misleading.

What really happened was this. Somebody at United had the bright idea of buying some tracksuits on the cheap, and when they arrived I was appalled to discover they had pockets in the trousers. What's the problem? Pretty soon the lads were burying their hands in these pockets during training, and I thought that was diabolical. Rather than fostering the image of a team of fit young athletes preparing to achieve excellence, it created a lackadaisical impression which I felt was wholly inappropriate. So I introduced a rule: anybody found with their hands in their pockets during training had to do ten press-ups on the spot. Anybody, whether it was the youngest trainee or the most seasoned international. As a result, people stopped doing it, not least because serial pranksters such as Shay and Nobby kept their eyes peeled, and if they saw a hand in a pocket they would shout about it at the top of their voices. So it was a fun thing, and all the lads joined in with the laugh, no problems.

Now on the day Alex mentioned, it was dry and sunny; certainly we were not standing in a quagmire, as he recalled. Earlier that morning, Bobby had asked if he could leave training a little early as he had a meeting to attend. I said: 'Yes, that's fine, but I'd like a word with

Struggling to control their grief at my departure are, left to right: Bobby Charlton, Denis Law, George Best, Sir Matt Busby, Brian Kidd, Paddy Crerand and David Sadler.

If I had been able to sign these three young players, I sincerely believe I would have made a success of my time in charge of Manchester United. Left to right are Colin Todd of Sunderland, Luton Town's Malcolm Macdonald and Mick Mills of Ipswich Town, all of whom went on to enjoy top-class careers.

everybody together at the end, so go and get changed while we're having a kick-in at the end of the session, then come back and join us before you nip off.' It should be patently obvious that I wouldn't have said that, and Bobby wouldn't have done it, if it had been raining or muddy. As it was, Bobby returned to the dressing room and changed into his suit, then came back out while we were discussing our plans for the next match.

As the chat continued, Bobby slipped his hands absent-mindedly into his suit pockets. Next thing I know, Shay and Nobby – both close mates of his – crept up behind him, clapped their hands and nabbed him. What could I say except: 'Bobby, they've caught you out, pal. Hands in your pockets, that's ten press-ups.' So he did them, albeit with a rueful grin on his face, joining in with the joke even if he was not deliriously happy at being caught out by the lads. Now, if I was trying to belittle Bobby Charlton, something I would never have contemplated under any circumstances, that would have been a particularly pathetic way to do it, and I told Alex Stepney so when his book was published.

It was serialised in a newspaper, which made the situation worse by spreading this scurrilous material even wider, and I thought about suing them. That was how strongly I felt about it. It was a nasty little story because it reflected really badly on both Bobby and myself, making me look petty and Bobby appear weak, and it simply wasn't true. I loath the type of journalism that allows such injustices to happen and I was extremely upset with Alex. But in later years we got used to each other, good sense prevailed on both sides and now there are no problems between us.

Though that rotten tale of the Charlton press-ups has been repeated frequently with the wrong emphasis, I'm delighted to report that it never remotely threatened a breakdown of my long-lasting relationship with Bobby. We understood each other far too well for that to have been a possibility. True, there was a time towards the end of my managerial stint when he wasn't happy with the way things were going, and he said so, but there wasn't a moment when I felt our friendship had been damaged. When I was in charge there had to be some demarcation line, but before and after that we have been very close. Every Christmas Eve he comes to my home in Timperley with his wife, Norma, and we exchange family presents, the same as ever. I hope that will never change.

In general, I'd say that none of the minor rifts which developed between myself and several of the players have been lasting ones. It was said that when the going was getting tough in the autumn of 1970, and possibly even before that, the likes of Alex, Willie Morgan and Paddy Crerand went to Sir Matt to complain about me behind my back. If they did then, obviously, it wasn't an ideal situation, but Sir Matt never mentioned it to me, so I can't vouch for it. I just don't know the truth. All I do know is that I was always loyal to every footballer on the staff at Old Trafford. I took the view that we were all United men working in a common cause, and that if we continued to pull together then we could work our way through the problems that beset us.

Only once did I have genuine cause to wonder if everyone else shared my belief in our solidarity. That was when Michael Parkinson, writing in the *Sunday Times*, quoted an unnamed United player as saying that even if I'd been given a million pounds to spend then I would have wasted it because I was such a bad manager. Now I thought that was below the belt, especially as the individual involved didn't have the courage to voice this opinion to my face.

One question often asked of me about those tumultuous times is a particularly awkward one. Did I feel I had the full respect and backing of all the players all the time? Sadly, the honest answer has to be: not really. In football you have to earn respect by winning things, by having a lengthy history of success, and it helps immeasurably if you cut a charismatic figure. Matt Busby, of course, was the perfect model for any aspiring manager, but an extremely difficult act to follow, especially for someone like me who had been one of the lads for so long. Matt had so much knowledge, but he was also an immensely mature character with that wonderful deep voice. He had about him a certain aura, a magnetic presence, which exuded calmness and reassurance. In contrast, I was not particularly mature, my voice was not remarkable in any way except for being loud and I was not renowned for my serenity – indeed, some might have called me excitable!

Thus the overall impact on the players of Matt Busby and myself offered about as vivid a contrast as it was possible to imagine. That might not have made a scrap of difference if we'd been winning everything in sight, but as we weren't I think my comparative lack of obvious gravitas provided an easy target for critics. But what could I do? I had to be true to myself. Although I could always behave correctly when the occasion demanded, I couldn't acquire instant maturity. If you like a joke, then inevitably there are going to be times when you appear a little immature. That's the way I have always been.

For all that, it cheesed me off enormously when people questioned what I had done in the game. In fact, barring obvious exceptions like Charlton, Law and Best, I had done more by the age of 20 than most others at the club. Though I've always been known for making my voice heard, that's merely a manifestation of my outgoing personality rather than an indication of conceit, and I genuinely dislike trumpeting my own attainments. However, I refuse to be damned as an insignificant non-achiever when, palpably, it's not the case. I became the proud possessor of a League Championship medal when I was still in my teens, and I was in an England team, usually as the skipper, every year between the ages of 14 and 22. I'm not comparing myself directly to anybody, but Jack Charlton hadn't been picked for England at any level until he was only a few weeks shy of his 30th birthday, and Nobby Stiles didn't win his first full cap until he was nearly 23. They are remembered as tip-top international players, and rightly so, but who knows what I might have gone on to achieve if I hadn't been seriously injured at the tender age of 22? I don't think I'm being arrogant to suggest that I might have been on the threshold of a long and glorious career. I'm not saying I would have become an England regular, but I was in with a chance; certainly I had plenty to go at. I know I played in the same position as Duncan Edwards and I'm not daft enough to believe for a moment that, had he lived, I was ever going to be selected in front of him. But Dunc was so great that he could have played anywhere, and he might have made another position his own.

Then there were my coaching qualifications, both with England and Manchester United. I had been involved in winning a World Cup and a European Cup, not as the boss on either occasion but my small contribution was valued and trusted by two such great men as Alf Ramsey and Matt Busby. So I'm absolutely clear on this point: when Manchester United did Wilf McGuinness the honour of picking him to be their chief coach, and then their manager, they were not selecting a footballing nobody.

Another criticism that has been laid at my door was that I was too keen to get out the blackboard and blind the players with footballing science. That's rubbish. Yes, I used that method to illustrate strategy from time to time, but people forget, or choose not to remember, that Matt was not averse to using a tactical board. It might surprise a few outsiders who buy into the image of Matt merely telling his men to go out and enjoy themselves, to play 'off the cuff'. In fact, he might have said that before the game on a Saturday, when he wouldn't have wanted to block his players' minds with detail, but on the Friday he was immensely thorough in his preparation, going through our opponents man by man, discussing strengths and weaknesses and issuing individual advice to every member of our team. Generally speaking, my approach was the same as Matt's, with no more blackboard and no less, so while I am ready to admit that I made some mistakes, that wasn't one of them. On a lighter note, Denis Law used to reckon he was glad Matt's tactical talk was on Friday, because he'd forgotten every word by Saturday! Of course, that wasn't true, because Denis was the ultimate professional, an attitude which helped him to make the most of his astonishing natural ability throughout his long and fabulous career.

When I was forced to step down as manager of Manchester United, the ultimate job in the game as far as I was concerned, I was hurt, and I can't begin to describe how deeply. I felt I was suffering from a wound which no one in football could heal. But Sir Matt Busby and the board of directors were not ogres. They knew that United was my life, and though they had relieved me of my first-team duties, there was no attempt to cut me adrift from Old Trafford. I was told I could go back to coaching the reserves, though now it would be alongside the new incumbent Bill Foulkes, and at first I accepted. I needed time to come to terms with what had happened, and their offer gave me just that.

There was so much that I wanted to get straight in my mind. For instance, had I made the most of the magnificent footballers I'd had at my disposal? Well, in all honesty I don't see that I could have done a lot more than I did in that area. When I took over, a lot of them were going past their peak, or had already passed it. I'm thinking here of Bill and Shay, Bobby and Paddy. Then there was the crippling extent to which Denis and Nobby were handicapped by long-standing injuries. Quite simply, they were not the performers who had excelled so spectacularly throughout most of the previous decade. Add them up – that's six key members of my team. Now I'm not saying they were all beyond the pale, far from it in several cases, but none of them could fully exert the compelling influence that they had in their prime.

I knew I was very much a learner, but I felt I was working alongside the perfect man from whom to absorb wisdom, a man who had done it all, a man whom I respected, even loved. The way I saw it was that if I needed new players then Sir Matt would talk to me about it. His role was to advise and I was happy to accept his advice. If, for example, he had deemed that it was time to replace Bobby, and had added that there was a lad at, say, Blackpool whom he believed capable of doing the business, then I would have acted on that opinion immediately.

But it transpired that this whole area of responsibility was very grey. I feel now that perhaps there were many occasions when he kept his counsel because he didn't want to interfere. I thought at the time we were communicating freely, but perhaps that wasn't the case, albeit for the best of motives. He didn't want to ride roughshod over me, and I didn't want to be seen running to him every time there was a decision to be made. Was this a recipe for confusion? Maybe it was, though I never felt in the least bit inhibited, either by his continued physical presence at the club or by the psychological weight of his achievement over the previous quarter of a century.

What made the situation even more difficult to work through was that there were times when the team played brilliantly, such as at Anfield in December 1969. On afternoons like that I felt we were on the right track, and Matt must have concluded that there was still plenty of life in his old boys.

Should United have bit the bullet and either appointed an experienced, proven manager – and I'm sure they did make enquiries for the likes of Jock Stein and Don Revie – or given me full responsibility? Either way there would have been no doubt about who was in charge. However, I think Matt would have feared for his staff if an established outsider came in. The likelihood is that Revie, Stein or any other highflier would have wanted to draft in his own people, thus costing faithful retainers such as Jimmy Murphy, Jack Crompton and John Aston Snr their livelihoods. As for giving me *carte blanche*, I don't think that was a viable option. I needed guidance at that early stage of my managerial development and I welcomed his presence at my shoulder. I think I might have gone crackers if I'd been left wholly to my own devices. So, on balance, I think United came very close to getting it right. If only the responsibilities had not been quite so blurred, I remain sure to this day that we could have arrived at an arrangement that could have brought success, leading to an ultimate full transfer of power.

But there remain questions to which I don't have the answer. Why didn't Matt recognise that the latest wave of United youngsters, lads such as Steve James, Paul Edwards, Carlo Sartori, Don Givens, Tommy O'Neil and the rest, were not of sufficient stature to replace the fading heroes? Why didn't he see that the likes of Colin Todd, Mick Mills and Malcolm Macdonald, all rising stars, were needed – and needed urgently – if the Old Trafford empire he had nurtured so lovingly and inspirationally was not to slip towards inevitable decline?

Indeed, the issue of transfer funds is an extremely vexed one and it begs perhaps the most telling question of them all. Why was only one player – an ageing Scottish defender whom I did not rate particularly highly – bought during my reign, but then each of my successors, from Frank O'Farrell right through to Alex Ferguson, was handed a pot of gold to improve the team?

I am not making any accusations here, but it's fascinating to list the expenditure of each United manager in the first 18 months of his tenure, the amount of time granted to me. Frank O'Farrell brought in Martin Buchan, Ian Storey-Moore, Wyn Davies, Ted MacDougall and Trevor Anderson at a combined cost of £570,000. Then it was Tommy Docherty's turn and he recruited Alex Forsyth, George Graham, Jim Holton, Lou Macari, Mick Martin, Gerry Daly, Stewart Houston, Jim McCalliog and Stuart Pearson for a combined £830,000. Dave Sexton settled for a mere three newcomers, but the arrivals of Joe Jordan, Gordon McQueen and Micky Thomas resulted in a bill of £1.15 million. Then came Ron Atkinson, who was joined by Frank Stapleton, Remi Moses, Bryan Robson and Paul McGrath, who between them set United back more than £3 million. Finally there was Alex Ferguson, who shelled out £2.85 million for Viv Anderson, Brian McClair, Jim Leighton and Lee Sharpe in his first season and a half at the helm.

Looked at in that light, the £80,000 expended on Ian Ure in August 1969 looks modest, indeed. I don't want to labour the point, and I understand perfectly well that I was a novice in comparison to these men, but a neutral observer might feel it peculiar that the least experienced of United's post-Busby managers should be expected to make the team thrive with the lowest injection of new resources. I'm not suggesting for a moment that I should have been handed a blank cheque but, bearing in mind that the final decisions on transfer targets would have been made by Matt Busby, I think I would have stood a better chance of success if the ageing side could have been bolstered by new talent.

It's instructive, too, when evaluating the strength of the squad bequeathed by Matt, that despite all the money he spent, Frank O'Farrell, the fellow who arrived after me, was sacked within 18 months. Then his ambitious successor, Tommy Docherty, led United to relegation from the top flight in his first full campaign. Of course, the Doc brought them back up at the first attempt and created an exciting side which almost won the League title and went on to lift the FA Cup, and that demonstrates to me the value of patience. Though my team was disconcertingly close to the foot of the First Division table when I was relieved of my duties in December 1970, maybe if I'd been given the time which Tommy subsequently enjoyed then I, too, would have brought success to Old Trafford. Personally, I am convinced that I could have proved myself as United boss if I had been able to see out the three years of my contract, and been backed with cash in the transfer market as all United's subsequent managers have been. Hand on heart, I harbour not a trace of bitterness – life's far too short for that, you have to move on – but I have to admit that it is frustrating that I can never know for sure.

I have said that I was hurt by my removal from office, and I know that my pain was shared by Matt Busby. When he broke the news he was as gentle as it is possible to imagine in such traumatic circumstances. No one had wanted it to work more than him. His family, too, were wonderful to me in the immediate aftermath, which did something to soften the blow. When I attended the Middlesbrough cup tie, Matt's children, Sandy and Sheena, could not have been kinder. It was important to me to know that they, as well as the family of Jimmy Murphy, cared about me so genuinely.

Of course, when Matt resumed the reins for the remainder of 1970/71, although we went out of the FA Cup our League results picked up immediately and United rose to finish eighth in the table. People who don't know me might assume that I was disappointed by that, out of pure pique, but I wasn't. I was delighted and relieved because, as I keep emphasising, I still loved United and the last thing I wanted was to be associated with the unthinkable calamity of their first demotion since the war.

However, for all my affection for the place, I couldn't go back to a job with the reserves. It would be idle to deny that pride played a part in my decision to leave, but it wasn't the only factor. For one thing, Bill Foulkes was now coaching the reserves and you can't have two people in charge of one team. I went along to one game against Burnley in January but I felt like a spare part. I wasn't truly at the centre of things, it didn't feel right, so there was only one thing I could do. Also I couldn't possibly have been involved in such a great servant to United as Bill being moved down to, say, the 'A' team. In the end I stayed for a few weeks, just to stabilise my thoughts, get my priorities in order, sort out my compensation package and complete the purchase of my club house in Timperley.

With all the upheaval I can't hide the fact that it was a desperate and confusing period in my life, but then in early February Bolton came in for me with an offer to work alongside Nat Lofthouse at Burnden Park. He would have been general manager and I'd have been team boss, an arrangement which had rather a familiar ring to it. I met the chairman beside the swimming pool of his luxury home, chatted with him and Nat about the prospects, and although we all felt the club was on the verge of relegation from the Second Division, they had some terrific youngsters in the pipeline and there seemed no reason why they couldn't bounce back to a bright future. I told them I'd sleep on it, and went home to discuss the idea with Beryl. In some ways it would have been ideal because we wouldn't have had to move house. Then again, maybe I needed a complete change of environment, and Bolton was a bit too close to Manchester for comfort. There was also the nagging fear that I would be in a situation similar to the one at Old Trafford, where I would be dividing the load with an iconic figure – after all, Nat was, and remains, Mr Bolton. Thus there was the possibility that once more there would be grey areas over individual responsibilities, a scenario which I was convinced had proved fatally detrimental to my efforts with United.

Whatever else, I couldn't face a repeat of that, and so we declined the opportunity to remain in the north-west.

I was grateful for the invitation, though, because it made me feel wanted and lifted my spirits at a time when they had sunk uncharacteristically low. Then a press man asked me if I'd be interested in going to Greece, which did appeal, especially when I heard the sums of money involved. Suddenly I was thinking that leaving United wasn't the end of everything after all. As I had told the kids who had faced rejection from Old Trafford in my days as manager, the world was indeed a massive place, and now I had the chance to sample another corner of it.

Before then, I was confronted by the possibility of big bucks nearer to home if I was prepared to dish dirt on Manchester United. But no matter how hefty the fees brandished in my direction by various newspapers who wanted to portray me as a sacrifical lamb, an innocent victim hung out to dry by United – and some of them amounted to five figures, an absolute fortune in those days – there was never any way I was going to accept them. The way I saw it, the very fact that I had been selected by Matt Busby as his successor was an honour beyond measure. My position was that I had given it a go with all my heart, made mistakes, but not done too badly in the circumstances, and while I believed the club might have given me a little more time, I wasn't going to whine about it.

I can't hide the fact that it was a supremely harrowing period, but eventually I could take a lighter view. Now, as I make my rounds of the after-dinner speaking circuit, I offer my listeners a cheerful version of events: 'I was in charge of United for four seasons – summer, autumn, winter and spring – and summer was the most successful!' Back in 1971 maybe I wasn't quite as cavalier, but I did realise that it was time to get on with the rest of my life.

Chapter 17
GOING GREEK

APART FROM two of my players being jailed for joining in a riot and all my hair falling out, my first year in Greece didn't go too badly! Of course, I'm being flippant, and I must be careful not to give the wrong impression. In fact, my three seasons in the Greek sun were memorable for all the right reasons, despite the hot-headed nature of certain local footballers and my own sudden onset of baldness. There was considerable success on the pitch, which brought me professional fulfilment at a point in my career when it was desperately needed, and the McGuinness family enjoyed a glorious lifestyle while striking up friendships that will endure for the rest of our lives.

Having made up my mind that Bolton was not the right option for me, I was pondering on which direction to take in April 1971 against a background of hectic family life, with Beryl having lost her father in January and our fourth child expected in September. Also to consider was an offer from Sir Alf Ramsey, who had been tremendously supportive in the wake of my Old Trafford trauma.

As soon as he heard of my removal he was on the phone, urging me to keep my chin up and boosting my confidence by telling me how much I still had to offer the game. He added that an FA squad was off to Australia that summer and asked me to go along to do some coaching, together with Ronnie Suart, the former Blackpool manager. As he put it, this would keep me in the frame when permanent posts became available. It was a timely and typically kind intervention by one of the great men of football, who was often misunderstood by the public, many of whom believed he could be cold and unfeeling. They couldn't have been more wrong, as my experience in my time of turmoil demonstrated aptly.

Later that spring, with my future still undecided, came the start of my Greek adventure in the form of overtures from the First Division Aris Salonika. It appealed on first hearing and after an initial meeting in London with Dr Hadji Georgiou, the president of Aris and a gynaecologist who eventually went into politics – I don't know what the connection is there – I was invited to Salonika for a look around.

The background was that Panathinaikos, the Athens-based club managed by Ferenc Puskas – a footballing legend through his stirring deeds for the Magnificent Magyars in the international arena and Real Madrid at club level – had confounded most pundits by reaching that season's European Cup Final, where they had performed bravely, losing by a mere 2-0 to mighty Ajax of Amsterdam. This had raised expectations of Greek sporting success and the colonels in the military junta then running the country were keen to encourage further glory. They believed that British coaches would bring unparalleled expertise and generate vast interest, so more and more jobs were becoming available. Billy Bingham, the former Northern Ireland boss destined eventually to take charge of Everton, was handed the reins of the Greek national team, there was Allan Ashman at Olympiakos, Les Shannon at PAOK, and John Mortimer and Jack Mansell were coaching in the country, too. As the 1970/71 season ended, Les Allen, who had played an important and often underrated part in Spurs' League and FA Cup double triumph of 1960/61, was just coming to the end of his contract with Aris. Now maybe Les felt like going home to England, or perhaps the club wanted a change. Either way, here was an enticing opportunity for me, not least because I was being offered the equivalent of £11,000 a year, nearly three times what I had been getting as manager of Manchester United.

I liked what I saw in Salonika. Though the training pitches consisted of hard-packed dirt – it was such a dry climate it was difficult to cultivate lush grass – I was impressed by the general set-up of the club. We would have the use of a beautiful villa, once the home of one of the ruling colonels, and there was a marvellous seaside resort just down the road. For a man with a young family – Anna was nine, Paul five, Clare two and John on the way – it was hard to imagine anything more attractive.

Still, it was a massive step and at the back of my mind was the thought that if I remained in England I might just land a job with the FA.

I had worked for them for seven or eight years, I got on extremely well with Sir Alf Ramsey and had grown close to his regular staff, Harold Shepherdson and Les Cocker. Ultimately, though, in view of my recent trauma at Old Trafford, it felt right to take a complete break from the domestic game and so, after talking it through thoroughly with Beryl and my parents, we decided to go Greek.

So I bid farewell to Manchester in July, leaving Beryl and the kids to follow in December, by which time our fourth child, John, would be born. I arrived in Salonika in time to supervise pre-season training at a camp in the hills, and immediately found myself in a furious argument with one of my fellow English coaches, Les Shannon of PAOK. We had both booked the same training pitch, which they were due to vacate at 6pm, and when they were still playing at 6.15 I strode on with my lads. Les took great exception to this 'invasion' and blasted at the Aris players in Greek.

Although I wasn't too proficient in the local lingo at that time, I managed to get the drift of what he was saying and blasted back at him in a mixture of pidgin Greek and ripest Blackley. Suffice it to say that he got the message, but he bore no grudges and soon we became the firmest of friends.

Football-wise, I was pleased with the standard of the Aris squad, which included a smattering of Greek internationals: Christidis was a terrific goalkeeper, Spiridon was a granite-tough centre-half in the mould of Bill Foulkes and Palas was a classy full-back. The whole group appeared receptive to my ideas and I set up my team to attack and to entertain, as I had been brought up to do by Matt Busby and Jimmy Murphy. Like them, I was a great believer in width and deployed two wingers and a centre-forward. Defensively I opted for a sweeper system – I liked the security of a spare man at the back – with the full-backs marking tightly when the opposition had the ball but always ready to overlap when we gained possession.

Whatever I did, it worked, because we got off to a flyer. Aris hadn't managed a single away victory during the previous term and finished in the bottom half of the table, so there was plenty of scope for improvement, which we achieved in dashing style on our first trip. We won 5-0 at Agalio on the outskirts of Athens, and on our return to Aris we were greeted at the airport by hundreds of ecstatic fans, who showered us with flowers and hung garlands around our necks. I could hardly believe my eyes; we'd only won one match but our supporters celebrated as if we'd lifted the League and Cup double. Soon I came to realise that the Greeks were amazingly emotional. They let you know exactly how they felt whether things had gone right or wrong, an honest, heartfelt outlook with which I was totally comfortable. I was quite happy to bask in the glow of this generous reception, but didn't let it go to my head, knowing that a few poor results could change the atmosphere dramatically.

Happily, that season I never experienced the other side of the coin as we exceeded everybody's expectations. Around the halfway stage we were top of the table and there was a delicious whiff of glory in the air, but we had played all the other top teams in the early months of the campaign and then had to contend with a series of demanding trips. Not surprisingly for a side which was still knitting together, we fell away a little in the second half but still did tremendously well to claim fourth spot behind the powerful Panathinaikos.

We gave a spirited account of ourselves in the cup, too, reaching the semi-final, where we were beaten 1-0 by Les Shannon's PAOK. However, it wasn't the result which attracted most of the headlines because after the referee refused us a penalty, some of our players lost their heads in spectacular manner. Fighting broke out at the end of the game, the referee was attacked – I must admit I had felt like throttling him myself when he hadn't given the spot-kick, which should have been a nailed-on certainty – and pretty soon the police were dealing with a full-scale riot. Two of my lads, both steady and likeable fellows in normal circumstances, went particularly wild, throwing punches at all and sundry, and they were arrested, then thrown in prison for the rest of the weekend.

Immediately after the game one of the ruling colonels phoned me to apologise for what might be termed typically Greek behaviour. I was mightily impressed that a member of the government had stepped in so decisively to resolve the controversy – I don't think it would have happened in England! – but all too soon I was not so happy when it was announced that the hot-tempered pair were to be banned for a year, a loss which would hit the side hard. Luckily the Greeks, a lovely people but so passionate, are as good at giving pardons as they are at handing out draconian sentences, and it wasn't long before the suspension was commuted to a much shorter span.

However, though I had kept a cool head throughout the game and its explosive finale, there was no disguising the fact that it was a tumultuously unsettling episode, and it might have had a bearing on my next problem, a distressingly personal one. A few weeks later I woke up one morning to find large tufts of my thick, black hair all over the pillow. Clearly something was radically wrong so I went to the club doctor and was referred to a specialist, who diagnosed alopecia, a miserable condition which can culminate in complete baldness. He couldn't tell me why my hair was falling out, only that the loss was usually as the result of a severe shock or trauma. For instance, the Olympic swimmer Duncan Goodhew attributed his hairless head to falling out of a tree during his childhood. Apparently it could be anything that happened in the last year so, in my case, it could have been my upsetting exit from Old Trafford, or perhaps the riot in Salonika.

Next I was dispatched to a second specialist for hormone treatment and he gave me a bit of a fright. It seemed I needed an injection and, as he prepared the syringe, he told me in his halting, rather comical English that a patient had died recently of hepatitis contracted from a dirty needle. However, as he held his needle over a naked flame, he assured me that I had no need to worry, but insisted that I should inform him of any anxieties I did have, as they could exacerbate my condition. The truth was, as he administered that hot needle, *he* was my only pressing worry, and there was no way I was returning for a second visit.

Now, though, I had a problem. The footballers, coaching staff and supporters of Aris Salonika were used to seeing Wilf McGuinness with a thick, healthy head of hair, and I had no desire to be transformed into an instant figure of fun by appearing suddenly as an egghead. So, in a desperate but not very wise attempt to cover my embarrassment, I thought I would find a wig. Big mistake.

I should have realised my folly when it proved impossible to find a man's wig, but instead I accepted a suggestion that a woman's rug, suitably trimmed, would meet my needs. When I had it fitted, Beryl was absolutely brilliant, totally understanding and supportive; she didn't take the mick at all and somehow managed to keep a straight face. The

Setting an example: I always loved training, and it was a pleasure to work out in the Greek sunshine.

That's me in the shades with my predecessor at Aris, Les Allen. In the bottom left-hand corner is Les's son, Clive. You might have heard of him …

players, however, were not so restrained and thought it was absolutely hilarious. I could see where they were coming from so I told them they could have a good cackle for a couple of days, but after that the joke was over, and anyone laughing at my wig would be fined.

That did the trick as the Aris players were not exactly millionaires, but clearly a situation in which the coach was liable to be ridiculed at any moment could not be satisfactory. In the event, the obvious solution presented itself after only a week. We were away to Olympiakos Volos, a club which Howard Kendall was destined to manage after he left Everton, and after about half an hour we scored an absolutely sensational goal. Everybody on our bench leapt to their feet and started jumping up and down in celebration. The fellow next to me, our director of football, was so excited that he grabbed me round the neck and started shaking me – and so vigorous was his celebration that it dislodged my wig, which was jerked from my head into the dust at our feet.

Of course, this produced pandemonium. My condition was not public knowledge and now, suddenly, our great goal was all but forgotten as everybody goggled at me and fell about laughing. One of our substitutes picked up the fallen hairpiece and I tried to muster a smidgin of dignity as I replaced it on my head, but I realised at that moment that the only viable course of action was to come clean and face the world in all my bald glory. After all, it was nothing to be ashamed of and, when the novelty value had worn off, I was sure people would quickly come to terms with it. And so they did. In no time at all everybody was concentrating on football again, and I felt a better man for coming out of the closet.

As I took stock at the end of my first season in Greece I felt I could be pretty pleased with the way things were working out. Professionally I had made an impact, so much so that pretty early in the campaign, when Aris were top of the table, I had been approached by Olympiakos, a much bigger club. We had just beaten them, they seemed unhappy with Allan Ashman as manager and they offered me his job. Although they didn't get as far as mentioning money, I knew the wages would be a considerable improvement on the already generous terms at Salonika, but there was no way I could have accepted their offer. I told them: 'You already have a manager, I have a contract with another club and I don't break contracts. Simple as that.' I believe they were stunned by my integrity, they might even have thought I was daft, but I was very happy with Aris. Of course, pretty soon they sacked Allan anyway and brought in a Greek-American, and I wouldn't have been human if I hadn't speculated what might have happened if I'd stepped up to the bigger club. In the final analysis, though, I was glad I had remained true to my principles. There have to be certain things in life that money can't buy.

On the domestic front, too, I was content. At first I lived on my own in a hotel and planned our move into the villa, which happened after John's birth back in Manchester in September. I must admit I'm not great at solo living, I'm too used to my home comforts, but all the while I had in front of me the vision of being permanently reunited with my family within a few months. I wasn't with Beryl for the birth of John – in those days, fathers weren't expected to be quite so attentive – but I did take a week off to spend some time with mother and baby. The people at Aris were brilliant, packing me off with gifts for my little newcomer.

It was fantastic when Beryl, Anna, Paul, Clare, John and Beryl's mother Ann came out to join me at the villa in December. Life was very good. The climate was beautiful and, because of the heat, our two-hour training session didn't start until 5pm. As I was employed purely as the coach I had no administrative duties, so with working hours which stretched from 4pm to 8pm, including preparation and planning, that left me with the day to myself. That said, I have always loved my work, I have never been a skiver, but that didn't stop me taking advantage of a smashing social scene in an idyllic location. We became very pally with Les Shannon and his partner, Maureen, and with Jack and Moira Mansell, and fitted in very well with our neighbours, who all occupied lovely villas overlooking the sea. There were loads of parties, whist drives and community get-togethers, I tried never to miss a school sports day, I spent lots of time with the kids, we enjoyed the open-air cinemas and, of course, there was the traditional Greek siesta to respect. Quite a few of my players and members of the Aris committee spoke English, I got to know my interpreters pretty well and also made plenty of new Greek friends. Really, it was a little paradise for me, though it was harder for Beryl. While I had my job and the footballers to mix with, she had four children to look after which was a huge responsibility, and she was particularly grateful to Maureen for her help and friendship,

Who's that handsome fella with the luxuriant mop of lovely dark hair? I felt pretty happy with the way I looked – and then my wig fell off!

Les Shannon and I got off on the wrong foot, but soon he and his partner, Maureen, became two of our closest friends.

especially at weekends. But she never complained, she's not that sort of person. Whatever I've done in my life, I've always known that I couldn't have been luckier in my choice of wife.

Having become established happily in Salonika, I approached my second season with confidence and once again Aris did pretty well, finishing in the top half of the table and beating the powerful Turkish side, Besiktas, in the Baltic Cup. That went down brilliantly with our fans because the Greeks and the Turks don't get on too well on the football field, a bit like the English and the Scots, and any victory over the neighbours is greeted rapturously.

But change was on the horizon. My contract was for two years and Dr Georgiou, the man who had recruited me, was stepping down as club president in the summer of 1973. As his departure approached, I was told that his replacement, the owner of a major sports newspaper, wanted to bring in his own coach so I would be surplus to requirements. There were no hard feelings, just as there had been none when I'd replaced Les Allen. That's how things worked in Greece. If Dr Georgiou had stayed, then so would I.

However, the McGuinnesses were enjoying their sojourn in the Greek sun and, although we always intended to return to England at some point, we were not ready to do so yet. Thus the word went round that I was looking for employment and I was offered the reins of Panachaiki in Patras, some 100 miles outside Athens. They were a smaller club but had qualified for the UEFA Cup, which was a huge inducement to me, having relished the atmosphere of European competition in my United days.

Unfortunately, a few of the better players were injured shortly before my arrival, but still I had Drambis, a Greek international left winger, and we enjoyed a pretty decent season, finishing sixth in the league table. Our moment of sweetest glory, though, arrived in the UEFA Cup, in which we managed to beat GK Graz of Austria in both legs of our first-round tie, going through 3-1 on aggregate. Our next opponents were the powerful FC Twente, who were in the process of finishing as runners-up in the Dutch League, and we did tremendously well to hold them to 1-1 in the first leg in Patras. Sadly they overwhelmed us in Holland, putting us to the sword 7-0, but I was philosophical about the outcome, knowing that we would have had to have punched well above our weright to have obtained any joy from such a testing encounter.

Away from the football, it's fair to say that we were not so well placed as we had been in Salonika. Patras is a much smaller place, and this time we had no villa. Instead we were installed in a new apartment at the top of a towering block. You could call it a penthouse, which sounds very glamorous, but the glamour tends to wear a bit thin when you've got four youngsters to get up and down on a regular basis. Once again, Beryl was an uncomplaining heroine, making life easy for me while working prodigiously hard to keep the family home ticking over. As ever, I owed her so much.

On the positive side we weren't far away from some magnificent beaches, which the children loved – I must admit that I was quite partial to them myself, especially on Mondays when I had the whole day off – and we were only an hour away from Olympia, where the first Olympic Games were held, so there was plenty to see. Against that there was no English-speaking school so we had to bring over a tutor from England, and consequently the children didn't have many friends to play with.

In the end, what decided us to head for home in 1974 at the end of our third season in Greece was an accident to John, our youngest, who suffered a hernia while bouncing on our bed. Of course, there was plenty of good medical care available, but it made us feel vulnerable, we wanted to be close to our extended family. In addition, things were happening back home; people were getting married, life was moving on and we wanted to be part of it all again.

So ended our Greek adventure, but we left with no regrets and a deep store of happy memories. For instance, there was the time we couldn't find any Christmas trees, so together with Les Shannon and a fellow called Al, who happened to be the Australian vice-consul in Northern Greece, I went up to the mountainside above our homes and we cut down three fir trees using a handsaw. I shudder to think about the publicity which would have followed if the bosses of the two main local football clubs had been caught in the criminal act, and I don't think it would have helped a lot if the felons had been discovered transporting their booty in the car of an eminent consul official. But it was fantastic fun, our families all had trees for Christmas and there was no real harm done. I still chuckle now whenever I think about it, as I do about so many episodes from that time.

We had made good friends, been paid excellent money and enjoyed a lifestyle which many people would have envied. We had experienced a different culture and I felt I had more than held my own professionally, proving that it was safe to put me in charge of a football team. Now all I wanted was the chance to show what I could do in front of my own people.

Chapter 18
LET HIM DIE!

UNTHINKABLE THOUGH it would have been during any other period of my life, before or since, I had rather lost touch with Manchester United during my three seasons in the Aegean sun. Oh, I'd had periodic long-distance chats with Jimmy Murphy and David Meek, the journalist who looked after all matters concerning Old Trafford for the *Manchester Evening News* – David remains a close and loyal friend – but I no longer had my finger on the pulse on a day-to-day basis. Therefore I had missed out on the gory detail of the relegation trauma in 1973/74, and on my return in the following summer it felt distinctly surreal to see my beloved Busby Babes preparing for the 1974/75 campaign in the Second Division.

As it turned out, it did them no harm at all. Under Tommy Docherty they played scintillatingly attractive football and entertained royally on their way back to the top flight at the first time of asking. Genuinely, despite my traumatic departure from the club, I could not have been more delighted for them. Time had proved a great healer and I felt as excited as any other fan by the fabulous football being purveyed by the likes of Steve Coppell, Gordon Hill, Stuart Pearson, Lou Macari, Martin Buchan and company.

However, although we had returned to our home just down the road from Old Trafford at Timperley, I was no longer part of United and my immediate priority was to find work. There was no blinding rush because we had saved some money during our time in Greece, and I was able to feel my way back into the English scene thanks to Billy Bingham, who was now managing Everton. He invited me to join his squad at Bellefield, their training headquarters, once or twice a week and also he asked me to assess forthcoming opponents. I enjoyed my scouting expeditions, and

I am convinced that without my report on Plymouth Argyle, Billy's boys would never have won their FA Cup tie at Home Park!

All the while I was looking around for a suitable opening and received one or two offers. For instance, I could have gone to Turkey, but that was out of the question for family reasons, and also I was approached by Chicago Sting, before they gave the job to Bill Foulkes. The chance to work and live in the USA appealed in some ways, but having just got back to this country there was no way we were going to uproot again, so I set my sights closer to home.

Duly an opening presented itself at York City, whose boss Tom Johnston surprised many in the footballing fraternity by leaving the Second Division Minstermen to become general manager of Huddersfield Town, who were on the verge of dropping into the Fourth Division. That seemed an odd decision, but with all due respect to York, which is a lovely club in lots of ways, it didn't take me too long to follow Tom's reasoning after I became his successor. Quite simply, they had arrived at a place above their station, in terms of both finance and regular support.

These days I tell anyone who wants to listen that I managed York City in the Fourth Division, the Third Division and the Second Division in three consecutive seasons – but unfortunately in reverse order! When I took over in February, City were worryingly close to the wrong end of the table, but I was encouraged to find some decent players on the staff. We had two capable front-men in Jimmy Seal and Chris Jones, who were well served by a pair of experienced wingers, the former Nottingham Forest flyer Barry Lyons and Ian Butler, once of Hull. Then there was Barry Swallow, a redoubtable centre-half who had been around for years and Chris Topping, another strong defender; a steady goalkeeper in Graham Crawford and promising youngsters such as Chris Calvert and Brian Pollard.

For my first game we faced fellow relegation candidates Millwall at the old Den, a formidable place to visit at the best of times, but we battled bravely and came away with a 3-1 victory. That raised everybody's morale, setting the tone for a sequence of performances which saw us win or draw seven out of our last dozen games and rise to a creditable 15th place in the table at season's end, more than satisfactory in the circumstances.

One of our five defeats came at Old Trafford, where I thought we were extremely unlucky to lose by the odd goal in three to the champions elect. It felt overwhelmingly peculiar to be operating from the away dugout, but there was absolutely no question of divided loyalties. I was a York City man now, and I was very proud of how my team played. I think we deserved a point and the goal by Lou Macari which turned out to be the difference between the sides was an outrage. The little fella caught the ball in both hands, ran with it for ten yards and then drop-kicked it into our net – at least, that's how I remember it! Diabolical though that was, I wasn't too disappointed at the end. To me it was an immense achievement that my York City side was contesting a game closely with Manchester United, and by then I was certain that we had enough in our locker to avoid the drop.

I was profoundly moved, too, by the warmth of the reception I received at Old Trafford. The fans were fantastic, greeting me with genuine affection and appreciation, together with a dash of sympathy over the way I'd had to leave. They've always been good to me, from the first time I played for the youth team right up to the present day, when I wield the microphone in the hospitality lounges. It was great to bump into Matt Busby again, too, and he was very kind to me, wishing me well for my future, clearly delighted I had a job. Then there was Tommy Docherty, the current boss, who could not have made me more welcome. The Doc can be a contradictory customer because he says some outrageous things at times, but he can also be one of the most supportive men in football. When I had broken my leg all those years earlier, one of the first letters I received was from Tommy, outlining how he had made a complete recovery after breaking his own leg and predicting that I would do the same. It was a lovely touch because he was an established star at the time and I hardly knew him. You never forget generosity of spirit like that.

Talking of grand gestures, after I led York to safety at the end of that season, with six points to spare, the Bootham Crescent board decided to reward the players and staff with a communal holiday in Majorca. It was very generous of the directors, but organising the trip was not as straightforward as might be imagined. Football League rules state that if a club takes players abroad out of season, it must be to play a game, otherwise it's considered a treat and is taxable. Luckily Colchester

United, then managed by Jim Smith, were also exploring the possibilities of soaking up the sun so we arranged a friendly with them. Well, it was either Colchester or a team of hotel waiters! In the event it was a bizarre occasion, a goalless draw played out on a dirt pitch in front of no spectators at all. I can't imagine why for the life of me, but none of the tourists in Majorca that summer were the least bit interested in watching York City take on Jim's Essex boys.

Still, we all enjoyed getting away together after a hard winter's work. Okay, it wasn't at one of the island's more up-market locations, but it's the thought that counts – and it gave me an idea. I knew I was facing a bit of a struggle to re-sign several of our key players so I told the chairman, Bob Strachan, that we would never have a better opportunity than when they were all together having a good time, soaking up the Mediterranean sunshine at the club's expense. It worked like a treat with most of the lads, but Barry Swallow, our influential captain, was proving a hard nut to crack. Then I had a moment of inspiration – I remember it well because they didn't come along too often! I said to Barry: 'Just think, you'll be able to tell people that Wilf McGuinness has re-signed Charlton, he has re-signed Law, he has re-signed Best … and he has re-signed Swallow.' Barry thought for an instant, his face lit up and he said: 'Hand me the pen!'

That break in Majorca was memorable for more reasons than one. It was around the time of Brian Pollard's 21st birthday and a party was planned. What with the euphoria of escaping from relegation and the signing of the new deals, it was always going to be a lively do, but I thought I would add an extra dimension. I told the players that I would have to be excused for a couple of hours because my brother Larry was arriving from the USA and I had to pick him up at the airport. In fact, it wasn't Lawrence McGuinness who was going to make a grand entrance at our hotel, but his heavily disguised little brother. Now the snappiest dresser at our club was Cliff Calvert, so I took him into my confidence because I needed to borrow some of his sharpest, most modern gear. Cliff, God bless him, came up with the goods, which I concealed in my room. Then I bid a loud farewell to the boys before sneaking upstairs to get changed. On went a shirt with a fashionably high collar, a flashy suit, massive tie and high-heeled shoes. Obviously I had to do something about my shining pate, so out came my old Greek rug and, as a final touch, I slipped some white cardboard into my mouth to disguise my gappy front teeth.

Thus magnificently festooned, I wandered into the bar where the York party was gathering pace, and asked, in an exaggerated American accent: 'Howdy Folks. Mah name's Larry McGuinness. Is mah little brother Wilfie around?' No one seemed to twig that anything was amiss: 'You've just missed him, he's gone to meet you at the airport, come and join us till he gets back. It'll be quite a surprise for him.' By this time I felt my feet were well and truly under the table, so I offered to buy everyone a drink, and their response was quite humbling: 'That's more than your brother ever did!' they told me.

Then the drinks arrived and I spilt a tray of sparkling wine over several directors, but they were not a bit upset. In fact, they told me: 'Don't worry, it could have happened to anyone. You must let us pay.' I was just wondering how long I could keep up the deception when it came to a sudden end. Having become increasingly suspicious as my accent slipped a little, and maybe recognising Cliff's gear, Barry Swallow slipped behind me and lifted my wig. Two directors nearly fell to the floor with astonishment – it seemed they'd had no idea they were being wound up.

It was an absolutely hilarious situation, the sort of fun you can have at a football club when things are going well, though I've always believed it's crucial to have a laugh when the tide is flowing against you, too.

For instance, there was a time when York were having a bad run – can't remember exactly when, there were so many! – and the squad was jogging around the university playing field where we used to train on an unbelievably windy day. I was running with them, though the pack had got ahead of me, when I spotted a fallen branch and decided it was time for a laugh. So I threw myself to the ground, dragged the branch across my neck and screamed in mock agony, thinking they would rush to my aid. Some hope! When I glanced up, not moving my head, they were still jogging around, one or two glancing back but taking no notice of their manager lying on his back under half a tree. It seemed the prevailing notion was: 'Let him die!' Eventually it was Chris Topping who trotted back to see if I was dead or alive. Obviously, I made him captain on the spot! But seriously, it is important to inject some humour no matter how serious the team's plight and, believe me, ours was pretty serious for much of the time.

As I bedded in at Bootham Crescent, and the initial exhilaration at avoiding the drop wore off, the full extent of City's financial problems became evident. York is a tourist city with a rugby tradition, so we didn't attract great attendances, even when we were in the Second Division. The people who did come along to support us were great, loyal to the core, but there just wasn't enough of them. Tom Johnston deserved a mountain of praise for taking them to such heady heights, but I don't believe anyone could have kept them there in the long term and it became increasingly plain to me why he left when he did.

Duly in 1975/76, my first full season, we finished in 23rd place and suffered relegation, but even worse was in store. In 1976/77 we were rock bottom of the Third, and there seemed to be nothing I could do to reverse the slide as the realities of life in the lower echelons of the English game hit home. Truly, this was a different world to the one I had grown up in at Old Trafford.

Repeatedly it was drubbed into me at board meetings that if a bid came in for one of my players I must report it immediately because the club was desperate for money. I had to agree – it would have been dishonourable of me to conceal lucrative approaches – but it hurt me sorely as a football man to see so many of our finest talents leaving the club. Of course, I would state my views strongly, invariably pleading to keep the player, but the outcome was always the same – the directors would listen to me, conscientiously and sympathetically, and then they would vote to sell. It made me weep to bid farewell to the likes of Cliff Calvert, our classy young full-back, who joined Sheffield United for £55,000, and not because I could no longer borrow his gear! Financially

it made perfect sense, but it ruined the process of team-building and was overwhelmingly frustrating. On the positive side it gave me immense satisfaction to know that I had helped to nurture such excellent young performers as Gordon Staniforth, who I had signed from Hull for £7,000 and who was sold to Carlisle for around £120,000 after my own departure; the same applies to Brian Pollard, who was snapped up by Graham Taylor for Watford.

All I could do was seek to replenish my stock by bringing on more youngsters, but unfortunately we didn't have a tremendous crop during the mid-1970s, so my only means of recruitment was free transfers. I returned to Manchester United to sign centre-half Steve James and the utility man Tony Young, thinking that they had been taught the right way and therefore would be able to flourish at the lower level, but it didn't work out for either of them. The style of football proved a bit hectic for them and they never really adjusted to the drastic change in their footballing environment.

Throughout all this travail, it would have been easy to get downhearted, but there was a terrific atmosphere at the club and we always managed to smile. I had a happy relationship with the chairman, who liked a joke as much as I did.

Once, when York City were already a long way down the slippery slope, we were at a dinner and, in his speech, he was explaining the difference between a misfortune and a catastrophe. Then he caught sight of me at the end of the table and it gave him inspiration: 'For instance, if Wilf McGuinness, our manager, was to fall into the River Ouse it would be a misfortune. But if someone were to pull him out it would be a bloody catastrophe.' Of course, he didn't mean it – at least, I don't think he did.

Managing York City engendered a full range of emotions ...

York City treated me as well as they could, but the lack of funds was a constantly debilitating factor. For instance, in my final season they told me my coach, Clive Baker, would have to go because they could no longer afford to pay his wages. I was already doing a lot of the coaching myself, but I wanted to keep Clive because he was a good and loyal man, just the sort you need around you. I'm a great believer in contracts, in sticking them out to the end, but it crossed my mind to resign in protest at Clive's dismissal. However, he advised me to stay because making such a gesture would not have helped him, and he understood that I needed to make a living. So I did stay, but I was very hurt on Clive's behalf, as well as under-staffed. Now it was just myself, a physio and a lad looking after the reserves. We were ridiculously thin on the ground and the writing on the wall could not have been clearer.

The 1977/78 campaign in Division Four did not start well – we recorded only three wins in our first dozen games – and when Bob Strachan approached me with a serious expression on his face I had an inkling of what was coming. He was very honest and straightforward, telling me simply that the board had decided to try somebody else as manager. They realised that by selling so many players they had not given me a chance to gain promotion, but they had hoped to hold their own, gradually get the finances right and then build again. That hadn't happened. I knew he was sorry because we had got along so well, supporting each other through thick and thin (mostly thin). He had handed me a new contract after one of our relegations, and not too many employers would have done that. In the end I had no complaints and our parting was as amicable as it's possible to imagine in such sad circumstances.

When Bob broke the news of my dismissal, it didn't come as a surprise. People had been shouting at me from the terraces for some time, urging me to resign, but I was never going to do that. In my position, with a family to keep and nothing else to go to, I doubt if many of them would have handed in their cards. That said, I understood their feelings. They were paying hard-earned cash to watch us lose on a regular basis, and it could not go on.

Regrettably, towards the end there were a few unpleasant incidents involving disillusioned supporters. I used to have a left-hand drive Jaguar, a legacy of my time in Greece, and it became a familiar sight in

York, making me easily recognisable even when I was off duty. On one occasion a motor-cyclist pulled up beside me at traffic lights and started shouting vile abuse at me over the head of my nine-year old son Paul. This left me fuming, particularly as Paul was visibly shocked by the fellow's obscene outburst. After giving me his mouthful he zoomed off, but I caught up with him at the next set of lights, which were red. I leapt out of the car, ran up to him and grabbed him, then started giving him a piece of my mind. I told him if he wanted to shout at me then the time and place to do it was when I was managing the team at Bootham Crescent. How dare he behave in such a foul fashion when I was with my family! He was a teenager and was so shook up by my verbal onslaught that he fell off his bike. He climbed to his feet, still quaking in his boots and rode off with me following him, still in high dudgeon. I could hardly believe my eyes when he turned in at the local police station. I followed him in and we were all questioned, including poor Paul, and in the end there were no charges. It had been a distressing incident, but no damage was done. I do hope the motor-cyclist learned a lesson, though.

Another time when City were struggling, a group of youths came round to our house, knocked over a sundial and threw eggs at the windows. I raced out to confront them with Paul on my heels, and I managed to grab one. I hung on to him while the police were called, but when they arrived I didn't get the response I expected. On hearing the facts, the officer said: 'Well, you can't really blame them, can you?' Actually those weren't his precise words, but he did put the matter in perspective and I didn't press charges.

It was a bit like the female York fan who was arrested for running on the pitch at Bootham Crescent and kissing our scorer, Micky Cave. The magistrates excused her because it didn't happen very often! They thought it was understandable that she should show her glee in such barely precedented circumstances as City scoring a goal. As might be imagined, the press gave us more than a little stick after that. Looking back, I can see the funny side but, clearly, for loyal fans of the much-abused Minstermen, it was no laughing matter. As for me, I left York City as I arrived – fired with enthusiasm!

Chapter 19

MANCHESTER UNITED
SAVED MY LIFE

SURROUNDED BY a mob of hostile refugees and in genuine fear of being murdered, miles from civilisation on the edge of a mountainous desert in one of the most volatile regions in the world … somehow this wasn't quite how I had envisaged life as a football coach. Indeed, the thought of confronting a foul-mouthed motor-cyclist or a gang of disenchanted young York fans seemed positively enchanting by comparison. But how did it all come to this?

Well, when I was out of work in the late autumn of 1977, with a wife and four children to feed and precious little to spend at the supermarket, I was approached about working in Jordan. It seemed that the country's military team, comprising 90 per-cent of the national side, was in need of a coach for a prestigious tournament in Syria, and they had a yen for an Englishman to take charge. Word came to me through Alan Wade, the English FA's director of coaching, who knew I was at a loose end and thought I might be just the man for such a challenging assignment. I had got to know Alan through my work with England and I both liked him and respected his judgement. He thought it was an opportunity worth taking and so, in my situation, I reckon I had little alternative but to accept.

It was never going to be a particularly joyful jaunt because there was no way I could have taken the family. Though I was no longer with York City, we still had a lovely house at Hobgate in Acomb and the children were well established at their various schools. It wouldn't have been fair to drag them away from their education and their friends, especially to such an unstable part of the world. I was well aware that with the conflict between Israel and many of the Arab countries constantly simmering, the Middle East could be an extremely perilous place to live and work, but I didn't dwell on that, reasoning that as a football man I would not become embroiled in politics.

In fact, the driving force was purely financial, even though there wasn't a vast amount of money involved. My rationale was that it was better than nothing and that as I would only be away from January to May then it was my duty to make the best of it.

When I arrived in the capital, Amman, I was met by a colonel who confirmed, with every appearance of sincere sympathy, that my wages would be horribly poor. But then he ushered me into his office, told me that I would need considerably more than was mentioned in my contract and handed me a big bundle of banknotes. It was just the sort of greeting that would make anyone feel at home, except that it didn't appear particularly professional.

After that he showed me to my billet in the officers' barracks – no fancy hotels for Wilf on this trip – and introduced me to an interpreter who would help me communicate with the players. Unfortunately he was hopeless at putting across football ideas, such as how to work a short corner – he actually told the boys to go and stand in a corner, which caused quite a bit of confusion! – and I had to swap him almost immediately. Luckily one of the players understood English and took over his duties, after which we all got on extremely well. They knew all about Manchester United and England, they even knew me by reputation, and they were gratifyingly receptive to my ideas.

So long as I was occupied on the training ground I was fine, and also I had some terrific times at the British Embassy social club, mostly playing cards, watching films, having a drink or swimming. But I missed my family dreadfully and there were long stretches when I was damnably lonely. I was never a great one for my own company. I wouldn't say I suffered depression but there were moments when I was very low and I took up smoking again, which wasn't very clever having given up the weed only a short while earlier. Also I dabbled in gambling, nothing heavy but a complete waste of money and time, and an indication that I was far from happy with life.

One saving grace was sight-seeing, and I did enjoy the Dead Sea, although it was doing the tourist bit which might have got me killed. I had been allotted a car to drive around Amman and one day I decided to vary the routine, setting out across country to visit some famous ruins at Jerash. I'm not averse to a bit of exploration when I'm on holiday so I looked at my map and spotted a dam high up in the hills, and decided to make for that on my way back. It was well off the main road in desolate countryside but that only added to the appeal – or so I thought. However, as I drove slowly down the single street of a scruffy village in the middle of nowhere, people began rushing out of the houses and crowding round the car. Pretty soon I was forced to stop and then the villagers started rocking the vehicle from side to side as though they were trying to turn it over. Their faces were distorted with anger, and although I couldn't understand a word of what they were shouting, I was pretty sure they weren't enquiring after my health. By this time a feeling of vague apprehension was turning into one of blind terror, so I wound down my window and played my only trump card. I raised my voice and told them, as firmly as I could: 'I come from England … I'm a footballer … Manchester United … At those last two words a few expressions changed, tentative smiles replacing ugly aggression, but still I was very worried, surrounded by a menacing throng of some 200 people who seemed distinctly peeved by my presence.

But it was my lucky day. Somewhere near the back of the melee was one couple who spoke English and they pushed forward to question me. They wanted to know who I was and what I was doing in their settlement. I explained as clearly as I could and they told me I had taken my life in my hands by straying into what turned out to be a Palestinian refugee camp, especially as I was driving an army vehicle. Hell, what a fool I'd been. I had thought my car was a funny colour, kind of a gun-metal grey, but had not dreamed that it could lead to me being mistaken for a military policeman.

Fortunately, thanks not a little to those two magic words 'Manchester United', I was allowed to depart peacefully, albeit with a dire warning ringing in my ears as to the potential consequences if ever I was so careless again. In fairness to myself, when I had been handed the keys to my car I hadn't been warned not to venture into the outback, but I was now. Evidently it had been assumed that I would confine myself to Amman, but now the military laid down the law, telling me I might not be so lucky the next time. Believe me, I needed no second bidding.

On the football front, my efforts were far more warmly appreciated. Expectations for our showing in the tournament, in the Syrian capital of Damascus, had not been high, so when we beat a Palestinian side in the first match everyone in our camp was utterly delighted. Results went downhill after that, but there was philosophical recognition that we were facing teams from the likes of Saudi Arabia and Syria who had access to far greater resources. In the end the Jordanians were so pleased with my efforts that later I was offered the chance to return, but there was never a chance of that. It wasn't so much my narrow escape from dismemberment by a howling mob which deterred me, but I just couldn't face the loneliness again.

However, although I was ecstatic to be reunited with Beryl, Anna, Paul, Clare and John in May 1978, I did feel a little as if the weight of the world was resting on my shoulders as I looked around for employment. Okay, I was a former manager of Manchester United, with the status that entails, but life had moved on since my painful Old Trafford exit more than seven years earlier, and now I was not exactly being deluged with offers. But then, out of the blue, I had a call from Ken Houghton, who had just been promoted from youth development officer to become boss of Hull City and wanted me to become his number-two.

The Boothferry Park club was still reeling from the effects of recent relegation from the Second Division, which had resulted in the sacking of manager Bobby Collins, the former Leeds and Scotland midfield general, but I saw huge potential at the club and had no hesitation in accepting Ken's timely offer. Humberside represented a vast catchment area for supporters; the Needlers, who were in control, furnished enviable stability while looking to progress steadily; there was plenty of tradition about the place, not least because the great Raich Carter had been both player and manager there; and the current staff were first-rate. True, it meant a round-trip of 100 miles each day from York but I was back with my loved ones, and in no doubt that my new situation had the edge on life in Amman.

Another thing I liked about the club was that so many of the staff were former Hull City players. Ken himself had been a fine striker for the Tigers, while Chris Chilton, who had a coaching role, and Ken Wagstaff, who was often at the club, were both goal-scoring legends

Working with the Jordanian military team, virtually the national side, was very rewarding, but it led to one truly hair-raising experience.

I had some good times with Hull City, but my sojourn at Boothferry Park ended on a sour note. This was one of the better days, with manager Ken Houghton (left), director Ian Blakey, and coach Andy Davidson (right). I could not have worked with nicer men than Ken and Andy.

and among the most popular of all Boothferry Park old boys. Then there was Andy Davidson, an outwardly flinty Scot but with the proverbial heart of gold, who was part of the fabric after spending more than three decades at Hull as player and coach. In fact, to this day he still holds City's all-time appearance record.

As we approached 1978/79 the optimism was fuelled by that summer's £60,000 purchase of the gifted young marksman Keith Edwards from Sheffield United, and the newcomer didn't disappoint, banging in 25 League and FA Cup goals that term as we finished in a highly promising eighth place. Keith would never have won any prizes for his work-rate or tackling but he was a born sniffer, brilliant at turning and shooting in confined spaces, and proved a vast asset.

Contemplating my future at the end of that campaign, I was more than happy. The work was fun, the people were terrific and I thought the prospects were bright. Even the travelling wasn't the drawback it might have been because I used to give a lift from York to one of the juniors, a nice lad by the name of Steve McClaren – you might have heard of him. At that point, Steve was a smooth young midfielder, skilful, precise, never in a hurry, more of a creator than a destroyer. He went on to a worthy career for the Tigers, as well as serving a handful of other clubs, without ever quite hitting the heights as a player. However, he became a sought-after coach, served as right-hand man to Sir Alex Ferguson when Manchester United won their unique treble in 1998/99 and then, when England dispensed with the services of Sven-Goran Eriksson, my former passenger took the reins of our national team. Unfortunately Steve experienced a turbulent ride as England boss and then he was dismissed, but I wish him well. He suffered from strong criticism early in his reign, but he battled on gamely and deserves credit for that.

Yet again, I stray from my subject. Back at Boothferry in 1979, we made an unexpectedly poor start to the new season and things began to turn sour. I could understand the board hoping for better results, but I'm convinced we had the foundations of something special. If only they had exercised a little more patience, realised that their club needed to walk before it could run, and made the appropriate comparatively modest investment on several new players, then they might have reaped enormous rewards. That didn't happen, though, and in early December, on the back of an horrendous 7-2 drubbing at Brentford, they sacked Ken Houghton, myself and Andy Davidson.

It was a demoralising body blow to me, of course, but I was particularly upset for the others. I hadn't been there too long and was a big enough boy to understand that these things happen in professional football. But the rest were Hull City through and through; Andy Davidson, in particular, had given his working life to the club since enlisting as a homesick teenager in 1947. Yet now they didn't even want to pay off our contracts, which I thought was appalling. After all, if another club had come in for us then Hull would have demanded compensation. I felt it was a disgraceful way to treat loyal servants and I have to say that the Hull directors disappointed me deeply.

My own sorry circumstances were rendered even more lamentable because of my own stupidity. In the October, on my 42nd birthday, I had been stopped by the police while driving in my Jaguar between Hull and York when I had been drinking. I know it was foolish of me, but people kept offering me drinks and I kept accepting them. Nowadays drink-driving is socially taboo, quite rightly. But in 1979, while obviously it was just as dangerous, attitudes were rather different, society was more tolerant, even if the practice was illegal. I can declare with total honesty that it wasn't a regular thing with me, but it did happen and it was the wrong thing. We all make mistakes and this was one of my biggest. Thank God nobody was hurt physically because of my irresponsibility. I admit that I fully deserved my one-year driving ban and I was utterly ashamed of myself.

It was a situation which did little to help my jaded state of mind around Christmas that year. I was out of work again, I'd sold my beloved Jaguar because it was no further use to me and I was reduced to pedalling around York on my bike. Happy new year? I didn't think so. By nature I'm an eternal optimist, but at this point I was feeling more than a little down in the dumps, so much so that I considered a future outside football. One option was taking a pub – a time-honoured occupation for old footballers – and I even went on a preparation course at a place near Darlington, but around the time when I would have had to make up my mind I was saved by a call from an old pal which took me back to my north Manchester roots.

In July 1980 Fourth Division Bury, not too far from where I grew up, were looking for a new boss. I had applied for the job but they turned me down in favour of Jim Iley, whom I had got to know pretty well when he was in charge of Barnsley and I was running York. We had often had a chat about our respective problems and discovered we were on the same wavelength. Now when he asked me if I wanted to look after the Shakers' reserves I jumped at the chance. It was a bit of a wrench to sell our house in York, which we loved, but we sorted that quickly and with the proceeds we bought our present house, back in Timperley. We had come full circle and were back on our home patch after a decade of travelling. I was only halfway through my driving ban but the Bury coach Micky Pickup, who lived in Congleton, Cheshire, agreed to give me daily lifts so that was fine. True, the wages were not brilliant, but I was just delighted to stay in the game at a club where my services were valued.

I spent 11 years at Gigg Lane, and I loved it there. We never rose higher than the old Third Division, but the people were great, absolutely the salt of the earth. Of course, we could have done with twice as many supporters but the ones we had were superb. I'll cherish my memories of that homely little club as long as I live.

Not unexpectedly, Bury's perennial difficulty was shortage of cash, as experienced by any minnow eking out an existence in the shadows of several giants. As a result, cost-cutting was pretty much a constant and one of the first victims during my stay proved to be poor Micky Pickup. When he left there was a bit of restructuring and I became trainer to both first and second teams, essentially Jim Iley's number-two. Effectively it worked out that I had taken Micky's job, but I have to stress that the situation was not of my instigation, though that didn't stop me feeling bad about it after all his generosity to me.

At small clubs everybody has to muck in, but that was something I relished, dating back to my days of helping Jack Crompton to carry the training skips for Manchester United. One of my most important duties at Gigg Lane was feeding the cat, Friday, with whom I struck up a warm rapport. I was very upset when she died, not least because I think I'd have had a job for life if she'd survived!

Football-wise, too, I was content with Bury. Some people thought Jim Iley was a tad eccentric, but I got on with him, and he always wanted his teams to entertain, so we were singing from the same hymnsheet. In our first season together, with a side including such terrific footballers as centre-half Paul Hilton, striker Craig Madden and a young rough-round-the-edges goalkeeper name of Neville Southall, we finished halfway up the Fourth Division. In 1981/82, having sold Neville – I had recommended him to United, among others, but he was destined for superstardom at Goodison Park – we moved up to ninth, then the following term we progressed to fifth, missing out on promotion by a mere two points, even though money was tighter than ever.

It was monumentally frustrating, therefore, that having made such encouraging strides on the pitch, the continual lack of funds produced its inevitable consequence in 1983/84. In October, having held West Ham to a respectable 2-1 victory at Gigg Lane in the first leg of a League Cup encounter, we crashed 10-0 in the Upton Park return. In later years I could joke about it; for instance, I would point out that it was a very even game – there were five goals in each half! Then there was my merciless quip at the expense of one of our big defenders. As I put it, he looked like Tarzan, played like Jane . . and smelt like Cheetah. I added that he had a stutter yet he was the man in charge of the offside trap! We can laugh about it now but at the time it was anything but funny, and in February 1984 the deteriorating sitiuation cost poor Jim Iley his job.

Given my experience, it was not surprising that I should be asked to step in as caretaker, which made me wonder: did I still want to manage a League club? In all honesty, I was torn in two. I was still as hopelessly in love with the game as ever, but I had to admit to myself that it was a luxury to know that when things went wrong, as long as I was only a member of the supporting cast I would not be the first man to be dismissed.

In the event, I stood in for a month until Bury appointed Martin Dobson as player-boss, which was a tremendous coup. Martin was a cool, classy footballer, a real thoroughbred who had been unlucky to collect no more than five England caps during his prime with Burnley and Everton, and a lovely fella. As is the custom with most new bosses, he brought his own coach with him – in this case Frank Casper, like Martin one of the best-loved names in Turf Moor history – and that meant a change of role for me. Now I concentrated on physiotherapy. I already had qualifications for the treatment and management of injuries, and now I was made responsible for anything which didn't demand treatment by a doctor.

Martin proved a huge influence as a player, and also used his connections to bring in some other high-quality performers, such as the Welsh international Leighton James, another former Burnley hero who had also starred on the wing for Derby County. He was a trifle cocky and I can recall a Fourth Division full-back saying to him: 'I'm not bothered by you James, I know you.' Quick as a flash, Leighton responded: 'No you don't, I've never played this low before!'

With such quality at his disposal, Martin guided Bury to fourth place and promotion in 1984/85, though we found the going to be much tougher in the third tier. Still, we reached the fifth round of the FA Cup before going out to Watford in 1985/86, and League finishes of 20th, 16th, 14th and 13th indicated steady improvement, which was remarkable in view of the financial restrictions under which we were compelled to operate.

There was one highlight with a special resonance for me. In the 1987/88 League Cup competition, we beat Preston, Sheffield United and Queen's Park Rangers on the way to a fourth-round showdown with Manchester United. We were drawn at home but because of crowd restrictions and ongoing ground improvements at Gigg Lane, the game was switched to Old Trafford, where we went within an ace of bringing down my former employers. After a tight first period, Jamie Hoyland put us in front early in the second half but then, with Bryan Robson in typically inspirational form, United reeled us in with strikes by Norman Whiteside and Brian McClair. As I've told Robbo and Alex Ferguson many times since, they were lucky to sneak a win that night!

Meanwhile Martin Dobson seemed to be growing ever more assured in management and I was disappointed when a disagreement between him and the chairman, Terry Robinson, precipitated his departure in the spring of 1989. The upshot was that coach Derek Fazackerley, supported by Yours Truly, took up the reins on a temporary basis, our first game ending in a 6-0 home hammering by Huddersfield. That was the start of a dismal springtime sequence which saw us slip into the second half of the table, particularly upsetting as we had started the New Year with real hopes of promotion.

The next boss was Sam Ellis, a hard man but very fair, although sometimes his iron discipline rubbed people up the wrong way. But whatever people thought about his approach, they couldn't argue with his success in taking Bury to the play-offs in his first and only full season. We lost to Tranmere over two legs, but that shouldn't obscure the scale of his achievement on slender resources. Sadly but understandably, after a key financial backer cut the size of his support and the entire squad was placed on the transfer list in the autumn of 1990, Sam left to become Peter Reid's assistant at Manchester City.

As it turned out, my time was up, too. After a lifetime in football, and the last decade at Gigg Lane, I was suffering excruciating pain in my hip and was forced to have a replacement operation. While recuperating in hospital, looking for something to cheer me up, it duly arrived in the form of an hilarious message from the chairman, with whom I always enjoyed a congenial relationship. This is what he had written: 'Wish you a speedy recovery. Look forward to seeing you back at Gigg Lane as soon as possible. This resolution was passed by the board – with three in favour, two against and four abstentions. Regards, Terry'.

That was typical of the lovely rapport which permeated the club, but by 1991 I knew that physically I was no longer up to the job and had no alternative but to step aside. Towards the end of Sam Ellis' reign I had been given a testimonial match, Bury against Manchester United at Gigg Lane, to mark my decade's service to the Shakers and that was generously supported by around 8,000 fans.

There was nothing I liked better than a bit of good-natured interaction with the supporters, especially the kids, with whom I had endless fun. When the last of my hair had disappeared, I was christened *Kojak* after the old TV cop played by Telly Savalas, and I relished playing up to the image by handing out lollipops – *Kojak's* trademark, for the uninitiated – before a match.

Often during the course of this book I have mentioned my love of United, but I have to say I will always retain deep affection for Bury, too. They have always had to fight for survival, and that is unlikely to change. I hope with all my heart that their struggle is successful because the professional football scene would be immeasurably poorer without the dear old Shakers.

I threw myself into life as Bury physio and I loved every minute of it, whether tending to stricken players or celebrating promotion with the lads. That's the victorious manager, Martin Dobson, on the left. Standing at the back, left to right, are Wayne Entwhistle, Joey Jakub, John Kerr and myself. In the middle are John Bramhall, Winston White, Kevin Young, Terry Pashley (looking back at me), Gary Butler and coaches Frank Casper and Ray Pointer. At the front are Andy Hill, Trevor Ross and Craig Madden.

Chapter 20
AFTER THE BALL

To a hopeless football addict like me, life after Gigg Lane might have been a colossal letdown. As it turned out there were three hugely enjoyable and fulfilling jobs waiting for me – all of which enabled me to remain close to the mainstream of the game, thus retaining a public profile as well as having a whole lot of fun. In 2008, nearly two decades on from the day I parted company with Bury, I am still as busy as I want to be – and that is very busy, indeed – combining my roles as an after-dinner speaker, a summariser for Manchester United Radio and a corporate host at Old Trafford for virtually all the club's home games.

By the early 1990s, I had already become accustomed to public speaking. My wages at Bury had not been brilliant – not their fault, like pretty well every small club they just couldn't afford to pay very much – so I had made a modest start on the after-dinner circuit to supplement my income.

I had loads of help and encouragement from some smashing people, such as the former top referee and magnificent master of ceremonies Neil Midgley – who was to die tragically young – and Fred Eyre, the ex-Manchester City apprentice who went on to so much success as a writer and broadcaster, but my big break came courtesy of Murray Birnie, a former engineer who had broken into the promotions business and who had already been extremely good to me as a member of my testimonial committee. Tommy Docherty, the most outspoken of my successors as manager of Manchester United, had been due to speak at a Gigg Lane function, but had been forced to drop out the day before the event. I was thrown in as a late substitute.

People who know me today might find it hard to credit, but I must admit that I was a trifle apprehensive at the prospect. Deep down, though, I believed I could do it. I might not be the world's greatest at my first attempt, but I knew I would get better with experience.

And so it proved. At that first dinner I told an Irish joke, which raised a few politically incorrect laughs, nothing malicious, and I was quite pleased. But at the end of the evening Murray pulled me to one side and told me to forget about the jokes. Leave them to the professional comedians, he told me, and it was good advice. I needed punchlines for my stories, and if they were funny it was a bonus, but I learned the lesson that what the audience wanted from me was football yarns. Everything I said needed to be based on what happened inside the game. I could embellish it a little bit, but the basis of reality had to be there.

I don't think I'm being big-headed when I say I took to the business pretty readily. It was a bit like the banter in the dressing room which I had always loved so much and in which most ex-players can more than hold their own. I suppose it always came naturally to me. I have never liked being serious for too long, and I always looked for *double entendres* in everyday conversation.

Certainly there is never any shortage of material. That turns up all the time as I live my life. For instance, one day at Bury I went in to see my chairman, Terry Robinson, to ask for a rise. He said he'd give me £5 a week, and I was not happy. '£5 a week?' I groaned. 'With all the things I do around this place – right down to feeding the club cat – I'm downright insulted.' Terry's instant reply was a gem: 'Well, we'll pay you monthly instead of weekly. Then you won't be insulted so often!" That was brilliant, and I lost no time in working it into my act.

Also I found it was really important to be able to engineer a laugh at my own expense. It gets the audience on your side if you can knock yourself a bit. Mind, I had to work hard at it, rehearsing for hours in front of a mirror at home, and taping my efforts to gauge how they sounded. At first I tested out one or two stories on Beryl, but she wasn't really impressed. It wasn't her thing, so I tried them out on other people who knew what was required and my feedback was gratifyingly positive.

A huge plus for me in this new occupation was associating with the many leading sportsmen of my own time and afterwards who were also

I was in charge of Manchester
United for four seasons: summer,
autumn, winter, spring …

on the circuit. One of the most colourful, of course, was (and remains) Tommy Doc, who specialises in references to our days in charge at Old Trafford. Of course, he's a bit of a rascal and he might open with something like: 'We both got the sack from Manchester United, but to this day I don't know whose wife Wilf was seeing.' Then he might add: 'I heard York City were looking for a manager and I quite fancied the job because it's a smashing little club – trouble was the physio's wife was the ugliest woman I've ever seen. So I recommended Wilf, who could have been her twin brother!' Of course, we know each other that well that we can insult each other with impunity.

Likewise I laugh along with everybody else when the comedian says, at the end of my speech, something like: 'Actually I played a bit of football myself, but I don't go on about it all night.' The punters love that sort of knockabout, and so do I.

There have been so many household names who have joined the after-dinner brigade. For instance, Bobby Charlton, Denis Law and George Best all did their bit, and they were all fascinating in their different ways, while often players who didn't rise so high in the game turn out to be magnificent speakers. Two of the very finest are Steve Kindon, who played for Burnley and Wolves, and Paul Fletcher, who also made his name at Turf Moor. Then there is Duncan McKenzie, who tells the hilarious tale of his first meeting with Brian Clough when he was joining Leeds United. Asked for his views on the place, Duncan remarked that there were so many talented ball-players in evidence. Clough replied: 'Yes, but there's one less than you think, young man!' Of course, that was just Brian's way of putting the confident newcomer in his place, and it's much to his credit that Duncan doesn't shrink from telling that tale, which always gets a good reception.

Others who have impressed me so much with their patter have been Ian St John, Norman Hunter and Tommy Smith, as well as a considerable former United contingent, including Nobby Stiles, Paddy Crerand and Alex Stepney. I have been honoured, also, to share billing with so many non-footballing greats: legendary boxers such as Henry Cooper, John Conteh, Barry McGuigan, Alan Minter and Jim Watt; rugby stars Gordon Brown, Phil Bennett, Willie John McBride, Gareth Chilcott and Jonathan Davies, and the former snooker world champion Dennis Taylor. Then there have been the cricketers – early ones like Fred Trueman, Mike Cowan, David Lloyd and Peter Parfitt, and more recently Geoff Miller and Ronnie Irani.

The one thing all these great names have in common is the ability to communicate the joy of their sport so vividly that it makes you want to go outside and start playing. I have been delivering after-dinner speeches for more than 20 years now, and although I don't do so many as I used to because of my other commitments, I still relish the camaraderie of the circuit, which has added a remarkably rich vein of enjoyment to my working life. Certainly, too, it has helped me to make a good living. As I told Mike Newlin of MBN Promotions, a fella who has helped me enormously down the years, I earned more speaking at one of his lunches than I did in a year playing for Manchester United and England.

Equally fulfilling throughout my fifties and sixties, and now into my early seventies, has been my work on local radio. It all started when, soon after I left Bury, I was asked to summarise at games for the BBC's Greater Manchester Radio. I started off with lower division encounters, maybe at Gigg Lane or Oldham's Boundary Park, but before too long I was a regular at Old Trafford. I worked with some terrific commentators such as Mike Sadler and Jonathan Pearce, now frequently heard on *Match of the Day*. Jonathan was always extremely vocal – not to put too fine a point in it, he screamed a lot of the time! – though I have never been slow to offer my opinion, either, so we hit it off pretty well together. As the reader might have gauged by now, I have never been accused of being shy. Sometimes when I was particularly outspoken it raised a few eyebrows, but I never found myself in serious trouble, and I like to think that I made my contribution to the entertainment. I tended to get some stick for having a slight Manchester United bias, a bit like Paddy Crerand these days, though in contrast to Paddy, I always thought my views were sensible! Jimmy Wagg was the presenter, and I have to say he was brilliant at the job, even though he was always a City man, which made the programme pretty Blue. Needless to say, I made it as Red as I possibly could. We used to have some fantastic exchanges and it was hugely enjoyable, even if it wasn't very well paid.

Apart from the *craic*, and the modest remuneration, my radio stints were also important for keeping me firmly within the United circle. I

I got to know George Best even better on the after-dinner circuit, and he was a really smashing person, warm, generous and intelligent. We only saw the down side of George when he'd had too much to drink.

What a pair – Jaap Stam and his dad …

One of the finest footballers ever to pull on an England shirt … and on the left is Sir Stanley Matthews. I'm only joking, of course. Stan was magic, in a class of his own.

The cream of Manchester: Sir Matt Busby holds centre stage, flanked by (left to right) Mike Summerbee, Nobby Stiles, Alex Ferguson, George Best, Francis Lee, comedian Mike King, myself, Colin Bell, Denis Law, former referee the late Neil Midgley, Bobby Charlton and Tommy Docherty.

Tommy Smith pulls a fast one, standing on tiptoe to make himself appear taller, a trick he learned from the late, great Bill Shankly. Left to right at an Old Trafford ceremony to honour Bobby Charlton are former Charlton Athletic attacker Bobby Ayre, Sir Tom Finney, myself, Tommy, Denis Law, Sir Bobby, Roger Hunt, Ian Callaghan and Bill Foulkes.

A quiet moment in the Old Trafford stands with Sir Matt in the early 1990s. He was a truly great man and he will be revered as long as there is a Manchester United.

went abroad for all the European games, regularly interviewing the likes of Ryan Giggs and David Beckham, spending time with their families, generally being in the swim. I loved every minute of it and built up a hoard of deathless memories, none more vivid than the spring night in Turin when United came back from the dead to beat Juventus, thus reaching the final of the European Cup for only the second time in their history.

That game is remembered, and rightly so, for the brilliant performances of Roy Keane and Paul Scholes, who both knew that they would miss the final through suspension, but kept going to see that United got there. But there is another scene from that fabulous occasion which keeps popping up in my head. At the end of the game I was with the rest of the press and radio lads, who were all scrambling to get into the dressing-room area for interviews. The trouble was they weren't letting anyone in; even the likes of David Beckham's dad, Ted, and the Nevilles' father, Neville, were being turned away. I didn't have much hope but I decided on a novel approach, marching up to the security men on the door and telling them I was Jaap Stam's dad. 'Oh, come on in Mr Stam' one of them said, no doubt noting the family resemblance!

I got to know all the young players very well, and they were a terrific bunch. The likes of Ryan and David would always help me with an interview, but to get anything out of Scholesy demanded something akin to a miracle. It wasn't that he was being awkward, just that he always fought shy of publicity, as he does to this day. Once he had agreed to speak to me for a video I was working on, but he still wasn't looking forward to it and when I arrived to meet him he slipped out the back way. The next day I waited by the back door, and he popped out of the front. It wasn't until the third attempt, when I was ferrying back and forth between the two entrances, that I managed to pin him down. That didn't put me off him, though. He's a lovely, family orientated lad who just wants to live a quiet life and let his football do the talking. There's nothing wrong with that. I don't think I'd have been like it, though, if the media had been as obsessed with football in my time as they are now. I'd have been more like David Beckham!

I thought all those lads were decent types, well mannered and respectful and I think Alex Ferguson did a brilliant job in seeing that their feet remained firmly on the ground. That said, no one should underestimate the influence of the youth coach, Eric Harrison. He saw they were brought up in football the right way, just as Matt Busby, Jimmy Murphy, Bert Whalley, Tom Curry and Bill Inglis did all those years ago for my generation. United was a family club then, and so it is now. Watching the likes of Beckham, Scholes and the rest develop was like watching the Busby Babes come through.

I firmly believe that so many former United players are now managers because of the terrific schooling they received here. The likes of Mark Hughes, Roy Keane, Steve Bruce, Bryan Robson, Paul Ince and the rest were encouraged to think deeply about the game; they learned a lot and now they are passing on their wisdom, which is a fantastic tribute to Alex and the rest of the United staff.

I feel hugely privileged to have been in the commentary box – first for GMR, then later for Manchester United Radio – for so many of the club's modern successes. There have been so many unforgettable occasions, though nothing quite compares to the run-up to the unique treble in the spring of 1999. Of course, the climax to the season in the Nou Camp was utterly unimaginable, and yet six weeks earlier I thought that for sheer drama it would be impossible to beat the FA Cup semi-final replay victory over Arsenal at Villa Park. That game had just about everything. There was a fabulous Beckham goal, Roy Keane's sending-off, and a lucky Arsenal equaliser before Phil Neville tipped over Ray Parlour in the last minute of normal time, conceding a penalty. It looked all over for United as Dennis Bergkamp ran up to take the spot-kick, but Peter Schmeichel dived the right way and we had come back from the dead.

As extra time began I hoped that Arsenal had been deflated by Peter's save, but he was carrying an injury which severely hampered his movement and the rest of the lads seemed out on their legs. About ten minutes from the end I was getting worried, and I recall saying on air: 'It's going to take something exceptional to win this now, a touch of genius.' And at that very moment Patrick Vieira laid off a tired square pass which was intercepted by Ryan Giggs, who went past five or six tackles to score a wonder goal. Along with every other United fan in the place, I hit the Villa park roof. I was so excited. I'm afraid I didn't come up with a classic comment to rival Kenneth Wolstenholme's 'They think it's all over … it is now' when England won the World Cup in

1966. I just shrieked at the top of my lungs: 'Yeeeeeeeeeees.' But I think the listeners got the message.

Afterwards I went down to the dressing rooms to talk to some of the players and their relatives and bumped iunto the Arsenal right-back Lee Dixon, who had been at Bury with me. He's a lovely lad and sharp as a tack but, understandably enough, he was feeling a bit low. As I walked with him towards his team coach, we talked about Giggy's goal, in which he had been involved, and gave him a commiserating clap on the shoulder as he climbed aboard to find his seat. As it turned out, the two club coaches had been parked next to each other and he had boarded the wrong one, which was full of gleeful United players. In full celebration mode, one of them shouted to him: 'Get off, you've lost.' He might have been crushed, but he wasn't, coming back instantly with: 'Sorry lads, I'm so used to getting on the winners' coach.' I thought that was brilliant in the circumstances, and typical of the lad.

After that, the rest of the season was just a dream for Manchester United and all their followers. The climax was 11 days in May when everything fell into place, and I can always say I was there, on the spot for every triumph, intimately and passionately involved. First we came from behind to beat Spurs at Old Trafford, winning the championship on the last Sunday afternoon of the League campaign. Next we defeated Newcastle at Wembley to claim our third League and FA Cup double of the decade, an incredible achievement in itself and one which set the scene perfectly for *the* game, *the* final, *the* most unforgettable footballing experience of my broadcasting career to date.

Even in retrospect, I feel a warm glow whenever I think of that wonderful trip to Barcelona. Lots of United's European Cup winners from 1968 were there, and there was a real community spirit, a feeling that we were all there to take home the trophy. Mind, it wasn't quite like that in the commentary box with the rest of the GMR team, which consisted of Jimmy Wagg (a Blue), Alan Buckley (another Blue) and Paul Hince (yet another ****** Blue!). There we were, all sat in a line with me heavily outnumbered but vociferously holding my own, when Paul remarked, some ten minutes into the game, that United might be struggling if Bayern Munich scored an early goal. A few seconds later they did just that from Mario Basler's free-kick, a real rubbish goal from our point of view. That was a miserable moment, especially with the three City men all smirking at me, and matters didn't improve as the game went on. United weren't at their best and deep in the second half, as the Germans hit both bar and post, the treble dream seemed on the verge of dying.

But then something happened which summed up for me the overwhelming determination of Alex Ferguson's men to lift that trophy. There was only around a minute left, we were 1-0 down and we got a throw-in in the outside-left position. Who took it? Our right-back Gary Neville, that's who, after sprinting the full width of the field to grab that ball! I caught a glimpse of his face, realised that he hadn't even thought of giving up, and somewhere inside me a little flame of hope began to flicker.

Almost immediately we won a corner and there was Peter Schmeichel running into their penalty area, like some old-time Viking bent on pillage and rape. That was enough to panic the Germans. Over went Beckham's corner and their full-back lost his nerve, slicing his clearance to Ryan Giggs on the edge of the box. Ryan shot for goal with his unfavoured right foot, and he made a mess of it, shanking it badly. But the gods were on our side and there was Teddy Sheringham to nick it just inside a post from six yards.

Salvation! I was on my feet and screaming, something along the lines of: 'Great, we've got extra time, we can do them now.' But I was wrong. We didn't get extra time. Bloody hell, we didn't need it! Before the referee could signal an end to normal time, away we went again and won another corner. Schmeichel didn't go up this time; we had something to lose now, but something to win, too.

I was beside myself with excitement as Beckham sent over his kick, Sheringham flicked it on and there was the blessed Ole Gunnar Solskjaer to volley it in from close range. I couldn't believe what I was seeing, my eyes must have been out on stalks. I was jumping up and down, still clutching my microphone but passing up another opportunity for a timeless Wolstenholme moment. All I could manage, at the very top of my voice, was: 'Yes! Yes! Yes!' Not exactly memorable when I look at it on paper in the cold light of day, but there was a world of emotion in those three brief explosions of sound. Certainly GMR reproduced it often enough in the years that followed, so I must have got something right.

I was jubilant; nothing could have been sweeter. It was the best moment in the entire history of Manchester United, and *I was there*, telling the folks back home about it, intimately involved. It didn't exactly puncture my bubble, either, that the three City lads alongside me were virtually dumbstruck. They were happy for me – at least I think they were! – but they knew they were never going to hear the last of it, and they haven't.

I was overjoyed for the United players, but even more I was elated for the fans. They were ecstatic. The game had seemed to be slipping away from us, and they were looking at a dismal anti-climax to a memorable season, when the world was turned upside down. It was nothing short of a miracle, something I shall remember until I breathe my last.

Afterwards, as I walked (on air) back towards my hotel, a coach with the players' wives came alongside and the girls, who were headed for the official banquet, insisted that I climb aboard. Actually I didn't have an invitation but when we reached the hotel the club chairman, Martin Edwards, said I was welcome to stay. It reminded me of the World Cup celebration in 1966, when Alf Ramsey insisted that I join the party.

I wasn't really dressed for it, I didn't even have a tie, but there was no way I was going to refuse that sort of opportunity. In the end I stayed with them all the way through the night, not returning to my own hotel until 10 o'clock in the morning. During the formal part of the jollifications I sat with the Schmeichels. Peter is a great man as well as United's best ever goalkeeper and his lovely family – wife Bente and children Kasper and Cecilie – all did their bit to make me feel welcome. Of course, young Kasper's a professional footballer in his own right now and I wish him all the best, even though it's Manchester City's net he's been guarding!

I had my photo taken with the European Cup, and luckily I had my own camera with me so I did a bit of happy snapping, too. My favourite shot is one of Martin Edwards, dancing on a table with Dwight Yorke while smoking a cigar. Well, if a chairman can't let his hair down after his club has won the European Cup, then when can he?

That night was the highlight of my extremely happy spell with GMR, a station for which I had a lot of affection and for which I stopped working only when my corporate hospitality commitments made it impossible for me to be available for the previews and phone-ins which

Take your partners for the European Cup boogie. Dwight Yorke and Martin Edwards cast their inhibitions (if they ever had any) to the wind on that unforgettable night in 1999. Exclusive photograph by W. McGuinness.

are a crucial part of the output. Happy to report, however, I have remained on the air, working for quite a few years under the friendly guidance of Matt Proctor for the club's own station. Matt's a smashing lad and we had a good laugh together until his retirement in 2008. I'll miss him but I'm looking forward to linking up with his replacement, who hasn't been named at the time of writing. I get on well, too, with the station's regular match commentator, David Hooton, even though I discern a certain City slant to some of his pronouncements. Never mind, I enjoy our arguments – in fact, I disagree with him whenever I can!

Radio has been kind to me, projecting me at a time when a new generation of United fans had probably never heard of me. I still love it when I'm on holiday and someone comes up to me and says: 'You're Wilf McGuinness. I'd recognise that voice anywhere.' Despite all my other matchday jobs, I intend to continue as long as they want me.

Equally fulfilling, in its own way, is my role as an Old Trafford hospitality host, one to which I was intoduced by Danny McGregor, who has now retired after a lot of successful years as the club's commercial manager. I have always been a social animal and my passion for Manchester United is no secret, so meeting and greeting people before home games is right up my alley. There are usually 20-odd suites in use on matchdays, and I tend to compere in the Europa, which caters for more than 200 diners. For a three-o'clock kick-off, people start turning up at 12 noon for drinks and a meal, they are entertained by a comedian and a magician, there is a quiz, there are former United heroes circulating among the tables, and the hospitality continues after the game, when usually a man of the match from either side pops in.

I have to admit that I love being part of the entertainment, part of the United scene. I get a kick out of being there, in the centre of it all, still involved at the age of 70. When someone asks me to sign something, I think to myself: 'Bloody hell, they still know who I am!'

Even more satisfying on a personal level is being part of the Manchester United Former Players Association, which was formed around a quarter of a century ago. We have managed to raise a great deal of money for charities, especially helping children who suffer from leukaemia, and at the time of writing we are contributing towards to equipping a special ward in the Manchester Children's Hospital. I was delighted to be in at the start of the organisation, along with the likes of Harry McShane, Charlie Mitten, Bill Foulkes, Laurie Cassidy, David Herd, David Sadler, Paddy Crerand and two men who sadly passed away in 2007, Warren Bradley and John Doherty. Warren was a lovely man, a terrific treasurer and a selfless worker for the cause for whom nothing was ever too much trouble.

Then there was John, as magnificent a chairman as it is possible to imagine, and the man who did more than anyone else to make the Association a success. John was a strong and forthright character, to put it mildly, and he was also very clever. He believed that things should be done in a certain way, and he didn't mess about. We used to have long discussions at our meetings when some people disagreed with him, but usually when we had finished he had got his way – and on most occasions that was because he was right.

Many hard-working individuals have played their part – notably David Sadler, our long-serving secretary and now the new chairman – but John was the main mover and shaker. He brought a lot of humour to his role, too – no one could deny that he used the English language to its ultimate extent. The Association, and the wider football community in Manchester, is much the poorer for his absence.

When we started, a lot of the Busby Babes were involved, and it's just possible that we were a tad old-fashioned for some of the younger element. Whatever else happens, it would be a tragedy if we ceased to be effective as a group, both in terms of our charity work and the glorious social framework it provides for our members. So the message is clear. Now is the time for our good young men and true – and there is no shortage of them in the Association – to set their own agenda.

Mention of the Babes brings me to the events staged by Manchester United on 6 February 2008 to mark the 50th anniversary of the Munich disaster. Having been present all day, and having talked to many relatives of the lads who died, I must say that the club did a wonderful job.

I can't begin to express how emotional I felt during the service at Old Trafford. As the memories came back, I could feel the tears welling up, and I know lots of people there felt just the same as me.

There were especially moving contributions from Sir Bobby Charlton, Harry Gregg, Nobby Stiles and my son, Paul, United's youth team coach. It was appropriate that he should speak at the ceremony because he represents the new generation of young footballers.

It would have been easy for the club to have got it wrong, to have gone over the top, but they didn't. They got it just right, as did the fans of both United and City at the Manchester derby the following Sunday, when they maintained an impeccable minute's silence. There was grief, of course, but there was pride, too, and a timeless dignity which did full justice to the lads who had lost their lives half a century earlier.

Chapter 21

SIR ALEX – THE FIRST 22 YEARS

W E DIDN'T know much about Alex Ferguson before his arrival at Old Trafford in November 1986. Certainly we knew precious little about his character. But what we did know was that he had ended the age-old Scottish dominance of Rangers and Celtic, transforming Aberdeen from an also-ran into a potent footballing power.

His start at Old Trafford was pretty ordinary. Success didn't happen at once. But it used to annoy me intensely when people were so impatient with him. When I had the job of managing Manchester United, I could have done with some more time, so I felt deeply for Alex's plight when things were not going according to plan. I pointed out how well he had done in Europe with Aberdeen, but still there were a lot of moaners who wanted to get rid of him. I felt they had it wrong. Surely it was only common sense that after nearly 20 years with more downs than ups following the departure of Sir Matt Busby, it was time for the club to exercise a little patience.

It's easy to be wise after the event, but I always liked the manner in which Alex Ferguson worked. I thought he treated people the right way. True, if you crossed him he would tell you what he thought, but there is nothing wrong with that. Over the years he has brought his Scottish friends to Manchester and invited old United hands like myself to join his celebrations. He has been warm and inclusive, always made us feel part of the scene, and I have appreciated that deeply.

Then, of course, there is the little matter of his ability to take a football club by the scruff of its neck and make it successful, not just over the course of one or two seasons but in the long term. As soon as he arrived he recognised that United's youth system was in desperate need of a radical overhaul and, aided brilliantly by Eric Harrison, who looked after the boys in his charge in the same inspired fashion as had Jimmy Murphy a generation earlier, Alex got things moving in the right direction. The pair of them taught youngsters how to be better players and better people; in short, they taught them the Manchester United way.

Together they were the first since Matt and Jimmy to bring on a wave of great young footballers at Old Trafford. They nurtured the talents of Giggs, Scholes, Beckham, Butt, the Nevilles and Brown, making them understand thay they could enjoy a fabulous life in the game but they had to behave. Alex and Eric were unstinting in the time and effort they would expend on the lads, but they wouldn't stand any messing round, making it crystal clear that if anybody stepped out of line then they could expect recrimination to descend on them like a ton of bricks.

In due course, these young men became millionaires, and then, no doubt, multi-millionaires, but still the United boss knew how to handle them, as well as the vastly expensive acquisitions on the transfer market that he continues to make. He knows these boys are financially secure for life, and that they could walk out if they became unduly upset with his methods, but still he remains the man in control, still he makes one or two shake at the knees when he needs to, and that is because they respect him utterly. For a regime such as Alex Ferguson's to succeed in the modern world, he has to be serially successful. As his phenomenal record in Manchester indicates – 20 major trophies in 22 seasons at the time of writing, with infinite power to add! – he is that and more. Thus he commands respect, both by sheer force of personality and by weight of silverware. Quite simply, he has no equal.

There are some who question his sureness in the transfer market, but I can't agree with them. For heaven's sake, we're talking here about the man who brought to Old Trafford the likes of Cantona, Schmeichel, Pallister, Bruce, Irwin, Hughes (well, he brought him back), Keane, Solskjaer, Stam, van Nistelrooy, Ronaldo, Rooney, Vidic and Tevez – I could go on. True, there have been a handful who haven't worked out, and his critics will never let him forget Juan Sebastian Veron, who was branded a £28 million misfit. Okay, that *was* a failure, but it was a great shame because the lad had fabulous ability, unbelievable skill on the

I could say that Rio is doing a fine impersonation of a mop, but he might say I'm only jealous. Back row, left to right: Norman Whiteside, Paddy Crerand, Paul Parker, Micky Thomas, Yours Truly, Lee Martin. Front row: Rio Ferdinand, Wayne Rooney, Cristiano Ronaldo, Ruud van Nistelrooy.

The first Premiership is in the bag and it's time to party. Left to right are Ryan Giggs, myself, Mick Hucknall, a pal of Mick's, Paul Ince and Paul Parker.

Past differences long forgotten, Norman Whiteside and Sir Alex face the camera with me at Old Trafford.

Three generations of United managers, Sir Matt, Sir Alex and me, entertain a pair lively guests at the Red Café, my twin grandsons James (left) and Tom.

ball, and I can see why Alex thought he would be the central midfielder to lift the team to another level. The Premiership catches out a lot of players with its relentless pace and ferocity, which denies them time to dwell on the ball, and that's what happened to the Argentinian. But no manager gets every transfer exactly right, that's a fact of football life, and no one can deny that the United boss is heavily in credit overall.

He is remarkable, too, in bringing on young lads from different cultures as surely as he helped the home-based Beckham generation to develop. We are already witnessing the maturing of Ronaldo. When he came to us he was described by a lot of people as a show pony whose best trick was diving, but now he is acknowledged as one of the best players in the world, if not the best. There is discernible improvement, also, with Tevez, Nani and Anderson, and no doubt others will follow.

Alex doesn't seem perturbed, either, by whatever unexpected complexities are placed in his way. The Tevez transfer, for instance, brought all manner of complicated worries, but he steered his way through them all and ended up with a boy who has the capacity to become an all-time great.

Equally, when he feels it's time for a player to move on, even when it isn't obvious to the rest of the world, then he makes it happen. Not everybody agreed with the exits of Stam, van Nistelrooy or Beckham, but Alex was decisive, and Manchester United have not exactly withered and died in the aftermath.

There is no doubt that his body of work since replacing Ron Atkinson is unrivalled. His main brief when he arrived was to end United's long wait for a League title. At the last count he has helped himself to ten Premierships in 16 years, an astonishing achievement. It gives me endless pleasure to cast my eye back over some of the glorious performers who have illuminated his teams, and it feels right to begin with Eric Cantona. I know there was a bit of luck involved in his signing, when Leeds rang up to inquire about Denis Irwin and ended up selling us the Frenchman for a song. Despite his remarkable natural gifts, he had never done particularly well in France and he had been inconsistent at Elland Road, but Old Trafford turned out to be Eric's spiritual home. He was the man who turned the key for us, transforming us from a very fine side into a great one. Our other terrific performers drew inspiration from playing alongside him, and he set a superb example in training which rubbed off on the youngsters. Truly the gods were smiling on Manchester United the day Eric Cantona joined the club.

Equally influential in his own way was Peter Schmeichel, as magnificent a goalkeeper as I have ever seen, and Bryan Robson was a born leader. At one time we all feared that he would be undone by the injuries which plagued him, often as a result of his courageous approach, but he overcame that hoodoo. The best thing I can say about Robbo is that he reminded me of Duncan Edwards – I'm not saying he was Dunc's equal, because no one was – and I can offer no higher praise than that.

Another who deserves to be mentioned in the same breath is Roy Keane. When we lost Robbo I thought it would be impossible to replace him, but then along came the Irishman. I can recall countless occasions when he lifted the team by personal example and changed a game, but the incident which stands out most vividly for me didn't even occur on the pitch. It took place in the tunnel at Highbury before one of our epic encounters with Arsenal. Roy felt that Patrick Vieira had stepped out of line by having a go verbally at Gary Neville, so he took it upon himself to intervene. He told Vieira, in so many words: 'Stop shooting your mouth off at Gary. If you have a problem, you take it up with me. We'll sort it out on the pitch.' And so he did, winning a series of tackles against the big Frenchman and inspiring United to yet another terrific victory against the north Londoners. That summed up Roy Keane for me. He matched his actions to his words. People talk about his nasty streak, but many great players had that. Take it from me that Denis Law upset a few in his time. With such men, if you take the best then you have to put up with the rest. If you're a fan you put up with it. You understand why opponents moan but, for my money, Roy Keane is one of the most heroic figures in United's history.

Having talked about Robbo and Roy, I feel I should mention Paul Ince, too. He tends to be overlooked these days when great United midfielders of the Ferguson era are discussed, and I think that's unjust. Okay, he wasn't quite on a par with those two, but who was? Some people say he got above himself, and that he became bossy, but even if he did, so what? He was a terrific player to have on your side and a massive influence as United lifted those early Premiership titles.

That team had so much heart and so many exceptional individuals. Take the centre of defence, where Steve Bruce and Gary Pallister were

Ball-winners both. Roy Keane and I had a certain amount in common, but not as much as I would have liked!

You needn't have dressed up, Eric! Enjoying a get-together with the French genius and former United winger Keith Gillespie.

He takes a lot of flak, but I'll always maintain that David Beckham is a lovely, decent lad. He could play a bit, too.

absolute bulwarks. When people think of such players, they tend to have little pictures in their brain, moments frozen in time that define the great footballers. In the case of Brucie, for me, it has to be heading his second goal against Sheffield Wednesday in the seventh minute of stoppage time in the spring of 1993. We had been a goal down, but Steve equalised close to the end of 90 minutes, then nodded the winner at about the time most supporters would have expected to be halfway home. That was the moment when most of us believed that we could finally end our championship drought – and so we did.

Similarly with Pally, I can visualise two golden moments at Anfield in April 1997 when he headed a couple of brilliant goals which virtually knocked Liverpool out of the title race and made us the red-hot favourites. Certainly it could be said that United won the title on Merseyside that season.

While we're on defenders, I must refer to Denis Irwin, a resolute teammate of Brucie and Pally who lasted into the new millennium and whose purchase from Oldham must go down as one of the best pieces of business Alex ever pulled off in the transfer market. He was one of the most consistent performers I can ever remember, carrying on United's tradition of outstanding full-backs which has included Johnny Carey, John Aston, Roger Byrne, Shay Brennan, Tony Dunne and Arthur Albiston.

As I write now, my head is beginning to spin with those precious little pictures that will stay with me forever: Cantona's sensational effort to win the 1996 FA Cup final, when he shot through a forest of Liverpool legs to break the deadlock just ahead of the final whistle; Mark Hughes' staggering volley when the ball dropped over his shoulder in an FA Cup semi-final against Oldham at Wembley, a goal which earned a replay and enabled United to go on to their first League and Cup double in 1994; Schmeichel's plunge to save Dennis Bergkamp's penalty in another semi-final, this time at Villa Park, on the way to the treble in 1999; and, leaping forward to March 2003, Ruud van Nistelrooy's astonishing slalom through the Fulham defence, climaxed by a clinical early finish, as United closed in on their eighth Premiership crown.

There are so many unperishable memories, too, of the class of '92, which a lot of people view as Alex Ferguson's masterpiece in this era of mega-expenditure on foreign stars. I'd known the Neville boys since their schooldays because I'd been at Bury with their dad, Neville Neville, when he was the Shakers' commercial manager. They were always out-standing sportsmen and while they were growing up, whenever they were playing either football or cricket I did my best to watch them. Gary, the older brother, was good at everything, but as the years went by it looked as if Phil would overtake him. He was an absolute natural. But Gary refused to come second at anything, and he worked so hard to do everything right, correct any faults and improve himself, that he has enjoyed a superb career. So has Phil, of course, and between them now they have more than 150 England caps, a staggering achievement. They are a credit to themselves and their family, which includes mother Jill, who played a lot of rounders, sister Tracy, a netball international, and dad Neville, a terrific cricketer. The Nevilles have taken some unfair stick from some critics down the years, but they don't deserve it. They've got a spark, they'll tell you exactly what they think, but there's nothing wrong with that. They're both smashing lads.

Nicky Butt is in a similar category, a local lad who will always give you everything. He's always positive, when he loses the ball he'll fight to get it back, he always supports team-mates when they have possession, he'll make goals and occasionally he'll score them. He's another positive character, and that's something I always like in a footballer, maybe because I think that has always been one of my own best qualities.

An altogether classier footballer but one with a similar down-to-earth attitude is Paul Scholes. Have you ever seen a more talented English attacking midfielder? I don't think I have. His passing, both long and short, is remarkably imaginative and invariably accurate; he's clever enough to dribble past opponents, but knows when a simple pass is the better option; he scores fabulous goals and tap-ins, and he's so brave his heart must be bigger than the rest of his body. I won't say too much about his tackling, but nobody's perfect! Paul brings a great deal to the team, which is never quite the same when he's missing. His life is all about football and family, rather than money and glamour. He is well loved by everybody at Old Trafford, and one of the most influential figures of the Ferguson reign.

You might say that Ryan Giggs hasn't done too badly, either! The brilliant Welshman has outstripped Bobby Charlton's Manchester United appearance record, finally passing the milestone on the last tumultuous night of the 2007/08 campaign. I know that Bobby had been genuinely hoping that Ryan *would* beat his mark, recognising how much he deserved that honour. He's been a credit to his profession for nearly two decades, a fabulous footballer on the pitch and a terrific ambassador for the game off it. I often see the players being asked for autographs in situations when the press aren't present, and I've never seen Ryan behave any way other than with extremely good grace. He's always been an absolute gentleman, doing everything he can for the fans, and showing that he has an impeccable set of values. We hear a lot of bad stuff about unfeasibly rich young footballers; well, Ryan Giggs offers a contrastingly wholesome role model.

Finally from that vintage, let me turn to David Beckham, who has had to take so much media flak down the years and I just can't see why. I think the world of him, and whenever anyone has a go at him I jump to his defence. I can't see that there's anything wrong with promoting yourself – I think I'd have been a Becks if I'd had the chance!

Anyone who thinks he is some sort of bighead couldn't be more wrong. He has a lot of attention and so much on his plate, but fundamentally he's the same modest lad who came to the club back in the early 1990s. When my son, Paul, was a junior coach at United and having his 30th birthday party, David turned up with the other lads, even though he was already a massive name by then. He's terrific, there's no side to him at all, and I can't see any reason why he should not make the most of his success. He's earned it himself, after all.

Other names crowd in, but this isn't supposed to be a who's who of Manchester United, so I'll confine myself to just a few brief mentions. Among those I have admired immensely during Alex's 22 years at the helm are Norman Whiteside, who was dripping with talent and left dozens of glorious memories; Brian McClair, one of Fergie's first signings, initially a prolific goal-scorer and then a selfless worker in midfield; Lee Sharpe, an exciting left winger with real star quality; Jaap Stam, who was like a seam of granite at centre-half – I could never understand why he left; Andy Cole, Dwight Yorke, Teddy Sheringham and Ole Gunnar Solskjaer, the four strikers who did so much to capture the treble in 1999 – what a quartet!

As for his current team, there seems to be positively no limit to what it can achieve. With such extravagantly gifted performers as Wayne

Rooney, Cristiano Ronaldo and Carlos Tevez in the vanguard, with youngsters like Anderson and Nani on the rise, with a multi-talented midfield bolstered immeasurably by the arrival of the workaholic Owen Hargreaves, and with a high-quality defence built around the redoubtable Nemanja Vidic, the still-improving Rio Ferdinand and local lad Wes Brown, I could not be more optimistic, particularly after that wet but wonderful night in Moscow.

Throughout much of the 2007/08 season United were playing some of the best football to be seen anywhere in the world, and I think that winning the Premier League and the European Cup was no more than their just deserts. Certainly there is no doubt that they were worthy domestic champions because they scored more goals than anyone else, had the best defensive record and served up the most spellbinding entertainment on a pretty consistent basis. Always Sir Alex's players wanted the ball, they never hid from it; they wanted to play and to thrill the crowds, just like the lads did in Sir Matt's day. Fantastic!

Regarding the Champions League, I felt before the final that we would score goals, and we created enough chances during a brilliant first-half display to be leading by two or three at the interval. But then Chelsea were lifted by an extremely fortunate equaliser, which inspired them to work hard and create openings of their own in the second period, which was very tense.

But I always thought we had the edge, certainly during extra time, although I have to admit my heart was pounding during the penalty shoot-out. I hadn't given up even when John Terry ran forward to take what would have been the winning kick if it had gone in. I remained positive – that's the way I am! – and I thought to myself: 'Well, he'll have to miss it.' And he did!

I was there with my son Paul, and at the end we were both standing on our seats, bouncing up and down. When Edwin van der Sar made his final save from Nicolas Anelka I practically hit the roof, hugging Paul and shouting my head off. It was marvellous to share the moment, too, with others from the academy staff who were alongside us, smashing fellows like Brian McClair, Jim Ryan, Tony Whelan and Mark Dempsey, who are all working very hard to nurture the next generation of United footballers. The people around us were all celebrating like crazy, including Ryan Giggs' mum and grandad, and Paul Scholes' folks. It was sheer pandemonium and I wouldn't have missed it for the world. Just like Sir Matt, Sir Alex makes United a family club, and this felt like a very special family celebration. I'm sure the fans felt that, too, and they have played a gigantic part in spurring the club to success in 2006/07 and 2007/08, particularly in Europe. For instance, their fervour was astonishing on that fabulous night when we beat Roma 7-1, and they have been fantastically generous to me whenever I have been on the pitch, as I am from time to time, for various ceremonies and presentations. I was thinking of them after the penalty drama against Chelsea as we made our way to United's party at a hotel in the centre of Moscow. I hope they all had as great a time as I did – I didn't leave until about eight o'oclock in the morning, by which time I was very tired but deliriously happy. Then I managed to snatch a couple of hours' sleep before heading for the airport, and when I finally climbed aboard the plane I still couldn't stop grinning like a Cheshire cat as the barely credible scenes of only a few hours earlier continued to flash vividly across my mind.

Remarkably, through it all, as the fabulous success story of the modern Manchester United continues to unfold, Sir Alex Ferguson, like Old Man River, just keeps rolling along. As a personality, there's a lot more to him than the majority of people realise. They see this red-faced Scot ranting at the referee, practically foaming at the mouth, and occasionally being banished to the stands for his pains. They don't see the generosity, humanity and genuine friendship he extends to so many who come into personal contact with him. Through painful experience, I believe I know better than most that his job is an enormously taxing one, and for him to last so long and to bring so many honours to the club, all the while retaining his sense of humour and his sanity, is little short of a miracle. If, as has been suggested, he is going to retire before he reaches the grand age of 70, then I hope it's only the day before. Long may he reign!

Chapter 22

ACROSS A CROWDED ROOM

FOOTBALL HAS been my obsession for as long as I can remember. It has engulfed my attention, consumed practically all of my waking hours, dictated my mood far more comprehensively than might be deemed healthy by well-balanced neutral observers. And yet, when I come to weigh up what has meant most to me during the seven decades I have spent on this earth, when I peer into the darkest recesses of my soul and make a hand-on-heart assessment of what truly matters to me, the game, precious as it has been, comes a distant second in my list of priorities.

I consider myself supremely fortunate in that I have always been blessed with a close-knit and loving family. First there were my parents and my brother, then my wife and children, now my grandchildren. They have been, and remain, infinitely more important to me than all the trophies and medals and appointments and sackings that have comprised my professional lot.

Having made that heartfelt declaration, I have to say it's funny how football was central to my meeting the girl with whom I was to spend the best years of my life. As a 19-year-old professional at Old Trafford, believing the world of football was at my feet, I was in buoyant mood as I headed for the Continental Club, opposite the Palace Theatre on Oxford Street in central Manchester, a popular haunt for footballers at the time. The occasion was my friend and fellow Busby Babe Eddie Colman's birthday party.

When we got to the Continental, it was pretty packed, and I started looking around for people I knew. Then suddenly, as I glanced casually

Two McGuinnesses get their hands on the European Cup. I'm proud that my son Paul, who is in charge of Manchester United's youth team, has totalled more years at Old Trafford than his dad.

Action Man: on holiday in Tenerife with my pal John Scrivner, who is clearly confident in my driving ability – or is he hanging on for dear life?

across that crowded room, my eyes lit on this lovely looking girl I had never seen before, and I was captivated. I edged nearer, but for some reason I didn't talk to her very much, which was uncharacteristic of me, because I was never the shy and retiring type.

There was something about her that made her different from the rest. Some of the girls there were real townies, night-club regulars, very good looking, but a little on the knowing side. This one wasn't like that at all. I was just overwhelmed by her sheer niceness – and I wasn't wrong.

I asked my pal Gordon Clayton, the United goalkeeper, who she was, and he told me it was Beryl Thorp, who worked with his girlfriend Pat (later to become his wife) at the Royal Exchange in Manchester. That night Beryl was out with Gordon's Pat and Eddie Colman's girlfriend, Marjorie. Now my priority was to see if there was a chance of taking Beryl to the pictures. That duly happened, and our relationship blossomed from there. What a lucky lad I was, and have been for the last half-century, because I could never have found a more loving, understanding and supportive wife.

We were married at St Aidan's Church, Wythenshawe, in July 1961, and our first child, Anna, was born in May 1962. In due course there followed Paul in March 1966, Clare in August 1969 and John, during our Greek sojourn, in September 1971.

Anna, who turned out to be an extrovert along the lines of her father, now works in the designer-clothes department of Selfridges in Manchester's Trafford Centre. She is the mother of smashing twin boys, 18-year-old Tom and James, whose dad is Steve.

Clare, who had a career in textiles and ceramics, lives in Philadelphia, USA, where her husband, Steve Roper, is a football coach. He was in the Loughborough University team with Paul, then came to visit us here and that's how he met Clare. Steve and Clare have given us a beautiful grandson, Matthew, who is a year old.

John, our youngest, was a good footballer who could have signed as an apprentice with York City. He was a skilful midfielder who, I'm convinced, could have made a living in the game, but he was more heavily into art than football. He studied at Birmingham University and now works for Cosgrove Hall, the animations company responsible for *Postman Pat* and, more recently, *Little Robots*. He is married to Rachel

Innocents abroad. The McGuinness family had a cracking time in Greece in the early 1970s. Left to right are John, Anna, Wilf, Beryl, Paul and Clare.

and they have two children, three-year-old Jack, and May, who was born in January 2008.

I've departed from chronological order, leaving our second-born, Paul, until last, because he took the McGuinness story full circle by joining Manchester United straight from school, and that seems a neat way to finish.

Paul was another midfielder who, although he occupied roughly the same part of the pitch as me, was not too similar as a player, being more skilful, more constructive and more likely to score goals. We had differing personalities, too – he was quieter and more polite than his altogether noisier dad.

Playing alongside the likes of Norman Whiteside, Mark Hughes, David Platt, Mark Higgins, Russell Beardsmore, Mark Dempsey and Graeme Hogg, he progressed pretty satisfactorily at first, doing well for United's 'A' team and reserves, but then came an agonising choice. He had to make up his mind between going to Loughborough University to obtain qualifications which might serve him well in later life, and staying at Old Trafford to pursue his dreams. Looking back, perhaps I made a mistake in not seeking qualifications and I knew how rocky the path could be for a youngster trying to make the grade at a big club, so maybe that influenced him.

Paul thought long and hard, and for a season tried to combine playing part-time in the reserves at United with studying PE and sports science at Loughborough before picking up a bit of League experience with Crewe Alexandra.

He spent four years at Loughborough, captaining the football club there for two of them, helping to win three inter-university championships and playing for Great Britain Universities, but even more importantly from his point of view he gained a group of lifelong friends. Then he was brought back to Manchester United as an experienced older head to skipper what was a very young reserve team.

There followed a loan spell at Brighton and a few games for Chester before he was encouraged by Alex Ferguson to get his coaching badges. So he did, and in due course he worked for United as youth welfare officer, then coached youngsters under Nobby Stiles at the club's Centre of Excellence. Paul turned out to be a natural at the work – after all, he'd grown up with football in his veins – and in time he took on more responsibility under Nobby, then began to climb higher up the ladder.

Ever since he has worked with United's young footballers, and if you add up his years employed by the club they come to more than mine. These days he is manager/coach of the youth team – he took them to the final of the FA Youth Cup in 2007. He loves his job and I think he's good at it, which gives me a great deal of pleasure. Paul is married to Lynda, and they have a son, Joseph, who is nine.

Though having a lad following me at Old Trafford means a lot to me, I am equally proud of all my children. I feel privileged to be the patriarch of such a wonderful family. Everybody should be proud of their children, they're unlucky if they're not, and I can honestly say that I count my blessings every time I look at mine.

The family ethos has been crucial to me all my life, both at home and at Old Trafford. My nearest and dearest haven't really had to vie with United for my affection and attention, of course, though sometimes it might have seemed like that because of the nature of my job. In all honesty, I feel Beryl deserves sympathy because I didn't pull more of my weight with household matters, but that's just the way it is in football and any other family man in the game will tell the same story. Luckily my basic relationships with my wife and children have always been strong, and I don't believe my absences have harmed them.

I must admit, though, that a placard I spotted at a recent game made me smile. It read: 'United, kids and wife, in that order!' For me, that wasn't quite true, although there were times when it wasn't quite untrue, either. Happily Beryl, Anna, Paul, Clare and John will know my tongue is not unadjacent to my cheek when I point out that such a sorry state of affairs was inevitable for any poor souls involved with a fellow like me, hopelessly devoted to Manchester United, man and Babe...

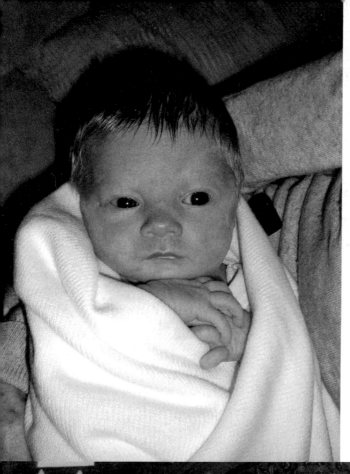

Opposite: The youth team: Beryl and I have been blessed with five smashing grandsons and a beautiful granddaughter. Here we are with the boys; left to right are James, Jack, Matthew, Joseph and Tom. Left: the newest McGuinness, our lovely baby May.

The first team: lining up with my wife and children at my 70th birthday bash. With me, left to right, are John, Anna, Beryl, Paul and Clare.

Wilf McGuinness
PLAYING STATISTICS

1953/54

First leg: 23 April 1954 v Wolverhampton Wanderers at Old Trafford.
Result and scorers: 4-4 (Edwards 2, Pegg 2 inc 1 pen).
Team: Hawksworth, Beswick, Rhodes, Colman, Harrop, McGuinness, Littler, Edwards, Charlton, Pegg, Scanlon.
Attendance: 18,246.

Second leg: 26 April 1954 v Wolverhampton Wanderers at Molineux.
Result and scorer: 1-0 (Pegg Pen).
Team: Hawksworth, Beswick, Rhodes, Colman, Harrop, McGuinness, Littler, Edwards, Charlton, Pegg, Scanlon.
Attendance: 28,651.

1954/55

First leg: 27 April 1955 v West Bromwich Albion at Old Trafford.
Result and scorers: 4-1 (Colman 2, Charlton, Beckett).
Team: Hawksworth, Queenan, Rhodes, Colman, Jones, McGuinness, Beckett, Brennan, Edwards, Charlton, Fidler.
Attendance: 16,696.

Second leg: 30 April 1955 v West Bromwich Albion at The Hawthorns.
Result and scorers: 3-0 (Charlton, Edwards, Cooke og).
Team: Hawksworth, Queenan, Rhodes, Colman, Jones, McGuinness, Beckett, Brennan, Edwards, Charlton, Fidler.
Attendance: 8,335.

1955/56

First leg: 30 April 1956 v Chesterfield at Old Trafford.
Result and scorers: 3-2 (Carolan, Charlton, Pearson).
Team: Hawksworth, Queenan, Jones, Carolan, Holland, McGuinness, Morgans, Pearson, Dawson, Charlton, Fidler.
Attendance: 25,544.

Second leg: 7 May 1956 v Chesterfield at Saltergate.
Result and scorer: 1-1 (Fidler).
Team: Hawksworth, Queenan, Jones, Carolan, Holland, McGuinness, Morgans, Pearson, Dawson, Charlton, Fidler.
Attendance: 15,838.

SENIOR CAREER

1955/56
Manchester United – 1st in Division 1

	LEAGUE		FA CUP		TOTAL	
	App	Gls	App	Gls	App	Gls
Geoff Bent	4	0	-	-	4	0
Johnny Berry	34	4	1	0	35	4
Jackie Blanchflower	18	3	-	-	18	3
Roger Byrne	39	3	1	0	40	3
Eddie Colman	25	0	1	0	26	0
Jack Crompton	1	0	-	-	1	0
John Doherty	16	4	1	0	17	4
Duncan Edwards	33	3	-	-	33	3
Bill Foulkes	26	0	1	0	27	0
Freddie Goodwin	8	0	-	-	8	0
Ian Greaves	15	0	-	-	15	0
Mark Jones	42	1	1	0	43	1
Eddie Lewis	4	1	-	-	4	1
Wilf McGuinness	**3**	**1**	**-**	**-**	**3**	**1**
David Pegg	35	9	1	0	36	9
Albert Scanlon	6	1	-	-	6	1
Johnny Scott	1	0	-	-	1	0
Tommy Taylor	33	25	1	0	34	25
Dennis Viollet	34	20	1	0	35	20
Colin Webster	15	4	-	-	15	4
Billy Whelan	13	4	-	-	13	4
Jeff Whitefoot	15	0	1	0	16	0
Walter Whitehurst	1	0	-	-	1	0
Ray Wood	41	0	1	0	42	0

1956/57

Manchester United – 1st in Division 1

	LEAGUE		FA CUP		EUROPE		TOTAL	
	App	Gls	App	Gls	App	Gls	App	Gls
Geoff Bent	6	0	-	-	-	-	6	0
Johnny Berry	40	8	5	4	8	2	53	14
Jackie Blanchflower	11	0	2	0	3	0	16	0
Roger Byrne	36	0	6	1	8	0	50	1
Bobby Charlton	14	10	2	1	1	1	17	12
Gordon Clayton	2	0	-	-	-	-	2	0
Eddie Colman	36	1	6	0	8	0	50	1
Ronnie Cope	2	0	-	-	-	-	2	0
Alex Dawson	3	3	-	-	-	-	3	3
John Doherty	3	0	-	-	-	-	3	0
Duncan Edwards	34	5	6	1	7	0	47	6
Bill Foulkes	39	0	6	0	8	0	53	0
Freddie Goodwin	6	0	-	-	-	-	6	0
Ian Greaves	3	0	-	-	-	-	3	0
Tony Hawksworth	1	0	-	-	-	-	1	0
Mark Jones	29	0	4	0	6	0	39	0
Wilf McGuinness	**13**	**0**	**1**	**0**	**1**	**0**	**15**	**0**
David Pegg	37	6	6	0	8	1	51	7
Albert Scanlon	5	2	-	-	-	-	5	2
Tommy Taylor	32	22	4	4	8	8	44	34
Dennis Viollet	27	16	5	0	6	9	38	25
Colin Webster	5	3	1	0	-	-	6	3
Billy Whelan	39	26	6	4	8	3	53	33
Ray Wood	39	0	6	0	8	0	53	0

1957/58
Manchester United – 9th in Division 1

	LEAGUE		FA CUP		EUROPE		TOTAL	
	App	Gls	App	Gls	App	Gls	App	Gls
Johnny Berry	20	4	-	-	3	1	23	5
Jackie Blanchflower	18	0	-	-	2	0	20	0
Seamus Brennan	5	0	2	3	-	-	7	3
Roger Byrne	26	0	2	0	6	0	34	0
Bobby Charlton	21	8	7	5	2	3	30	16
Eddie Colman	24	0	2	0	5	1	31	1
Ronnie Cope	13	0	6	0	2	0	21	0
Stan Crowther	11	0	5	0	2	0	18	0
Alex Dawson	12	5	6	5	-	-	18	10
John Doherty	1	1	-	-	-	-	1	1
Duncan Edwards	26	6	2	0	5	0	33	6
Bill Foulkes	42	0	8	0	8	0	58	0
David Gaskell	3	0	-	-	-	-	3	0
Freddie Goodwin	16	0	6	0	3	0	25	0
Ian Greaves	12	0	6	0	2	0	20	0
Harry Gregg	19	0	8	0	4	0	31	0
Bobby Harrop	5	0	1	0	-	-	6	0
Tommy Heron	1	0	-	-	-	-	1	0
Mark Jones	10	0	2	0	4	0	16	0
Peter Jones	1	0	-	-	-	-	1	0
Wilf McGuinness	**7**	**0**	**-**	**-**	**1**	**0**	**8**	**0**
Kenny Morgans	13	0	2	0	4	0	19	0
Mark Pearson	8	0	4	0	2	0	14	0
David Pegg	21	4	-	-	4	3	25	7
Albert Scanlon	9	3	2	0	3	0	14	3
Ernie Taylor	11	2	6	1	2	1	19	4
Tommy Taylor	25	16	2	0	6	3	33	19
Dennis Viollet	22	16	3	3	6	4	31	23
Colin Webster	20	6	6	1	5	1	31	8
Billy Whelan	20	12	-	-	3	2	23	14
Ray Wood	20	0	-	-	4	0	24	0

1958/59

Manchester United – 2nd in Division 1

	LEAGUE		FA CUP		TOTAL	
	App	Gls	App	Gls	App	Gls
Warren Bradley	24	12	1	0	25	12
Seamus Brennan	1	0	-	-	1	0
Joe Carolan	23	0	1	0	24	0
Bobby Charlton	38	29	1	0	39	29
Ronnie Cope	32	2	1	0	33	2
Stan Crowther	2	0	-	-	2	0
Alex Dawson	11	4	-	-	11	4
Bill Foulkes	32	0	1	0	33	0
Freddie Goodwin	42	6	1	0	43	6
Ian Greaves	34	0	-	-	34	0
Harry Gregg	41	0	1	0	42	0
Bobby Harrop	5	0	-	-	5	0
Reg Hunter	1	0	-	-	1	0
Wilf McGuinness	**39**	**1**	**1**	**0**	**40**	**1**
Kenny Morgans	2	0	-	-	2	0
Mark Pearson	4	1	-	-	4	1
Albert Quixall	33	4	1	0	34	4
Albert Scanlon	42	16	1	0	43	16
Ernie Taylor	11	0	-	-	11	0
Dennis Viollet	37	21	1	0	38	21
Colin Webster	7	5	-	-	7	5
Ray Wood	1	0	-	-	1	0

1959/60
Manchester United – 7th in Division 1

	LEAGUE		FA CUP		TOTAL	
	App	Gls	App	Gls	App	Gls
Warren Bradley	29	8	2	1	31	9
Seamus Brennan	29	0	3	0	32	0
Joe Carolan	41	0	3	0	44	0
Ronnie Cope	40	0	3	0	43	0
Alex Dawson	22	15	1	0	23	15
Bill Foulkes	42	0	3	0	45	0
David Gaskell	9	0	-	-	9	0
John Giles	10	2	-	-	10	2
Ian Greaves	2	0	-	-	2	0
Freddie Goodwin	18	1	1	1	19	2
Harry Gregg	33	0	3	0	36	0
Tommy Heron	1	0	-	-	1	0
Nobby Lawton	3	0	-	-	3	0
Wilf McGuinness	**19**	**0**	**-**	**-**	**19**	**0**
Mark Pearson	10	3	-	-	10	3
Albert Quixall	33	13	3	0	36	13
Maurice Setters	17	0	2	0	19	0
Dennis Viollet	36	32	3	0	39	32
Bobby Charlton	37	18	3	3	40	21
Albert Scanlon	31	7	3	1	34	8

SUMMARY

Manchester United

League: 81 games, 2 goals

FA Cup: 2 games, 0 goals

European Cup: 2 games, 0 goals

Total: 85 games, 2 goals

In addition there were more than 100 other games for Manchester United, at youth and reserve level and in friendlies.

ENGLAND

First cap: 4 October 1958 v Northern Ireland at Windsor Park, Belfast.
Result and scorers: 3-3 (Charlton 2, Finney). **Age**: 20.
Team: Colin McDonald (Burnley), Don Howe (West Bromwich Albion), Tommy Banks (Bolton Wanderers), Ronnie Clayton (Blackburn Rovers), Billy Wright (Wolverhampton Wanderers, captain), Wilf McGuinness (Manchester United), Peter Brabrook (Chelsea), Peter Broadbent (Wolverhampton Wanderers), Bobby Charlton (Manchester United), Johnny Haynes (Fulham), Tom Finney (Preston North End).

Second cap: 24 May 1959 v Mexico in Mexico City.
Result and scorer: 1-2 (Kevan). **Age**: 21.
Team: Eddie Hopkinson (Bolton Wanderers), Don Howe (West Bromwich Albion), Jimmy Armfield (Blackpool), Ronnie Clayton (Blackburn Rovers), Billy Wright (Wolverhampton Wanderers, captain), Wilf McGuinness (Manchester United), Doug Holden (Bolton Wanderers), Jimmy Greaves (Chelsea), Derek Kevan (West Bromwich Albion), Johnny Haynes (Fulham), Bobby Charlton (Manchester United).
Substitutes: Ron Flowers (Wolverhampton Wanderers) for McGuinness, Warren Bradley (Manchester United) for Holden.